YOU MUST LIKE CRICKET?

Soumya Bhattacharya grew up in London and Kolkata. His writing has been published in the *New York Times*, the *Sydney Morning Herald, Wisden, New Statesman*, the *Guardian* and the *Observer*. He is currently an editor on the *Hindustan Times*. He lives in Mumbai. This is his first book.

YOU MUST LIKE CRICKET?

Memoirs of an Indian Cricket Fan

Soumya Bhattacharya

YELLOW JERSEY PRESS
LONDON

Published by Yellow Jersey Press 2006

2 4 6 8 10 9 7 5 3 1

Copyright © Soumya Bhattacharya 2006

Soumya Bhattacharya has asserted his right under the Copyright, Designs and
Patents Act 1988 to be identified as the author of this work

First published in Great Britain in 2006 by
Yellow Jersey Press

Yellow Jersey Press
Random House, 20 Vauxhall Bridge Road,
London SW1V 2SA

Random House Australia (Pty) Limited
20 Alfred Street, Milsons Point, Sydney,
New South Wales 2061, Australia

Random House New Zealand Limited
18 Poland Road, Glenfield,
Auckland 10, New Zealand

Random House (Pty) Limited
Isle of Houghton, Corner of Boundary Road & Carse O'Gowrie,
Houghton, 2198, South Africa

Random House Publishers India Private Limited
301 World Trade Tower, Hotel Intercontinental Grand Complex,
Barakhamba Lane, New Delhi 110 001, India

The Random House Group Limited Reg. No. 954009

www.randomhouse.co.uk

A CIP catalogue record for this book
is available from the British Library

ISBN 9780224075213 (from Jan 2007)
ISBN 0224075217

Papers used by Random House are natural, recyclable products made
from wood grown in sustainable forests. The manufacturing processes
conform to the environmental regulations of the country of origin

Typeset by SX Composing DTP, Rayleigh, Essex
Printed and bound in Great Britain by
Clays Ltd, St Ives plc

For Oishi

There is a calm I haven't come to yet

'Disappear', REM

My moonstruck soul I now decide
To launch upon the whimsy tide

'Dream Song', Sukumar Ray
(translated from the Bengali
by Sukanta Chaudhuri)

Contents

YOU MUST LIKE CRICKET?

I

'Go, go, go, kill them!'

NOTHING IS LIKE that state of half wakefulness at seven in the morning after having stayed up late to watch India win a one-day international cricket match which you'd given up for lost. Absolutely nothing.

That's the trouble with writing about it.

It's not like waking up after great sex, the kind you've been wanting to have – *waiting* to have, with predatory intensity – for years and then suddenly found. It's not like the day after landing a first job or a flat or a car. It's not like waking up after you became a father for the first time.

You instinctively know what it is *not* like. But when you try to make sense of what it *is* like, you're struggling for analogies. You're pushed into a corner trying to find an equivalent experience – something similar in degree, if not in kind – to approximate that sense of wonder, of residual thrill, that ludicrous relief, that goofy grin and absent-minded air of the morning after. In a way, it stands to reason: you can only explain it to someone who knows quite what it means.

Let's just put this on record then. Watching India

clinch a tight one-day game is comparable with one thing: watching India win a Test match. (Now *that*, to think of it, is *better*.)

Maybe casting about for a comparison is going down the wrong road. Maybe describing those moments is a better idea.

So here I am early on a Sunday morning (some hours after watching the NatWest Trophy final between England and India in July 2002), fresh with lack of sleep, light-headed with no booze from the night before and feeling like (oh no, there I go again), well, like I've watched an incredible game of cricket in which we went and did just the opposite of what we're terribly good at doing: we went and won a match that was nearly lost instead of going and losing a game that we'd all but stitched up. (The 'they' and 'we' are already beginning to get mixed up. Never mind, it will happen more and more. It is one of the things that makes a fan a fan.)

This is not the last time I'll repeat the details to myself. There are friends who care about these things; there are relatives who don't but will be forced to listen to them; there are the newspaper reports to dissect – all of them; the highlights of the game to watch; the repeat telecast of the whole match the day after and then of course the video. From *how* far outside the off stump did Yuvraj Singh pick the one which he hoicked over widish mid-on? What was Tendulkar *doing*, letting Ashley Giles get him again?

The details then bear repetition. At least, they do for me.

Six hundred and fifty-one runs in ninety-nine overs and

three balls for the loss of thirteen wickets. Marcus
Trescothick got a hundred. Nasser Hussain got a hundred.
Mohammad Kaif nearly got one. Sourav Ganguly and
Virender Sehwag scored 106 runs in ninety-two balls.
Yuvraj and Kaif put on 121 runs in eighty-five minutes.
India got the last fifty-nine runs off fifty balls. India won –
their first championship win in the last ten attempts.

Statistics are like skeletons. How they come about is the
flesh and blood of the game.

But for those of us whose minds the day after a game
like this are photocopy machines gone berserk, spewing
out identical images over and over again, everything
counts: the skeleton, the flesh, the blood, the breath, the
life. We want the whole damn package. Cricket for us is as
alive as the person we share our lives with.

My wife is stirring. Her hair is short and mussed up. I
roll over on my side and kiss the nape of her neck. It's a
good-natured peck, not an invitation with erotic charge.
It is distracted. She knows. Years of living together tells
her this. She's been through this – gone through with this.
She's promised not to mind. Not the day after. (She will,
when this goes on, this distraction, this preoccupation
with things that are not on her radar, there to a lesser
extent but still there a week from now. But that is a week
from now.) For now, she chooses not to mind. She smiles,
faintly. A flutter of eyelids as she wakes, as she senses,
immediately that it's a Sunday but not quite a regular
Sunday. She remembers last night. The game. She gets
up and pads towards the bathroom.

Our daughter is still asleep. She sleeps on her stomach,
her face towards me. My heart lurches whenever I look at

her like this. I never cease to wonder that I have had
anything to do with her being there at all. I don't move
towards her as I usually do. I want time to myself before
the day begins to unfold, before its ebb and flow pulls me
away from this total recall.

I reach for a cigarette. The coffee can wait. I lie on my
back and watch the ceiling turn into a giant television
screen.

*   *   *

Trescothick and Hussain are savaging the Indian attack.
A second-wicket stand of 185 off 177 balls is taking the
match away from India. And this in a final at Lord's – that
most English of English grounds I've always thought of as
the real home of cricket. Here was where the empire
struck back in a moment charged with history and irony
in India's most unforgettable one-day wonder, the 1983
World Cup final. And now this, at the end of a summer in
which the team has played magnificently.

The big guns (Sourav, Dravid and Tendulkar) have
fired; the talent of the new lot (Sehwag, Kaif, Yuvraj and
Zaheer) is undisputed so far; the side seems to have grit, it
has shown resolve, the guys are holding their nerves in
tight matches. Why, India is playing like Australia, damn
it. So it is doubly galling to see all this being thrown away,
being crushed by two men who couldn't care less about
what it would mean for us to lose this final after having
lost the last nine we've played.

Chokers. Again.

Kumble gets Trescothick. Flintoff – the guy who had

taken off his shirt and waved it at the stands and done a bare-chested victory lap at Mumbai's Wankhede Stadium last year – has joined his skipper and is keeping the run rate at around six an over. Hussain gets his hundred, his first in seventy-two international games. He gestures to the press (who haven't been his biggest fans); he points to the number 3 on his shirt. He means that he is – contrary to what certain commentators think – good enough to bat one down for England. The match is becoming one-sided enough to allow for the drama of such personal statements.

A flurry of late wickets (two fall with the score at 312) but they reach 325. No team has chased as many runs to win a fifty-overs international game. Not yet, at least.

Everyone has written India off.

My mobile phone trills. The first text message arrives during the lunch break. (It's late evening in India.)

'Buried again?' a friend from Delhi asks. He is a guy who studied at the best law school in the country and then decided to become a journalist. We'd met as two rival reporters on the same beat. We had common interests – like cricket. We became friends. That was a decade ago.

Since then, he has left journalism and gone back to law. We still have common interests – like cricket. We are still friends. His wife – like mine – has no passion for the game. He seems to have given her a choice: he'll either hit the bottle or watch every game he chooses to. She has chosen the cricket. He does not mind. It is a choice that he has engineered.

I decide not to answer.

'You're fucking watching or what?'

The beep is insistent. It demands a response. 'This is the season for miracles', I type out for the effect of the words, for the oracular quality they seem to convey rather than for any other reason. I don't believe in happy endings. I think I'm too old even to allow myself hope. We are agnostics, both of us.

'Fuck you. Should have gone out for a film and dinner.'

Trescothick's century is being replayed on the screen. So is Hussain's. Where they got their runs from, how many balls they took, which bowler they plundered for how much off how many balls.

Television has made cricket more scientific, more arithmetical, among other things. It breaks down the whole; it resolves the game into the sum of its parts. It gives you insights you wouldn't get at the ground. (Did you know that this is the ninth time that Tendulkar was out in the third ball of an over? Wow.) Some of it is useful. More of it is meant for the number cruncher. A lot of it is junk.

Statistics, as the Indian player-turned-commentator Navjot Singh Sidhu tells us till I want to strangle him, are like bikinis: they reveal as much as they conceal.

It works. And it doesn't. Because the whole of cricket is much more than a sum of its parts.

I watch. Fascinated. Appalled. India bat in less than half an hour.

*　　*　　*

Sourav and Sehwag walk out in the gathering glare of the floodlights. One commentator remarks – again! – how closely Sehwag resembles Tendulkar. Both are short, stocky, happy to use the bat as a bludgeon, and possess more talent than an entire batting order put together.

Why won't they leave Sehwag alone? He comes across as a polite, modest, unassuming guy and he doesn't speak much about this comparison business, but it can't be fun to be told all the time that you are like somebody else.

As Salman Rushdie said after people told him, post-fatwa, to get his appearance altered and to make a fresh start, get a new life, 'I don't want somebody else's life, I want my own.'

The English newspapers have been saying that there are so many Indian flags in the crowd you can hardly believe India is playing away from home. It has been that kind of a summer, really, that kind of a trophy. It's not just that the support for India has been unequivocal. The exuberance of the fans has rippled across the grounds till it has become a wave.

Not many of these supporters have come from India. Travelling to away games is a luxury because few have the money to get past the pound-rupee conversion rate (more than Rs80 to the pound). Most of them are migrants, second generation British Indians, dancing the bhangra, draped in tricolours, unambiguous about where their loyalties, at least on the cricket pitch, lie.

Is Norman Tebbit watching?

We're off. And away. India love to crumble when faced with a colossal total. But this evening, the openers are playing as though this is the first innings of the game, as if they are setting the pace of the match.

The hundred comes up within fifteen overs. Sourav is

batting like his real opposition is Sehwag: he, as captain, must outscore the new star. But it's healthy competition and England are beginning to droop. Hussain has that murderous expression on his face.

On the off side, Rahul Dravid had once said, there is God, and then there is Sourav. It's one of those days when you begin to think that on the off side, there is Sourav, and then there is God.

Another text message. This time from Chirantan, one of my closest childhood friends. He lives in Delhi these days, so we don't watch cricket together any more. We grew up together, went to the Eden Gardens together; once he picked his way through a tangle of outstretched legs to spit on a spectator who was obstructing our view.

He is a serious bloke, Chirantan. Serious about his cricket. He is in Kolkata for a few days and we had planned to watch a bit of the final together. Like old times. Now that doesn't seem like such a good idea. We're going to lose, I think. But Chirantan is undeterred. He is on the road and is asking about the score. The roars coming from inside the houses of the middle-class neighbourhood through which he is driving tell him that India's reply has begun well.

The streets are deserted this Saturday evening. If you had taken a walk when the game began (as I did), you would have thought it was a public holiday. As the England innings progressed, the city seemed to turn in on itself, becoming quiet and introspective. You could hear the commentary from every television set inside every flat in every borough across the city.

In the impoverished neighbourhoods, where large

families can't afford their own TVs, money has been raised to hire sets for the duration of the tournament. It's common in Kolkata when championships like this one are on; it's imperative when India do as well as they have been doing in England this summer. Gaggles of unemployed anxious young men squat in front of rented televisions propped up on cardboard packing cases or wooden crates. These men are the most outspoken, the most boisterous and uninhibited of India supporters; there's no middle-class self-consciousness to cramp their style. Or their vocal support.

But the England innings has shut even them up. This is not the Indian team's fault, they think, because most of them believe, in the great tradition of the sport they follow, that cricket is a batsman's game, tailored for batsmen, won or lost by them.

Perversely, the bowlers get away with a lot. These fans will not blame the bowlers for allowing the opposition to pile up an intimidating total. No, it's the batsmen's fault. Why couldn't they have got the runs when the other side did? Not today, though. This is beyond us, they murmur, this is beyond any team.

'106 for 0,' I write back. And then, 'Sourav, Sehwag on mission impossible.'

The headline writer in me always takes over on occasions like this.

'Will reach your place in half an hour', comes the reply.

Suddenly it all begins to go horribly wrong. Tudor gets Sourav; Sehwag perishes to Giles; Dinesh Mongia comes and goes; Tendulkar looks out of sorts and is then done in by Giles; and Rahul 'The Wall' Dravid, so immaculate, so dependable, crumbles.

From 106 for 0 to 146 for 5. Half the side out with the addition of forty runs.

'Score? Score?' Chirantan asks.

I don't bother to reply.

'And we're throwing it away again', writes my lawyer friend from Delhi. It's hard to bear the torment.

On television, a sanctimonious commentator calls for more resolve and discipline. He might as well have said 'India need more balls', or perhaps, to borrow a line from Eddie Murphy, 'more testicular fortitude'. That's what he meant anyway.

I don't want Chirantan to come over now.

I want to suffer this agony on my own, in silence. I want to grit my teeth, mute the volume and watch till the bitter end.

It's funny, this. Watching cricket with other fans, in a cheering, arguing group is something I love when things are going fine. Then we become part of this backslapping, beer-swilling clique, high on locker-room humour and memories of other victories in other games. 'Remember Sharjah 1998?' 'Oh no, this is more like Old Trafford during the World Cup.' 'Come on, Kanpur in 1989 was more exciting.'

We speak in a code of our own, throwing out dates and names, games and grounds, and each one of us knows what the other means. On those occasions, there is enough bonhomie to go around. Watching India win a game on my own is never as much fun as watching it with people who are as overwhelmed by it as I am. It fosters a sense of belonging like few other things.

But at home alone, jumping up and down in front of the sofa as victory nears is embarrassing. It makes me feel self-conscious. On the other hand, jumping up and down along with a whole lot of other people or hugging complete strangers at the ground makes perfect sense. In the mind of the fan who is scenting victory, there is always security in numbers.

But what happens when the game is slipping away, when India are on the brink of getting thumped? Then I just want to hide away. Watching becomes a masochistic activity, a secret anguish. Watch I must but I must watch in the privacy of my living room. It's a strange sort of protectionism. I can't bear to hear the players being sworn at. And I can't suffer the blackness of my mood being lightened by a casual remark, a stray joke. A perverse pleasure can still be a pleasure.

Defeat is not meant to be taken lightly. Whoever said you needed to be objective about the game? Whoever said it was *just* a game anyway?

The 150 has come up – still for five wickets – and I am about to call Chirantan to tell him that we ought to wait till the Test matches start. The bell rings. He is here.

'Tendulkar out?' he asks as he comes through the door. The collective groan from inside the houses as he drove past has confirmed his worst fears.

I don't reply. He flops down on the sofa.

Yuvraj Singh and Mohammad Kaif have come together. With 180 runs to get in twenty-six overs, they are cobbling together what the commentators call 'a semblance of resistance'. Yuvraj cover drives to the fence. Kaif pulls backward of square for four. These two are not taking any chances. We aren't seeing wild slogs here but percentage play, sensible cricket shots which are finding the gaps. Hussain still looks relaxed. In the pavilion, as the camera zooms on his face, Sourav's face is not even grim: it is empty.

What must it be like when you know that the cameras are zooming and a billion people across the world can see your private anguish? It happens only to sportspersons, perhaps, this live beaming of torment to the homes of so many strangers.

Giles's spell is coming to an end. Yuvraj – who is playing with a chipped bone in his finger – picks Giles's last ball early and carts it over midwicket for six. Twelve overs after the two came in, Tudor gets the treatment from Yuvraj: another six over midwicket. Things suddenly explode. Flintoff goes for three consecutive fours in the next over and Tudor is pulled again for six in the over after that.

Runs are coming in a flurry. So are the text messages. Channel 4 is showing the game in the UK and Indian friends who live there now are getting into the act.

The six-year-old in the house next to ours – you can see their living room through our window – is squealing, little fists punching the air and then slamming down hard on the divan on which he sits watching.

Chirantan is yelling, giving the springs of our old sofa a hard time. '*Chalo, chalo, chalo! Shesh kore dao!*' ('Go, go, go! Kill them!')

What is it, this paradox of watching sport, of turning an essentially passive pastime into something so active? In no other form of entertainment are we so much on the margins while being so much at the heart of the action, so utterly powerless to do anything about anything out there and yet so engaged with it, so keen to shape the course of events with our enthusiasm. Can you imagine going to a play and exhorting (insert your favourite actor's name) to act better? Could you seriously believe that your urgent plea will actually have any effect?

Kaif drives Tudor between cover and extra cover. Neither fielder has the chance to move as the ball rockets to the fence. Yuvraj pulls Paul Collingwood to the fence off the front foot, and then does it again to Ronnie Irani.

I am silent, a stone-faced counterpoint to Chirantan's stomping, screaming optimism. My stomach is constricted, the wall of my chest seems to be pushing upwards. It hurts. I always feel uneasy on these occasions. I cannot share my friend's hopefulness. V. S. Naipaul pinned down this anxiety most memorably – although in a completely different context – in his novel *The Enigma of Arrival*. He called it 'a dream of glory together with a general pessimism, a wishing to hope and a nervousness about hoping'. And so it is with me. I fear that if I dare to hope, what I fear will come to pass.

But the target has shrunk to less than sixty. I pump my fists and do a little jig for the first time. Not hoping for a miracle, not being carried away on the groundswell of this enormous optimism, is hard to resist.

No sooner do I sit down than what I fear happens.

Collingwood holds one back a little, Yuvraj picks the length wrong and tries to send it sailing above midwicket. The ball arches upwards in a parabola, Tudor gets underneath it and hangs on. The spell is broken.

Fifty-nine runs to get in fifty balls.

If you were to make a list of guys you would trust to bat for your life, not one of the men to follow would be on it.

I'm cursing myself. The rest of the room is quiet. Through my window, I can see my little neighbour sitting quite still. Only my lawyer pal is busy with the keypad of his mobile. The message arrives as Harbhajan takes guard. 'Do you still believe in miracles?'

I believe in Mohammad Kaif. The young man is so unfazed tonight, he maintains his composure with such grace that I won't be surprised to learn that he had an ice bucket strapped to his head beneath his helmet.

He rotates the strike, scampers the singles, keeps talking to Harbhajan, finds the gaps. India are inching forward. The gulf between the runs to get and the balls in which to get them is closing.

Harbhajan sticks around for a while, stodgy and cavalier by turns. Then Flintoff shatters his stumps. Kumble goes for a duck. Zaheer Khan is in and, with Ashish Nehra to follow, India have twelve to get.

Kaif is unperturbed. 'Mohammad scales the mountain', the *Wisden* website will report the next day and Kaif is up there, where the air is rarefied and breathing is difficult, just a few steps more to go before he can plant the flag at the peak.

And then we are in the final over and with four balls left and four runs still to get, Kaif finds the gap on the off side. We hold our breaths for the moment that the ball speeds across the green. It reaches the fence. Chirantan has knocked me to the ground and Sourav has leapt up, taken off his shirt and is waving it wildly, now he is on the field and on top of Kaif, the firecrackers are going off all around us in the streets of Kolkata and the noise of the supporters at Lord's is deafening.

A text message is coming in but it's not my lawyer friend. He has phoned. I'm on three phones at the same time – the one in the living room, the one in the bedroom and the mobile – and I'm saying the same thing, 'Yes, yes, it's fucking crazy, it's Lord's again, like nineteen years ago,' and the anguish and the agony of all those lost finals, the label of 'Chokers, again', are buried beneath the exultation and the tumult and all those voices from all those parts of the world saying 'We did it, we did it' over and over again.

* * *

Now, in the stillness of the morning, as I hear the water from the shower hit the tiles on the bathroom floor and watch my daughter turn over on her back and look as if she will wake, now is the time to think of things beyond the pitch, beyond the rerun of the images which have filled my wakeful night.

For a cricket match is nothing without its subtext. Its backstory is always a part of the real story. How about this for starters? An Indian captain takes off his shirt, and standing bare-chested on the balcony of Lord's he waves it with wild abandon. It's a gesture of reprisal directed at Flintoff who did much the same thing in Mumbai a year before. But the media will choose to see more in this than was perhaps intended. They'll question whether it is

'proper' for the skipper – an ambassador for a billion
people – to do what he has done.

But hell, Sourav is an ambassador for a new, young
generation of cricketers and cricket fans; he is tough,
aggressive and articulate. He is unlike any of his
predecessors. He is not humble, polite, undemonstrative,
middle class. Indian cricket has always had about it a sense
of elegant puckishness; about splitting cover and extra
cover without either fielder moving. It has always been
about silk. It has taken Ganguly to put the steel into it.

He sticks by his men and makes hard choices (dropping
a bowler like Anil Kumble, who has taken more than 450
Test wickets, if he feels he has a better – or more effective
on a particular day and under particular circumstances –
spinner at his disposal). And if he swears at his guys on the
pitch, they know that he bears them no grudges off it. His
men know he will never sell them down the river at a
selection committee meeting.

These are assets that are historically rare in Indian
cricket. Cricket teams in India have always been riven by
factionalism; factions of class (in the 1930s, when the
Maharajah of Vizianagram was the skipper, he is said to
have treated players from lesser lineage like little more
than his personal attendants), of regions, of loyalties.

Here now is the emergence of a new meritocracy. For
the first time we are seeing a captain stand behind his
players and the players stick up for the captain. Mansur
Ali Khan Pataudi, one of India's most successful and
adventurous skippers, once memorably said that a captain
can either lead from the front or push from behind.
Sourav has managed to do both.

If one can't recall any Indian captain waving his shirt from the Lord's balcony, one also can't think of any other Indian skipper who would throw his match-winning player to the ground in a rugby tackle and proceed to squeeze the breath out of him in a delighted embrace. Sourav has fostered a rare sense of togetherness. Watch this team play volleyball before the cricket begins. Notice them go into a huddle after the fall of every wicket. And you will begin to get a sense of why this side, when it is at the top of its game, is greater than the sum of its parts.

Here is another coincidence. At the very ground at which India won the 1983 World Cup final and first announced to the world that it could be as good as any nation in limited-overs international cricket, we now see them proclaim that they have a new outfit of spirited young guys who will be the future of the sport in this country. (To make the coincidence sweeter, the two who took India to victory – Yuvraj and Kaif – had won an Under-19 World Cup for their country not so many years before.)

For someone like me, who has grown up watching India lose more games than they have won, it is not just the victory itself that matters. It is the manner of it. It suggests that India are beginning to play their cricket differently. That they can absorb pressure, believe in themselves, be dauntless and ruthless.

Fans tend to make too much of one win (just as they tend to make too much of one defeat) but somehow this one really does have about it a sense of things to come. It means a lot to people like us who first started following cricket in the early or mid-1970s. It also means that my daughter or her friends, when they begin to watch India play, are likely to see a different India play.

If it lasts – and will it? That we can never know, only hope and see over the years – it implies a paradigm shift. (Already, in the spring of 2006, as this book is being wound up, the star cast of Indian cricket has changed. Ganguly is no longer captain. Tendulkar is not the player he once was. The narrative of cricket is continually evolving.) It is impossible to see things coming. Things change, the reality changes. But for fans, these individual moments of joy remain like reference points of truth and beauty within a larger story.

*   *   *

Cricket gives me – has given me for as long as I can remember – a sense of time: a certain feeling or event in my life is referenced with the memory of a particular game. It also gives me a sense of place. This may be an extraordinarily blinkered way to look at the world (and you have to be extraordinarily blinkered to have Queen's Park Oval flash across your mind the moment someone says Trinidad), but I think of cities in terms of their cricket grounds. It is the most enduring geography lesson I have ever had and it brings closer and makes familiar places with which I have little acquaintance. It is, I have found, something which gives my life a coordinate, a kind of centre amid the changing clutter of daily life with which it is so tough to keep up.

But most of all, perhaps, cricket gives me a sense of myself. They say you only get a sense of yourself when you see yourself in relation to another. Cricket is that great other.

It's like a relationship, this thing between the fan and his sport, some say. Well, only those who are not fans say that. Because it is not like any relationship that I've ever known. (It may be odd to be thinking about all this on the day after a historic win, but then historic wins are, well, historic because they don't come along too often. Usually, there is the routine stuff. And given that we are talking about Indian cricket, the routine stuff does not involve much winning.)

On the average day, it is a relationship that is too full of shame and humiliation, too unrequited and too committed at the same time, too like a one-way street. If my wife had let me down half as many times as India have on the pitch, I would have walked out on her. But when it comes to the game, I can never, however great the disappointment in the last match and however certain I am of impending doom in this one, bring myself to turn away.

Can you?

If you can, you are not one of us. Which, come to think of it, is not such a bad thing. Because you are spared the painful pleasure of being a masochist. All fans – the ones like me who *need* sport to give a sort of shape to life – are masochists. What else can you be when you switch on the TV at three o'clock in the morning knowing that your team is going to get a pasting – *again*?

For those of us who are too far gone, gone far enough in fact to embrace torment (we lost three-nil against Zimbabwe? No matter, throw us a defeat against

Bangladesh. We'll still watch. We'll be able to take it), it's not a choice. It's a compulsion. Addiction does not have rationality at its heart.

The pact between a fan and his team is sacrosanct. It cannot be broken. It is not like the colas or the cars or the credit cards or the car tyres the players endorse. Don't like it? Flush it down the toilet. Sell it off. Exchange it for something better. Buy a new one.

When things go wrong on the pitch, some of us go on mock funeral processions. Some of us threaten players' families. (The first gesture is banal; the second despicable. But morality or ethics is not the issue here; it seldom is when you are talking about addiction.) Still, few of us can stay away when our players walk out on to the field. Were we able to do that, TV ratings would slip and channels would not pay millions for satellite rights, companies would hesitate before pumping in billions to sponsor the team and soft-drink majors would worry about putting their money where the nation's heart isn't. The fact that they have not suggests that there are millions out there like me. Sometimes it feels like a brotherhood of misery.

Every fan realises this: feeling miserable is part of the deal. But riding the misery and sticking with it *is* the deal. You can't support another team (Namibia?), or suddenly be passionate about another sport (ice hockey?). It's this or nothing. And nothing is so much worse.

The morning after winning, though, is different – perhaps because it is so rare.

*   *   *

My wife emerges from the shower, draped in a couple of king-size towels. Her hair is lank, plastered on her skull. She looks achingly beautiful. I have never told her this though I suppose I am telling her now. Smell of soap and shampoo and body lotion. She catches me staring at her in the mirror. 'Are we going out for lunch or are you going to watch the highlights?' she asks. She thinks this is normal now; she has allowed for – and accommodated – the kink into the rhythm of this Sunday.

Before I can answer, the mobile begins to trill.

'Feels like a hangover.' Another friend.

Oh no it doesn't. I smile to myself. I type out my response quickly. 'Feels like nothing else on earth.'

2

'How does Sachin Tendulkar pronounce his name?'

IN THE AUTUMN of 1993, I spent a while as an intern at the London *Times*'s offices in Pennington Street. A friend of a family friend of ours in Kolkata, a veteran cricket writer, had given me a letter of introduction to the paper's Sports Editor. I was in London nearing the end of a journalism course and this was an opportunity like no other to gain what everyone in India called 'invaluable experience'.

It was one of the most memorable periods of my time in London. I revelled in the sense of self-importance it gave me. (Afterwards, I would often say, 'At *The Times*, they would have sweepstakes during an important football game'; or 'At *The Times*, some of the writers often work from home'; or 'At *The Times*, they always asked me . . .' – statements which were sometimes true, just as often made-up, but always prefaced with that phrase, 'At *The Times*'. This practice stopped only when I realised that a) people thought I was a crashing bore, and b) they didn't give a damn about how things were done at *The Times* anyway.)

I loved the hum and the busyness and the clutter of the

office, the talk of well-connected, experienced journalists and the subsidised canteen where I would have my lunch with plastic cutlery. I loved, I now admit with more than a fair amount of guilt, the array of telephones from which I could make frequent calls back home – a rare luxury which seemed more delightful because it was so furtive.

And of course I loved the assignments I used to be sent on. Finally, after the mock-ups I had had to do at journalism school, this was the real thing.

That autumn, Nigel Short was playing Garry Kasparov for the world chess championship. I was sent to one of the games to write a colour piece. I arrived outrageously early at the Savoy in my eagerness to get my first ever accreditation card – a blue name tag with black typed letters. I stood there in the foyer fingering the card's edges.

Suddenly I saw a small, lean man, familiar from his photos on the dust jackets of the books that lined the shelves of my room as a student. I couldn't believe my luck. I shuffled towards him.

'No, they haven't left any message, sir,' the thickset man from across the counter was saying. 'We don't have your name on this list. But I'll check again. Who did you say you were again?'

'Martin Amis.'

'Ah.' Thickset sucked the end of his ballpoint pen. 'Any proof of identification, sir?'

Amis shrugged. He looked bored. Then he produced his driver's licence.

As the official prepared Amis's name tag, I sidled up to him and extended my hand.

He was friendly and kind and looked pleased as I

babbled something about how I'd read everything he had
written. 'Oh, *The Rachel Papers*. I feel a little embarrassed
about it now. But I was young then, only twenty-three,
Soumya,' he said peering at my tag to get my name.

Soo-me-ah. That's how he pronounced it.

'It's pronounced Show-mo,' I said. 'Not phonetic.'

'Oh. Sou-mo.'

'No. The "s" is soft. As in "sugar".'

'I see. And is it always like that with Indian names?'

'No, not always.'

The tag was ready and Amis was clipping it on.

'So how does Sa-shin Tendulkar pronounce his name?'

'Sachin. You've got the "s" right. But the "ch" is
different. It's like in "champion".'

Amis smiled. Already, even while we were speaking, I
was rerunning the sequence of events inside my head,
planning how I would tell it in my letters home to my
friends. I was also, at the same time, running on fast
forward, imagining how Amis and I would become best
friends and have a drink together after a game of tennis.
This was experience, I thought then. This was what I had
come to London *for*. Later in the evening, he even gave
me his telephone number. Over the following weeks – to
my shame – I even called. On several occasions. I
invariably got his answering machine.

Afterwards, when the glamour had worn off, what
struck me most about that first conversation was how it
seemed to epitomise the English view of Indians. It would
be repeated time and again over the years. It's a surefire
conversational opener, a safe, neutral topic. If you're
Indian, you must be crazy about cricket.

Some of it has to do with the fact that it is the only game that India is really ever any good at. If you're Brazilian, you must be crazy about football. It is a stereotype we all acknowledge. Whenever I meet anyone from Brazil, I always ask why so many of their footballers have various versions of the name Ronaldo. One Brazilian woman I met in Mauritius replied, 'Dunno. I don't really watch football. I've lived in Baltimore all my life.'

India has been playing international cricket since 1932 but, in a way, it all started with the 1983 World Cup. The fact was that India did not merely win the tournament; it was the year which marked the beginning of India as a cricket superpower – and the gradual shifting of the game's heart, soul and bank balance from Lord's to Kolkata.

The image of India as a nation fixated on cricket became sharper during the 1990s. This was the decade in which perhaps the single most significant social change of recent years occurred in India: the arrival of satellite television. Cricket's viewing figures shot up, of course, but it wasn't merely about the numbers of people watching. Satellite TV made the game far more accessible and far more plentiful for the average fan. He could now, from his living room, just as easily watch the Ashes as the match being played in his hometown.

As viewing figures grew and the game became stronger, everybody wanted a part of it. Cricket was making incredible amounts of money from advertising and TV rights. In no time, and in a tournament being played outside India, billboards of Indian companies could be seen in the stadium. By the time the World Cup came around in England in 1999, several of the main sponsors – Hero Honda, LG, Pepsi and Emirates Airways – were targeting subcontinental audiences.

This, of course, was a period in which cricket was being marketed as a global game. With tournaments in non-Test playing nations like Canada and the Netherlands, the sport's reach was widening. The subcontinent played the key role in expanding its frontiers. India began to wield more clout in the running of the game as a whole. Jagmohan Dalmiya, one of its shrewdest administrators, became boss of the International Cricket Council.

Today, in the first decade of the new century, much of the money that keeps cricket financially healthy comes from India. According to *Time Asia*, of the $45 million that the England and Wales Cricket Board received for the right to show the 1999 World Cup, India and Sri Lanka accounted for more than half. And that was small beer. In the next round of deals, the ICC received $550 million for sponsorship and broadcast rights to two World Cups (2003 and 2007) and three champions trophies. This would not have been possible without advertising and satellite-TV money from the subcontinent. A huge chunk of the 1.25 billion global television audience for the South African World Cup was Indian.

TV gave the Indian fan not merely a more diverse menu; it offered his obsession wings. Suddenly, we were exposed to fandom in the international sense: faces painted in the country's colours, banners and placards, the Mexican wave and the chants. Seeing what our counterparts did in other parts of the world gave us a template. Young people going to the grounds in India or watching the game from their living rooms realised for the first time that there existed a code of conduct for supporters, liable to be adapted differently according to the demands of each ground or team, but a code of conduct nonetheless. (The Bharat Army, an indefatigable – and indefatigably good-humoured – band of expatriate Indian supporters who danced the bhangra at cricket grounds, was modelled on the Barmy Army.) Before long, fans – and players – from this part of the world began to realise that they were more crucial to the health and the future of the game than they had hitherto believed.

Nearly three decades ago, I considered any cricket played on the subcontinent as an approximation of the real thing. *That* happened on English cricket grounds. A seven-year-old Indian today believes that the game played on his home ground is the genuine stuff; all else is merely a watered-down version, a pale imitation of it.

The manner in which India has made cricket its very own – in terms of the money it generates, the frenzy it engenders and its intrusion into every area of public life, from pop culture to politics – is a marker of India's post-colonial present. Like the English language itself, cricket was a game that was made popular in India by the British. And like the English language, it has, over the years, been appropriated by Indians in a very Indian way. It is not just that cricket now touches more hearts and fosters more excitement in India than in the land of its birth. Even the enthusiasm – its pitch, texture and unbridled overflow – is very different on the subcontinent. (Multiply by one million the kind of atmosphere you get at an India game at an English ground and you are beginning to get there.)

The empire has taken England's national game, sub-
verted accepted notions of how fans respond to it and
turned it into something that is its very own.

When *Time Asia* ran a feature on the eve of the 1999
World Cup, it stumbled upon a touching, funny anecdote
that exemplifies how deep this idea of cricket being an
essentially Indian sport has now taken root. The magazine interviewed a young boy, Sukhdev, who played, in
front of an admiring, unemployed audience, a serious
game of cricket in the shadows of Delhi's Red Fort.
'[Sukhdev] is confused about where the game originated;
he believes it began in the subcontinent. "The English,"
he says, "must have stolen it from us."'

The advertising industry – always a prism through
which social trends are reflected – was one of the first to
cash in on this. A slew of brands began to use cricketers as
ambassadors. And as they successfully raised the sales of
colas or credit cards, they began to be seen as sure bets for
commercial success, even if the products they advertised
had little to do with the game. Driven by the millions he
made from endorsements, Sachin Tendulkar became the
world's richest cricketer. Cricket was no longer a game
any more. It had become Cricket Inc.

Followers sensed that the cricket pitch was one arena
(perhaps the *only* arena) in which India could hold its own
against the rest of the world. It is a situation which has not
much changed in the twenty-first century.

Today, India is an emerging economic superpower.
Jeffrey Sachs, special advisor to UN Secretary General
Kofi Annan on millennial development goals, said in a
recent interview that 'India is poised to become one of the

three large economies of the world. By the mid century I think India could overtake the US by absolute size.'

But this is only part of the story. Seventy-two per cent of India's population still lives in the hinterland, many of them in shocking deprivation. That is why, despite its growing global status in information technology, India has, according to a recent study, eighty-four television sets per thousand people (America has 938); why it has 7.2 personal computers for every thousand people (Australia has 564.5); and why the internet reaches only two per cent of the population (in Malaysia, that figure is thirty-four per cent).

The gulf between the educated, urban elite and their fellow countrymen in the vast rural hinterland is widening by the day. Cricket has become their only common ground. For the urban rich, more than anything else, cricket has fostered a strong sense of national identity. For many people my age or younger, who have grown up in an independent country and are too distanced from the pangs of either Partition or the thrill of not being under Raj rule, the game has become the most triumphant mirror of the ideas of nation and patriotism.

But for millions of Indians (the ones who live on minimum wages, never take holidays, have no other avenue of entertainment and can only afford merely a community television on which to watch the matches), exulting in the success of eleven men on a green field is as close as they will ever get to success. These Indians are not proud of their city/town/village, their politicians, their backgrounds, their careers; they have little to look forward to in terms of what their country might have to

offer them or what they might be able to give themselves.
They have only the cricket.

Any outsider on a visit to India can see them – watching
the game on their community TV, standing in a huddle
with their noses pressed to the window of an electronics
store, attending a victory procession after the game is
won. They can see what all this is about. And they will go
back home and talk about it in wonder.

*   *   *

In the winter of 1993, I surprised myself for the first time
in my life with the intensity of my obsession: on impulse,
I took a plane from London to watch the final of a limited-
overs tournament back home in Kolkata. And yet, it was
not quite entirely on impulse. It might have been madness
(a lot of people told me that it was certifiably loony, that a
passion for the game was acceptable, likeable even in an
innocent, pleasant way, but travelling from London to
Kolkata to watch a game was taking it a bit too far) but
there was some sort of method to it.

On the occasion of its diamond jubilee, the Cricket
Association of Bengal had put together a one-day
championship involving India, Sri Lanka, West Indies,
South Africa and Zimbabwe. It was called the Hero Cup.
The final, scheduled for 27 November at the Eden
Gardens, would cap three weeks of high-quality cricket.

At first, it had just seemed like a nice idea. Then, as I
began to think about it, it became clear that my longing to
be there need not remain merely a longing; it could
actually be done. Not very long after I first thought of it,

going back home for the cricket seemed the *only* course of action open to me.

Perhaps it was because I had not watched much cricket involving my country for a long time. (India had played only Sri Lanka in Tests during 1993.) But when I decided to buy my ticket I had no idea that India would actually make the final. So it must have had more to do with watching cricket *in* India than watching India play.

The distance I had put between myself and cricket in India in physical terms had strengthened the emotional bond between myself and the game; it had sharpened my desire to see the game in India, to see, with new eyes, how much of what I said about it to my English friends was accurate.

Haven't people done more inexplicable – and worse – things on a whim?

It was quite a price to pay, it turned out, for a whim. Especially for someone who ate only a banana for lunch every day for a month to raise the money for the ticket. The travel agent, a Bangladeshi, had his cramped, airless office off the Bayswater Road. He sat behind a chipped Formica desk and swivelled around to the calendar tacked up behind him when he heard my request.

The chair squeaked when he turned. One of the wheels did not work. The venetian blinds at the other end of the room were crooked. One of the slats was missing, letting in the feeble November sunlight.

He scratched his chin and said it would be difficult, getting a ticket now, at such short notice in the winter when so many Indians were travelling back home, and asked if it would do to leave a fortnight later. When I explained that I didn't merely want to go but in fact *had* to go on precisely the date I said, he conceded that it could be arranged, through great enterprise and resourcefulness on his part. Besides, as a fellow Asian, he promised me a discount. He booked me into an Aeroflot plane from Heathrow to Dum Dum airport.

Only later, when I compared prices with Bengalis that I knew in London, did I realise that he had ripped me off. But that afternoon, as I walked out of the agent's office and into the stream of traffic on the Bayswater Road, my heart was singing. I had a ticket to the final at the Eden.

My parents were aghast when I told them. Many of my friends back home thought it was some kind of a joke. But those I knew in England did not find my plan as outrageous as I had imagined they would. My tutor, an Australian who was a member of the MCC, felt the break would do me good. And that this was as good an excuse to go home as any.

Now it seems to me that what I was doing was, in a way, expected of me by the people I had come to know in England. It fitted the notion that they had of the Indian cricket fan who would go to any lengths to satisfy his desire to watch a match at his home ground. It made them feel vindicated; it confirmed what they thought they knew: if you're Indian, you must be crazy about cricket.

*　　*　　*

To make my homecoming sweeter, India reached the final. But the real cracker of a match – the match that became part of Indian one-day cricket lore and added to

the myth that Sachin Tendulkar was already becoming –
was the game India played against South Africa at the
Eden on 24 November.

I was on the plane at the time.

I heard and read all about it once I'd landed. In fact,
my parents – who by the time I arrived had overcome
their reservations about my trip and were overjoyed at
this sudden opportunity to see me again – recounted the
details to me as we drove home from the airport.

I saw the rerun later on TV. South Africa fielded first.
India ran up a meagre 195 in the full quota of fifty overs.
Mohammad Azharuddin, in sublime touch throughout
the championship, scored ninety off 118 balls in that
cavalier-careless-caressing manner that only he had with
the bat. (It was so calming, so de-stressing to watch him.
It always is, I suppose, when you see something so awfully
difficult being made to appear so ludicrously simple.)

When the visitors began their reply, Anil Kumble and
Ajay Jadeja quickly pegged them back. And despite a
valiant sixty-two from Hudson, South Africa came into
the final five overs needing forty-five to win the game. But
they fought back, and with one over left they needed just
six to win. As skipper Azharuddin and the seniors – Kapil
Dev, Prabhakar – went into a huddle to decide who
should bowl those final make-or-break six balls,
audacious, unfazed-by-the-big-occasion Tendulkar, only
twenty-two, walked up and asked for the ball.

Azharuddin gave it to him, though it was never
absolutely clear if he did so because he had pretty much
run out of options, because it was a tactical master stroke
or because he was too taken aback by Tendulkar's guts.

In any event, Sachin had the ball. Fannie de Villiers was run out off the first delivery coming back for a second run, and South Africa's last batsman, Donald, came in. Sachin bowled three consecutive dot balls. Off the fifth, Donald and McMillan scampered a single. McMillan managed only one off the final ball, leaving India winners by two runs.

Those three successive dot balls, the nerve, the gall, the extraordinary steeliness to take on that final over in front of a capacity crowd in such a game, these were the blocks that went into building Tendulkar the hero. Valiant. Selfless. A doer at the death.

After that game, no final could come close in terms of the excitement. And the match itself was a bit of an anticlimax.

India batted first on a crumbling wicket and, after a good start, lost their way in the middle overs. Azharuddin stroked a cameo of thirty-eight and Vinod Kambli (who has now left cricket to make a career for himself in India's other mass passion, films) held the innings together with a sixty-eight from ninety balls. India reached 225 for 7 and when the West Indies came in, 100,000 spectators at the Eden were looking forward to a contest.

Brian Lara's dismissal opened the floodgates. From 57 for 1, the Caribbeans went on to lose their remaining nine wickets for only sixty-six more runs. Anil Kumble picked up the last six wickets for four runs, in six overs and two balls.

In the end, India won by 102 runs. Not too many people minded that it had been so one-sided. The chanting and the singing that began in the stands of the

Eden carried on well into the night in streets across the city.

We would not recognise how much we would cherish this win (and for how long we would have to do so) until a few years later. It was the last tournament victory India would manage at the Eden in the twentieth century. And this would be (perhaps because India won so convincingly) the last time for many years that a big game would end in Kolkata without crowd disruption.

In my case, nothing was about to take the sheen off the joy of watching India win, especially having travelled thousands of miles merely to see a final at home. It seemed like something a schoolboy dared not have wished for had he been imagining the perfect end to a fairy-tale quest.

But there were disturbing undercurrents to my happiness.

Lying awake in bed that night, I tried to figure out how closely the Eden that I had seen that afternoon had mirrored the ground, cricket culture and ethos that I so enthusiastically spoke about to my friends in London. In November 1993, the Eden Gardens was still recognisable as the stadium of my childhood. There was no electronic scoreboard; no fibreglass roof; no new stand above the sightscreen opposite the pavilion; no air-conditioned boxes for corporate bigwigs.

Still, things seemed to have changed since I had last watched cricket there. Then it struck me that perhaps they hadn't. Perhaps I had simply failed to notice the changes before. Or more plausibly, perhaps I had edited them out of my memories because they were so unwelcome.

The bloodthirsty cries of '*Jeetega jeetega, India jeetega*' ('India will win, India must win'); the rapid consultation with the radio commentary to check a player's name; the booing when a perfectly good ball was not scored off; the applause for the slashed four that just eluded the out-stretched finger of the fielder at third man: all these had not been mentioned in my accounts abroad of a prelapsarian Eden. I suspect I knew that the serpent had already slithered into the garden; I had chosen not to notice it.

There were other reasons for my selective representation. I had not, for instance, ever mentioned the growing number of unruly spectators in the members' stands to the right and left of the pavilion. I mean, who's bothered about them? Not an Englishman who wanted a picture of cricket in India. Those details were too minor, too insignificant, not part of the larger picture, I'd thought. Best to gloss over them.

My stories, I now realise, were a means of escape. I was expected to narrate – excitedly – tales of charm and fervour and clean, wholesome enthusiasm about cricket on the subcontinent. And that is what I had done. I had been playing my part by conforming to the notion of the stereotype. I had chosen the easier route. (In a place so far from home, with people I knew so little about, it had seemed the *only* route.) By trying to present the stereotype, I had become a stereotype.

In a sense, of course, I'd been deluding myself. But it had been partly because somewhere beneath the threshold of my consciousness, I had wanted it to be true. Just so. The correspondence between the ideal and the reality.

But that night at home, with the delirium of the victory just beginning to wear off, in the familiar darkness and the comfortable shadows of the room in which I had spent so many years of my life, I knew that things were not quite what I often made them out to be.

It was a great help, that realisation, that ticking over of the scoreboard of reality. Because when in later years the Eden officially fell from grace – again and again – and when crowds stopped play and the idea of this being cricket's paradise in the subcontinent was gone for ever, I was ready for it.

I had been waiting. But when it came, it was still hard to take.

* * *

The bunks are slatted planks of rough wood from which the paint has long peeled. The lights – the few of them that have not been stolen from behind their wire casings – do not work. The floor is so strewn with the detritus of unhealthy mini meals – greasy paper packets, bits of decaying raw onion, squidgy dices of tomato, decapitated shells of peanuts – that you have to pick your way gingerly to get to the toilet, the door of which swings open with every judder of the train.

Second-class travel on the Indian railways is all about endurance and stoic fortitude. And about not having enough money to go first class or in the air-conditioned compartments.

It is the autumn of 1989. Along with a few resilient and intrepid friends (all as short of cash as high on the desire

to go backpacking), I am returning to Kolkata after a
fortnight of travel in the hill stations of north India. The
train trundles through the heart of Uttar Pradesh, India's
largest state. We have, all of us, slept fitfully. We are, all of
us, tired of the slumming of the past fortnight and of each
other's company.

For once, we are looking forward to going home.

A group of six young men gets on at one of the stations.
Before we can react to their intrusion, they have pushed
us aside – the shoulder thrust is admirably effective in
such circumstances, especially when it is combined with
the surprise factor – and occupied most of the space that
had been allotted to us. They are travelling without
reservations. Aggression, we soon realise, is the only
capital they have. They want to cash in on that.

Pushed into corners, bristling with impotent rage and
eager to retaliate without having the means to do so, we
attempt a feeble retort or two. They elicit more aggression. It is the rule of the street fight. (Only, there's hardly
any fight here. Or at least not much of a fightback.) Get
the first blow in, keep up the pressure, instil fear in the
heart of your opponent. Fear will be your strongest ally. If
your opponent fears you, you can get away with pretty
much anything, never mind whose side the law is on.

We are terrified of this rowdy bunch of north Indian
men, barely older than us but appearing so much more
formidable, so much more menacing and well equipped.
It's hardly a contest. They abuse us for no other reason
than that they can. They keep pushing us, keep squeezing
us out of our seats so that eventually we feel grateful for a
few square centimetres.

And then, one of my friends performs a miracle. I still don't know how he managed the manoeuvre: bending forward and extracting a transistor from a backpack without toppling off his precarious perch. But he does – with rather a flourish; I remember the flourish – and begins to twiddle the knobs.

India are playing England in a one-day match at Kanpur, not very far from the area through which we are passing. The commentary comes on.

The effect is spectacular. I don't know if you have seen those films in which explorers win over tribes by showing them colourful trinkets. The effect that the radio had on our unwanted guests was exactly the same.

Thank heavens for Chetan Sharma. I have never otherwise – either before or after this particular incident – had cause to say these words. (And by the way, thank heavens for not having had to say 'thank heavens for Chetan Sharma' ever again.)

Krishnamachari Srikkanth, as mercurial in his captaincy as in his batting (and not even as occasionally inspired), had gambled by sending Sharma in at the fall of the second wicket.

Which was when the commentary came on in our crowded compartment, amid the unequal battle.

Everything goes quiet for a while. It's hard to tell what has more surprised our fellow travellers: that we have managed to conjure up a radio; or that a penultimate-over slogger has walked in at the fall of the second wicket.

Then, as Sharma puts on 105 for the third wicket with Sidhu (sixty-one from sixty-seven balls), our invaders begin to behave as though they are our guests. They back off and create space for us to sit (one of them actually squats on the floor – a gesture that is accompanied by a request to turn up the volume of the transistor) and before long we are behaving like an amiable bunch of teenagers listening to cricket commentary at a street corner.

By the time Sidhu is run out and Vengsarkar comes in, India have reached 170. Sharma is on his way to an improbable century. He hits, he misses, he is dropped, he narrowly escapes being run out.

One of the young men is unscrewing the cap of a bottle of cheap rum and holding it out for me. That sort of rum raises quite a stink but it is possible, now, to pass it off as the scent of victory.

Vengsarkar sticks around long enough to bring India within a boundary of triumph. Kapil Dev, ever the buccaneer, sends the first ball he faces rocketing to the fence. Scores level.

One of the youths is doing the bhangra. I am clapping. So are my friends, though it is not immediately clear – and still is not after more than a decade and a half has passed – whether it has more to do with the relief of approaching victory or with the relief of having defused a particularly nasty situation.

With a four off Gooch, Sharma reaches his century – off ninety-six balls with eight fours and a six – and wins the game for India.

We pass the bottle around. Before they get off some hours later, the six young men give us their addresses and phone numbers. They leave us with standing invitations to look them up should we ever visit their hometown.

*　*　*

Perhaps sport's biggest gift to its followers is the sense of belonging and togetherness that fandom engenders. All through the 2003 World Cup, I thrilled to the notion of following the cricket on the internet with people from different time zones, people who were mad enough to want to catch the latest news of Pakistan and Holland at seven in the morning and exchange comments about the proceedings. This sort of behaviour (I mean, a New Zealander following Pakistan versus Holland at seven in the morning?) lies at the heart of being a cricket obsessive. And the fact that there are so many of us makes us all feel that much better.

A hankering for this sense of togetherness makes us want to go to the stadium. It's why watching a game at the pub has always been so popular in England; why watching it with a lot of others in restaurants or bars or on the street in front of a television propped up on cardboard boxes is becoming just as popular in India.

Feeling part of a tribe makes us feel less odd, less mad, less of a curiosity. It makes waking up on match day with an empty feeling in the pit of the stomach seem, well, normal. Being an addict is only fun when people around you aren't on the wagon.

* * *

Everyone says cricket is like a religion in India. It isn't. Religion led to the partition of India (into India and Pakistan) more than half a century ago. It led to riots in Mumbai in which thousands of people died. It led to a pogrom against Muslims in Gujarat in this century.

Religion has led to some of the deepest scars that India carries in its heart. Cricket is the balm that heals.

Cricket is not like a religion in India. But if there is something – hypothetically – that makes the nation one, that thing ought to be likened to cricket.

At one time, it was Hindi movies. Assemble a roomful of Indians. Carefully select your candidates so that they come from different parts of the country, have different mother tongues, dissimilar backgrounds and belong to social classes that are so different that they will find it impossible to imagine the life of the man or woman sitting opposite. Once upon a time all the disparities would dissolve as soon as the topic of the latest Amitabh Bachchan blockbuster came up. (As a matter of fact, in such circumstances, the subject of the Amitabh Bachchan movie would never casually *come up*; it would be deliberately raised because it was the only thing both sides would – could – ever have in common.)

All that has changed since the late 1990s. Bollywood movies are no longer as inclusive in their appeal as they once used to be. Many film-makers tailor their films according to the audience they want to reach. The movies that are a hit with the educated, affluent urban audience who go to watch them in gleaming multiplexes are not the movies which have successful runs in the small towns and villages. Both kinds of cinema belong to Bollywood (they are both mainstream, popular, mass-market entertainment) but the one sort has next to nothing in common with the other. As the young actor Zayed Khan admitted in a newspaper interview, 'There are people who pay Rs20 to watch a film [in the hinterland] and people who pay Rs200 [in the urban multiplexes]. They can't possibly like the same sort of film, can they?'

These days, what your roomful of Indians will have in common will be a game. Cricket, already a consuming – and ever growing – passion, has swallowed up the space that Bollywood once occupied in India's collective consciousness.

But cricket isn't *like* Bollywood. And it certainly isn't *like* religion. Cricket is unlike anything else in India. It is its only analogy.

3

'How can a grown man drop his pants like this?'

Three reasons why cricket bats and balls made of paper are just great: their source is inexhaustible; they require no investment (they are just about free, actually); and they do their bit for recycling and the environment.

My parents are not the most eco-friendly of people (my father is the sort of man who drives to the park for his morning walk and thinks that 'going green' is a polite way to talk about jealousy) but it was paper bats and balls when it was time for my cricket education to begin.

I was a little over four years old then and we lived in a subsidised first-floor flat on Bolsover Street in west London. It was close to the Royal National Orthopaedic Hospital, where my father was working for a year. The address was posh but it wasn't really a reflection of our bank balance. My parents later told me that they had to scrounge for everything that year. There was little money for luxuries. There was so little money, in fact, that buying a small cricket bat for your child seemed like a luxury.

Hence my mother's brainwave with used sheets of paper.

Making the balls is simple enough. You need to scrunch the paper up tightly, turning loose ends inwards and packing them in so that the ball becomes as airtight as possible. Then you tie a piece of twine around it, taking care to snip off loose ends of the thread. The bats are more complicated. The paper is crushed and twisted to make the grip. It has to be broadened further down for the blade. And then the ends need to be smoothed and lightly cut to attain the shape of the bottom of the bat. Three decades on, my mother can still make those bats. They look strikingly real. And they aren't half bad for thwacking a paper ball.

This was my first encounter with cricket. And that Bolsover Street flat – so close to Lord's – was where the encounter took place. Unlike most other Bengalis, my father did not perform the initiation rites for me: he was away at work most of the time. My mum did. The other, more compelling reasons were that my mother was – unusually for most middle-class women in the pre-satellite TV generation – an authentic cricket freak: and she needed to give me something that would keep me quiet.

I insist I remember the flat – especially the strip of carpet between the sofa and the TV which became my first pitch. My parents, however, tell me that I am passing off as memory what I remember of the stories they have told me over the years. (Have they ever told me about the indentations on the carpet where the previous occupants must have kept some item of furniture – a heavy-legged stool or table, perhaps? Or the corner of the room where the wallpaper, just above the TV, was a shiny rectangle because our predecessors had hung a picture there?)

For me, the television itself was an object of fascination. I used to stare at it, unblinking, even after it had been switched off, watching the screen lose its glow, become a dimming pinpoint of light and then turn utterly blank. There was no television in India at the time – that you could press a switch and get moving pictures and sound simultaneously seemed magical. And it was through the TV in the summer of 1974 that I was properly introduced to cricket.

Watching the cricket on TV with my mother (trying to match it to the game she'd taught me on the carpet) seemed like an immensely important thing to do. It wasn't like having *Play School* or *Scooby Doo* on – mum would watch with me but I knew she was doing it out of a sense of kindness or duty. When cricket was on TV, she genuinely *wanted* to watch. Sitting there side by side (before or after practising in the living room) was an activity that drew us together like no other. When we watched *Play School* it seemed as though my mother was stooping to my level; watching cricket gave me a sense of expanding, of rising to the occasion and growing (growing *up*).

So that first summer was wonderful. Apart from the actual cricket. Which, as far as India were concerned, was appalling.

When India arrived in England, it had a team that seemed to be at the peak of its prowess. Over the previous three years, the Indians had beaten the West Indies in the West Indies and England at home and away.

My parents, who had not been in England for India's victory in 1971, were looking forward to the series. From my mother's excited exclamations and hurried preparation of lunch on the first morning of the first Test at Old Trafford, I gathered that something very special was about to unfold.

India lost the first Test by 113 runs.

By the time the team came to London for the second Test at Lord's, my parents' exuberance had subsided somewhat. Before the series began, they had been smirking as they went about their daily rounds: hospital, grocer's, newsagent's, school, supermarket. 'Just wait. Wadekar and his men are here. They'll show you a thing or two about cricket.' That first Test had wiped the smile off their faces.

In retrospect, especially given how the summer turned out, I feel so sorry for them – this couple in their thirties from one of the world's poorest countries clinging on to the hope that eleven men in white would let them hold their heads high in the land in which they now lived. They came from a country which had none of Britain's creature comforts and affluence. Here, they were there as poor relations in every sense. And they were often faced – despite the best and kindly efforts of many of the English friends they had made – with contempt and condescension. Cricket would help them to get level.

Somehow, my parents had expected the Indian cricket team to exemplify the best of what India had to offer. They wanted to see the empire strike back.

The Lord's Test told them that they would have to wait a while longer. England won by an innings and 285 runs. And the summer of 1974 became the 'Summer of 42'.

England won the toss and batted, rattling up 629,

powered by centuries from Amiss, skipper Denness and
Greig. India replied with 302 and followed on. No one
had expected the capitulation to be so abject. With only
Solkar reaching double figures (eighteen), the Indians
were all out for forty-two in the second innings.

The defining moment of the summer had come. For
my parents, it was shocking. Did the fact that the
humiliation was happening merely a few postal districts
away as they watched it on live TV make it any worse?
They didn't say. It was, though I didn't identify it as such
then, my first taste of the bitterness and the sense of
betrayal that a sporting defeat can engender.

I do know that for the rest of the summer, my parents
never brought up cricket when they spoke to English
people. But the guys at the hospital, grocer's, newsagent's,
school and supermarket were only too keen to talk about
it. 'Don't worry. It was too cold. Your spinners couldn't
grip the ball. It will be better in Edgbaston.'

It wasn't. India lost this one by an innings and seventy-
eight runs, making it a three-nil whitewash.

Unlike my parents, at the time I felt no shame. There's
something about children that makes them want to be on
the winning side. (Well, adults do that too. Only, they
don't always admit to it.) As a four-year-old living in
England, I had no specific fondness for India. I knew that
was where I came from but I had neither any vivid
memory of it nor any particular association with it. Home
was where your parents were. India's loss on the pitch
didn't result in a loss of prestige for me as it did for my
parents. The notions of nation, pride and belonging still
meant nothing to me. I saw my parents were hurt but

couldn't quite understand what the fuss was all about. More than Gavaskar or Wadekar, I was keen to watch Denness or Lloyd or Amiss bat. They were the ones who got the runs, so they were more fun to watch. It made perfect sense.

Two important things from that summer. First, cricket and I had made friends, though we hadn't yet gone all the way. It was fun but just another thing one did in the summer holidays. (It would be a few years before it would become all I did: the rest of life was what happened between overs.)

Secondly, I found my first cricketing hero: Mike Denness. It was a fleeting fling and did not last beyond that year. But I still have something to show for it: it's what my mother calls my 'Mike Denness jumper'. It's a V-necked chocolate and beige thing. After the end of the series, Denness gave a TV interview wearing it and I made my mother knit an almost identical one for me. It's still inside a suitcase, stuffed with mothballs. My mum plans to give it to my daughter once she finds her first cricket hero.

It's my relic from the 'Summer of 42'.

*　*　*

Bankura, a small town several hundred kilometres away from Kolkata, is remarkable only for being unremarkable. Or at least that is how it used to be in the mid-1970s, when we moved back to India. A little over a year after my introduction to cricket, a little over a year after living in the city of Lord's and the Oval, I found myself in a town many hours' train journey from the nearest international cricket stadium (the Eden Gardens in Kolkata) and where the only link with live cricket was a short-wave radio set I was incredibly privileged to possess.

Bankura: if you pronounce it right, in the proper Bengali way (not the way the English spelling on this page suggests you pronounce it), the name, with its emphasised nasal consonant and the rolled 'r' at the end, sounds – for want of a more apposite word – provincial.

I hated the name when I first heard it. I hated it even more when I learnt that we would be stuck there for at least a couple of years.

'Sounds awful,' I told my mother. I think what I really meant was that it did not sound like London at all.

You'd imagine that the friendship that I was just beginning to forge with cricket – in the desultory, casual, okay-I-might-be-interested-if-we-took-this-further way that most of my enduring friendships in life have begun – would just shrivel up and die in an environment that had everything to discourage its growth.

Quite the opposite.

My lifelong affair with cricket blossomed in Bankura not despite the lack of real action but *because* of it. Testosterone-crazed adolescents may not be getting any but they can't help thinking about it all the time ('If the wank mags are this good, how much better can sex be? How many *times* better?'). Just so with me and cricket. I became obsessed with the game through radio commentary and pictures in black-and-white magazines and heroic re-enactments of whole Tests in our backyard ('If listening to a match at Lord's can be like this, how much better would it be sitting there on a summer afternoon, with the slope at the Nursery End in front of me?').

In Bankura, I too fell in love, but it wasn't quite the heady, blood-pumping thing conjured up by pulp fiction or frothy movies. There was an element of inevitability about it, prompted, I suspect, by the lack of any other choice.

You didn't go out with friends in Bankura (there was nowhere to go to). You didn't watch TV (there was no television). You didn't listen to music (there was no music store to buy tapes from). You didn't go to the cinema (there was one cinema in the town and not once, in the two years that I spent there, did they show anything remotely resembling a film which my parents would let me see). You didn't read much (the two bookstores sold school textbooks. Anything else had to be brought back from Kolkata on our occasional visits).

Under the circumstances, the only avenue of entertainment was cricket. Even though I was nowhere close to the real action, at least I had the radio, newspapers, magazines. They were enough to keep me up to date. More than that, they told me everything I could want to know. For a six-year-old boy in Bankura, cricket was perhaps the only thing you could say that of.

Not surprising, then, that that boy would grow up to be a little dysfunctional. His world view would be shaped by something which is (as cricket's detractors love to say again and again) *just* a game.

To me, cricket wasn't *just* a game then – and hasn't been ever since. It was life.

* * *

There is a theory in contemporary Indian cricket to explain why most of the current crop of young players – Virender Sehwag, Harbhajan Singh, Mohammad Kaif, for instance – come from satellite towns or small villages and not, as it once used to be, the big cities.

The logic goes like this: unlike children in the big cities, boys from the suburbs and the countryside have no other outlet for their energy (no discos, no shopping, no video games, etc.), so they turn to cricket with unbridled enthusiasm. It is a theory I am utterly convinced by. For me, more than anything else, it has the ring of lived experience. The Najafgarh of Sehwag's childhood echoes the Bankura of mine. (The fact that Sehwag rebelled against the unrelieved tedium of his surroundings to become what he has become – one of the world's most attractive batsmen – and that I have rebelled against the experience to become what I have become – an obsessed moron who starts every time the Tube passes the Oval station – just goes to show why we have so many more critics than players.)

*   *   *

My parents' money went much further in this nondescript town than it ever had in London. We lived in a huge but badly planned single-storey house with an overgrown yard (the landlady had promised to have it weeded, cleaned and trimmed before we moved in). To the right of the yard was a driveway perfectly placed to become my first outdoor pitch.

My earliest memory of listening to cricket on the radio

is inseparable from my memory of this house – and this yard and this strip of ground that passed for a pitch. I remember sitting hunched forward on a cane chair in the living room, the red, untiled floor cool beneath my feet, the looping branch of a guava tree and a formation of homeward-bound crows like smudged lines against a darkening sky. In front of me was an old Grundig radio: a wedding present my parents had carried with them to wherever their fairly peripatetic married life had taken them.

The radio was more useful to them in Bankura than it had been anywhere else. (They, too, had no cinema to go to, no music stores to visit, no new books to buy, no clubs or bars at the weekend.) My father would twiddle the knob till he got the BBC. Short Wave 2, I remember. The voice of the commentators on *Test Match Special* floated into the room, transforming it, and transporting us all.

Fred Trueman, Henry Blofeld, Brian Johnston, Don Mosey, Christopher Martin-Jenkins: I knew their names and their voices by heart. After I had thought about it enough (not difficult, there wasn't anything else I thought about as much), I attached faces and gaits and characteristics to them. I was certain I would be able to recognise any of them if I passed them on the street. (When I first saw a picture of CMJ, I realised, with a shock, that he didn't look a bit like what I had imagined. It was one of my first small lessons in the gulf between imagination and reality.)

I did not always understand the reasons for their sudden boisterous laughter, nor the jokes that led up to it. But the tone of humorous bewilderment during 'Richards, believe it or not, nought' was not beyond me. In those evenings in the gathering gloom of a backwater town in Bengal, they conjured up for me a beautiful notion of the game. And if I saw the game more through English eyes than Indian ones, there was double-edged irony to it: the curious clash of colonial and post-colonial values that I did not even comprehend.

By the end of that summer – the summer of 1976, when Viv Richards, single-handed, had taken it upon himself to dismember the England bowling (829 runs in four matches at an average of 118.43) after a certain pre-series remark from an Englishman in which the words 'grovel' and 'West Indians' had been used in close proximity – I knew the English grounds as though I had been to each one. All those grounds had become for me a sylvan utopia unsullied by reality.

Years later, as a student in Britain, I was taken to Lord's for the first time. I had been up the night before in a frenzy of excitement, and had dressed with great care in the morning. I still have a picture of myself in a tweed jacket (as English as I could make myself), maroon tie and white shirt, leaning against a board which said 'No standing when there is bowling at the other end', my face creased in the kind of grin that becomes the idiotic or the deranged.

Once we'd been through the Long Room and emerged on to the balcony of the members' bar (more photo-ops: from here, I could see the players' balcony from where Kapil Dev had held aloft the Prudential Cup in 1983) and I realised that the tour was over and that that was all there was to it, it all seemed terribly anticlimactic. The ground was not bathed in the sort of sunshine with which I had presumed Lord's always to be awash. (As a matter of fact, it rained for a large part of the day and we didn't get to see much cricket.) The grass did not seem as green as I had thought it would be. The slope at the Nursery End seemed to have a less of a gradient than I had imagined. What, I ask myself now, did I expect? A hill inside a cricket field?

And the players – county players playing an insignificant match on a rain-spattered afternoon – seemed to be going about their jobs with as much enthusiasm as the milkman doing his rounds in the morning. (Where was the veneration, the genuflection at the shrine of the game?) I wonder now what it was that would have made me happy. And I don't know the answer.

Lord's had been a construct of my imagination. It was a construct bred by the isolation in which I had listened to the radio commentary; by the clipped tones and accents which were so removed from my own; the remoteness of a place so far away that it was in a completely different time zone: and my fervent desire (beneath the threshold of my consciousness but no less strong for being so) to fashion another world, somewhere I could escape to from the surroundings I found myself in in the summer of 1976.

Now, at Lord's at the beginning of the 1994 county season, the *real* reality had stepped in.

* * *

Of course, much had changed in the intervening eighteen years. Perhaps, most noticeably, in the amount of cricket being played. In 1975, for instance, the world saw seventeen Tests. Three decades on, in 2005, that number was up to forty-three. Another example. In the 1970s, India played thirteen one-day internationals; in the 1980s, 155; in the 1990s, it was 257.

This surfeit has killed the sharpness of our memories. I still remember, in vivid detail, India's tour of the West Indies in 1976. Especially the third Test in Port of Spain: sitting up in bed till the small hours with my fingers curled around a mug of Bournvita and Dicky Rutnagur and Sushil Doshi on All India Radio; Brijesh Patel racing to his forty-nine not out during that incredible 400-plus run chase after Gavaskar and Vishwanath had scored centuries to lay the foundations for victory.

In contrast, when I try to recall India's 1996 tour of the Caribbean and the match that we ought to have won but collapsed and lost instead, I can't. Without looking at the scorecard, all I can say with any certainty was that Tendulkar was captain. And yet every ball of that Test was beamed live to my living room. I had watched. And I have forgotten. It has become one among the hundreds of matches that we see every year now. When my daughter watches cricket, she can, by flicking the remote, switch seamlessly between Brisbane and Bridgetown, Harare and Hyderabad. The rarity has vanished.

Along with the rarity, the preciousness and worth of a great performance have also diminished. Too many runs are scored now, too many wickets taken for even the most dedicated follower to keep track. (In the 1980s, Indian batsmen scored seventeen centuries in one-day internationals. In the 1990s, that number more than trebled.) With the spiralling numbers, we have had a spiralling number of superlatives; they have become the currency of daily use. For commentators now, every shot is magnificent, every catch is superb, every ball a beauty. Restraint and understatement, never easy qualities to achieve, have been wantonly sacrificed in the pursuit of excitement.

And there are the casualties too. Now that so much cricket is broadcast live, we are in the danger of losing something precious, namely imagination – the gift that still enables us to visualise Stan McCabe's 232 by reading Neville Cardus's description, the gift that made me fall in love with the game, the gift that makes us all become fans.

However, there may be signs of a revival. The delicious paradox is that while technology was once responsible for imagination's banishment, technology may be responsible for its return. And it is cricket commentary on the internet that has made this possible.

Like radio and unlike TV, ball-by-ball commentary on the net manages to create the notion of an inviolable world. It requires the fan to invest thought; it demands of him complete engagement and intelligence for its full enjoyment. From the words that keep coming up on the screen – furiously typed, with a sense of urgency that comes with the commentator trying to keep the reader up to date all the time (more difficult even than radio: it takes more time to write than to speak) – the fan has to conjure up his notion of what is happening on the pitch.

Television tells it like it is in real time; what you see on the screen is what you get. When you are following cricket on the internet, the report is coming to you at a remove: not only is there a time lapse between the report and the

events it describes but it is always filtered through the
eyes, brain and hand of the guy who is writing it. Far more
than watching cricket, listening to it (or reading a ball-by-
ball) engenders a rapport between the fan and the
commentator (or reporter). And if immediacy is, in a
sense, sacrificed, intimacy is gained.

Intimacy is the common denominator between radio
and the internet. But the net takes the idea of inclusiveness
further. It expands on the idea of sharing between
commentator and listener and creates a whole chat room
full of cricket-obsessed people.

Intimacy, inclusiveness and imagination: for me, these
are the things that make an obsession full-blown. I don't
know how many six-year-olds are cementing their love
affairs with the game by following it on the internet.

But they and I will be family.

*   *   *

In his absorbing book *A Season with Verona* (travel writing,
cultural studies, analysis of mob psychology and football
fandom all packed into a season watching the Italian team
Hellas Veronas fight relegation from Serie A), Tim Parks
reflects on the etymology of the word 'fan'. It comes, he
says, from the Latin 'fanaticus', which means 'wor-
shipper'. The team becomes the god; the fans become,
during matches, a sort of zealot, a 'weekend Taliban'.

By the time we returned to Kolkata from Bankura, I
had become that sort of a Taliban, a full-fledged cricket
fundamentalist. And as in London, my mother stoked the
flames of this fanaticism.

She taught me fielding positions by sketching a rough approximation of a cricket field, pencilling in first slip, third man, square leg. She subscribed, on my behalf, to a weekly sports magazine called – unsurprisingly – *Sports Week*. My first scrapbook of cricket pictures – mostly in black and white, mostly rather grainy – was culled from this magazine. She helped me snip out the pictures (the only pair of scissors in the house were huge – you could use them as garden shears or as a murder weapon – and I was too young to be left alone with them), let me muck myself up with a pot of glue, suggested artistic angles at which I should place my clippings and finally wrote imaginative headlines and captions for each player page in variously coloured felt-tipped pens.

All the while, I honed my game. Batsmen were my idols. I spent hours impressing our landlady's grown-up son by shouldering arms to balls outside the off stump. (A rare Indian quality, though I say it myself.) There was nothing restrained and passive about the action of leaving the ball, though. I left balls not with a wary uncertainty but with a contemptuous glare, arms swirling in an ostentatious arabesque.

Bowlers were my villains, a notion strengthened by the West Indian pacers' intimidating performance against India in the 1976 series. The grace and fluidity of a fast bowler's run up, the guile and subtlety of a spinner's art were lost on me. Bowlers were there, in my view, to allow batsmen to be heroes, to assume centre stage, to appropriate for themselves the pivotal – and most memorable – moments in the narrative of a match. In the two years in Bankura, I had batted and batted whenever I played and cried and cried (and was deemed young enough to get away with it) if someone knocked over my stumps or caught an ill-timed, cross-batted swat.

By the time I arrived in Kolkata again, all I wanted to do was watch a proper batsman in action on an international cricket field.

The time wouldn't be long in coming.

*   *   *

Block J at the Eden Gardens is one of the worst places in the world to watch cricket. It runs from about wide midwicket to deep backward square leg if the batsman is at the pavilion end, so you are about as well placed to see the turn of a ball or the authenticity of a shout for leg before or the swiftness of a batsman's reflexes as he pivots for a short-arm pull as you would be standing on the road in front of the stadium. Before the 1987 World Cup final it was uncovered, leaving spectators exposed to the merciless midday sun. And the cheering, jeering, raucous crowd (those who had begged, borrowed or stolen for an inexpensive ticket to a day's cricket) were the kind of people that the members of the Cricket Association of Bengal, from their stands on either side of the pavilion, looked down upon with a mixture of contempt and deep-seated resentment. ('God, what do *they* want to come to the cricket for?')

None of which was of any consequence to me as I found myself on my concrete bench on 2 January 1979.

On one side of me was one of those irritating teenagers who seem to believe that because they are fat and need a hell of a lot of space to accommodate *both* their buttocks on the concrete, the boy next to him is obliged to sit with his knees pressed together *all* the time. On the other side was my aunt, who was exactly the kind of cricket follower that I, later on in life, would scornfully avoid while discussing cricket ('not a *real* fan, not one of us'; by then I had become a member of the Cricket Association of Bengal), but who had kindly volunteered to chaperone me on the final day of a Test match that had sparked to life. In front of me was a tall, broad and loud man who effectively blocked out my entire view. I had to stand on the seat to get any real sense of the play (and risk being pelted by oranges, abuse or worse) or else crouch forward till I practically had my head in a lock between the sides of the men sitting in front of me. My uncle (a *real* fan, I would admit then as well as later), who had actually got me the ticket, had not been able to get three seats side by side; he was on the other side of the ground.

Perhaps they weren't ideal circumstances for my baptism but I was determined not to let the small matter of being unable to watch the game take anything away from my sense of awe and occasion.

From where I was sitting, the players seemed like midgets. The faces were blurs: the only way you could tell who was who was from the thickness of a waist, the swinging of an arm or the tilt of a cap. But I chanted with the rest of the crowd, clapping till my palms were red and sore for days afterwards, screamed till my voice broke and felt, well, so *grown up* to be a part of this sea of grown-ups. Before coming to the ground for the first time, I had always watched cricket in the isolation of my home. It did

me good to see this mass hysteria; it was the first real
indication I had ever had that my obsession was not
unique.

But the main impression that first visit to the Eden
Gardens left me with was how *unreal* the whole spectacle
seemed. It was not like the game I watched on television.
There was the distance, of course, and the distortion – or
obfuscation – that distance breeds. But there was something else too: the vast number of people all around (I had
never seen 100,000 people together in one place before),
the roar, the glint of sunshine on an angled bat, the heat
which made you feel dizzy, the hovering cloud of cigarette
smoke and the sound of crackers.

In a curious inversion of the reality-illusion paradox,
the actual game in front of my eyes was only a reflection
– immensely enlarged in scale but diminished in terms of
individual components – of what was borne to me at
home across the airwaves. The TV pictures were more
real.

I don't remember much of what I saw. The West Indies
had come to India with Alvin Kallicharran as captain
(Kerry Packer had taken away the best of the best for his
WSC series). The first two Tests at Mumbai and Chennai
had been drawn and the Windies came to Kolkata more
with the intention of avoiding defeat than snatching
victory. That day, after the West Indies had reached 143
for 4 at tea chasing 335, the match suddenly opened up.
The Indian new-ball bowler Karsan Ghavri snapped up
three quick wickets but a dropped chance (Viswanath let
Marshall – and probably the match – slip through his
fingers) and fading light combined to rob India of victory.

None of this has stayed with me (I had to look it up). I can't really say why. Had India won, perhaps, it would have. (Winning is terribly important for a nine-year-old. Draws are never honourable or fair; they merely seem inconclusive, they merely seem like *not* winning.) Had I watched it on television, perhaps it would have.

My most enduring memory of that Test is of the Indian scorecard on the fourth day. It read 361 for 1 – Gavaskar 182 not out and Vengsarkar 157 not out.

'Look at that scoreboard,' my uncle said (we were watching television together), 'and never forget how pride makes your heart swell when you see something like that.'

He was right. I have never forgotten it. But the memory comes to me courtesy of the TV, not from my day at the Eden.

* * *

Actually, I do remember one incident from that day. And the emotion that accompanied it is still fresh: it was a sense of cringing shame.

On his way to a debonair forty-six, Kallicharran developed some sort of a problem with his box. The Indian fielders clustered around and, through the crack of space left between the men in front of me and then through the space between the loose circle that the fielders formed around the batsman, I saw the West Indies captain drop his trousers and fix his box.

I wanted to place a hand over my aunt's eyes. It seemed bizarre that no one else at the ground thought of it as anything but a minor stoppage in the run of play.

I looked down at my shoes. My aunt thought I had dropped something.

'How can a grown man drop his pants like this in front of so many people?' I squealed. My aunt smiled and ruffled my hair.

Clearly, I had a lot of growing up to do.

4
'Could I touch your hand just once?'

EVERY FANATIC KNOWS this – it's the moment he lives for. It's the moment I live for. It's the moment when the bass line kicks in, the instant when the drink has begun to take hold, the moment of sharp-edged clarity between feeling a little tipsy and losing oneself. It's the moment when you are floating, weightless, riding the high.

These moments are at the heart of our addiction. They are repeating, repeatable motifs we pursue in every binge. When these moments have arrived, we know we are there.

In sport, our heroes are these moments. They provide an intensity in the heart of a game we are already intense about. These are the players we most look forward to watching in the game we can't live without.

But the analogy doesn't hold all the way. Sometimes, heroes are bigger than the game they play. In fact, they seem bigger than anything else, ever. And that's what holds the key to our devotion.

* * *

I started playing cricket by myself soon after I arrived in Kolkata from Bankura. The idea must have come from the story I had heard about Bradman: belting the ball at a garage wall all day on his own in Bowral. I took that bit of lore, refined the system and modified it to suit my purposes.

There was a small strip of wall adjoining the front door of our house in Kolkata. To get to that door – and the wall – you had to pass through a large iron gate gnawed at by rust, and a small cement courtyard. On either side of the cement courtyard, there were two sections of overgrown mini-lawns and trees. The courtyard was my pitch; the lawns my outfield; and the wall my bowler. With my left hand on the grip of my bat, I would throw the ball at the wall with my right and, by the time the ball had rebounded, get into position to play it.

This wasn't just practice. These were proper Test matches. I batted for both sides; I played the role of a full-house audience (clapping and roaring within a stadium can be convincingly simulated by curling your tongue inwards till it touches your palate, gathering a fair bit of spittle and rolling it around rapidly inside your mouth and blowing out very hard through a narrowed mouth. It isn't as difficult as it sounds. And it really works: try it); and I was scorer and radio commentator. I was utterly unself-conscious about the bizarre sight I presented until one day I caught sight of an old woman who lived next door looking at me through the window with a mixture of amazement and alarm. The match was particularly exciting, and as India, with only a wicket in hand, needed ten runs to beat the West Indies, I'd become a little overwrought in my commentary. The old lady must have thought that I was demented. (I probably was. I certainly looked it.)

I used to cheat a lot in those matches. (I admit it, 'cheating' must seem rather a strange way of putting it, given that it was my game, and my rules – but that's how it felt to me.) Bowlers I had little time for ended up with pretty ragged figures by the time I had finished with them. Batsmen I was fond of almost always got big scores. India almost always won. I have never ever felt as omnipotent and powerful as when playing that game in the courtyard. I controlled not merely the pace of the match but held in my hands its fate, as well as the fates of all the players involved.

There was a certain skewered integrity to the cheating. I never allowed the same batsman too many big scores on the trot, and I tried to make India suffer the agony of an occasional defeat. In a way, this made sense. The bedrock of this entire elaborate charade was verisimilitude. I had to maintain a semblance of actuality for the game to seem *authentic* – and therefore, the victories to seem plausible and, most importantly, pleasurable – to myself. I had to be careful not to let fantasy and desire throw that completely out of the window. Not completely.

One Indian batsman used to score consistently heavily in my fixed matches – far more consistently than his record suggested. In real life, Gundappa Viswanath was one of Indian cricket's nearly men: he averaged 41.93, never a loser, no way, but never as much of a star as, say, Gavaskar or Kapil. He never really fulfilled the enormous talent that he so obviously had.

I thought I saw myself in him. Whenever we can't become achievers, we love to flatter ourselves with the delusion that we are at least *under*achievers; that, if nothing else, we have potential. It is so much better than being a *non-achiever*. His underachievement made Viswanath more human; at the same time, his achievements made him more of a hero.

Viswanath was hardly the obvious choice for a kid growing up in the 1970s. Sunil Gavaskar, Viswanath's brother-in-law and great friend, was the playground favourite. Picking Viswanath over Gavaskar was like choosing *The Queen is Dead* over *Sgt. Pepper's* or *Revolver* as the best album ever. I was loath to be as reverential towards Gavaskar as most cricket followers were. Viswanath was flawed, fallible and fickle; he was also, on his day, as divine with a bat as anyone could ever be. He was our symbol of the counterculture.

No one in India – and very few anywhere else in the world – has played the late cut as late or as fine as Viswanath. I can't think of anyone who played the shot that Viswanath made his trademark – the half cut, half drive square of the wicket – with as much impetuosity or impish cheek. Against super-quick bowlers a foot taller than he was, this five-foot-three-inch man would leap, *with both feet,* a good six inches in the air, to flash between point and cover. Watching it made you want to genuflect in front of him.

I unfailingly did.

But for every breathtaking shot, there seemed to be a corresponding soft dismissal. And the more I cared, the more it amused my family. They took every opportunity to kid me about it. Whenever my mother made ice cream at home, she etched 'G. R. Viswanath' on top of the slab of vanilla before serving it to us, the name of my hero sitting there ready to be cut into bits and eaten. This elaborate ritual would usually take place after another innings in which Viswanath had flopped, another occasion on which he had failed to match the form which he showed in my courtyard matches. Since this happened rather often, my mother had more opportunities to tease me – and test my loyalty – than I would have liked. I would howl with a sense of outrage and humiliation and often refuse to eat my portion. (A noble sacrifice in my scheme of things, second only to offering to give up watching cricket.) Soon, I found a way out. I would smudge Viswanath's name from the top of the slab before my mother could bring it to the table or, in a particularly black mood, replace it with 'S. M. Gavaskar' and scoop spoonfuls into my mouth. Everyone at home, of course, had decided to become a Gavaskar fan.

When I was eight, the same uncle who took me to the Eden Gardens had a daughter. We all used to live together in the sort of joint family that is becoming increasingly rare in India these days. As soon as my cousin had learnt to speak, I taught her the names of all the players in the Indian Test team.

I also taught her something else. In an endearing half lisp and without understanding a single word of what she was saying, she'd reel off a little chant I had made up. Roughly translated, it goes something like this: 'Gavaskar makes a duck every time he goes out to bat, Viswanath a century.' (This was patently untrue. Gavaskar made

about three times as many Test hundreds in his career as
Viswanath did.)

My family, of course, found a way to counter this. At
the end of January 1979, I came back from our annual
holiday to find a sheet of A4 paper pinned to the door of
my room. My uncle had left me a message: 'Gavaskar:
0 + 120: makes a duck? Viswanath: 100 − 91: makes a
century?' The Delhi Test against the West Indies had just
finished. Gavaskar – playing in the manner that he had in
the rest of the series – had made 120. Viswanath had
scored nine.

I tore the paper off the door and ripped it up. The
holiday had vanished in an instant. I knew I was back
home.

I never blamed Viswanath for all the humiliations that
I suffered for his failures on the pitch. I never found much
to blame him for at all. That is the way with heroes, or at
least the heroes we find in our childhood. It's impossible
to be objective about them. As I have grown older and
more cynical, I pretend that I am above the banalities of
hero worship. Nowadays, when things go wrong for a
player I like, I try to get criticisms in first before someone
can call me on it; I try to see things for what they are: a
bad shot is a bad shot, a lean trot a lean trot, it happens to
the best of us. I have learnt to assume an expression of
weary resignation, to develop a disdainful shrug and turn-
up of the lips.

But I know I am being disingenuous, trying to disown
my childlike devotion. The difference is, when you are a
kid and someone is running your idol down, you wipe his
face in the dirt with a ferocity that you reserve for little else

in life. Or you smudge his name from a block of vanilla and gulp it down as your eyes sting with tears.

It was not that Viswanath did not give me reason to cheer.

The bat, for him, was not so much bludgeon as brush. Some of his strokes will stay with me for ever. One of my most unforgettable images of him is from the first day of the Eden Gardens Test against Pakistan in February 1980. He came to the wicket with one ball left before lunch. Instead of patting it back, the little man cracked an audacious square cut that raced away to the boundary, the silly-point fielder looking both silly and pointless as he ducked for cover. It had been a good-length delivery; Viswanath made it look like a half-volley.

He gave us more substantial, more conventional gifts too. There was his double century against England in Chennai in 1981–2 (the first and last time he made a double hundred in Test cricket). His fighting ninety-seven against a rampaging Andy Roberts when the West Indies came to India in 1974–5. (I'd been too young to appreciate it but I took pride in the memory.) His match-winning 112 during India's fourth-innings chase of 403 against the West Indies in Port of Spain in 1976.

There was one incident which tells you all you need to know about Viswanath. During the 1980 Jubilee Test against England in Mumbai – his only Test as captain of India –he recalled Bob Taylor, whom the umpire had given out caught behind, back to the wicket. Taylor and Botham went on to add 171 runs. India lost the game.

But he had done what he thought was right. He was always humble, polite, he eschewed controversy, he

wasn't driven or ambitious – in short, he seemed a throw-
back to another era. By the closing years of his career, a
time in which cricket was beginning to acquire a ruthless,
competitive edge, he seemed positively anachronistic.

I can't even imagine him in today's professional
sporting world. Viswanath communicated such a sense of
sheer joy through his play, such elegance and good nature
that it is impossible to imagine him fettered by a mundane
commercial world of image, endorsements and
politicking.

And that was why we loved him. We sensed that he
conformed to our *notion* of the game; he epitomised the
schoolboy's idea of what cricket should be. Cricket is not all
about heroism, sacrifice, nobility, artistry and joy. It wasn't
even when Viswanath was playing. But how could we fail
to adore someone who made it look as though it was?

* * *

For many of us, sportsmen become prisoners of a
particular image. Whenever I think of Bjorn Borg now,
it's of him on his knees on Centre Court, in his striped Fila
shirt, clenched fists raised towards the sky after yet
another Wimbledon victory. My image of John McEnroe
is not of the graying, balding commentator (nor of the
graying, balding player of the late 1980s and early 1990s)
but of a scowling teenager, hair erupting from beneath a
flaming headband, racket in tailspin as his foot readies to
connect with it. I see Diego Maradona amid a shower of
confetti, biceps bulging as he holds aloft the Jules Rimet
trophy.

Ever since 25 June 1983, Kapil Dev has been defined by one image: white, even teeth beneath a thick moustache, a smile that can't quite make up its mind about whether to take what's happening seriously, his large hands wrapped around a trophy that no Indian had ever believed he'd get his hands on. India's captain with the 1983 World Cup. Kapil's Devils. World champions.

It is an image that is a tribute to Kapil; it is also one that does not do him justice.

Because Kapil Dev was more than a captain who pulled off the impossible, who scripted on behalf of an entire nation a drama magical enough to *still* seem, after twenty-three years, a fairy tale. He was a man who changed the course of Indian cricket. And the picture of him that every Indian fan remembers gives us no glimpse of that astonishing story.

I first saw him – on TV, in a highlights capsule – during his Test debut in Pakistan in 1978.

There he was, not yet twenty, rustic, untutored in the middle-class decorum at the heart of Indian cricket teams, that unprecedented thing in our history: a genuine fast bowler. For a country famous only for its batsmen and its spinners, this was, in itself, a phenomenon rare enough to take your breath away.

Here's another picture, from that first tour: Kapil runs in to bowl, gracefully gathering speed as he coils himself into a pre-delivery leap (another thing which we've never seen before: an Indian new-ball bowler *leaping* into the delivery stride, elegantly side-on, and then comes down hard on the deck with his left foot to release a perfect outswinger.

Kapil was a gift to Indian cricket because he revealed a side of the game that had been alien to us, a place where we'd never been. Also, and just as importantly, as his career flourished over the next decade and a half, he showed us just where we, as a cricketing nation, could go. We never knew where he would take us next. But we were always willing to let him take us there.

His biggest contribution to Indian cricket was not the matches he won, though he won many; it was not the 5,248 runs he scored, nor the 431 wickets he took, though that was a lot of runs and a lot of wickets – probably no Indian all-rounder will ever get close. The greatest thing about Kapil Dev Nikhanj was that he was, as Mukul Kesavan wrote in *Wisden Asia,* 'our talisman of hope and adventure'.

Kapil meant so much to so many of us for so long because he stretched boundaries, because he redefined what subcontinental cricket could mean, both on and off the pitch.

In 2001, seven years after he played his final Test, I spent three days with Kapil at a weekend golf do in Mauritius. The organisers had roped in a clutch of celebs – like Kapil – to play, and a clutch of hacks – like me – to write about it. My wife was then eight months pregnant. I turned the invitation down at first – I couldn't leave her on her own. But then I heard that Kapil was going to be there. There was nothing else for me to do: I gave in to temptation.

I had had one previous encounter with Kapil. (As far as Kapil knew, there had been no such meeting ever.) During the Pakistan-India Test at the Eden Gardens in 1980, I had

seen him waving at me from the players' balcony. I could
have sworn, despite the distance of several hundred feet,
that our eyes met, that he was waving at me. I believed this
so completely that I told friends and relatives the story
without a trace of self-consciousness, never imagining that
they would not believe me.

I have never heard the end of it. Till then, my parents
had not realised I was so far gone. Now they knew. And
they made sure that everyone else did too.

So the chance to actually spend a few days with him (in
the same hotel! On the same golf course! I could hear,
even while I was packing my bag to leave, the exclamation
marks as I recounted the experience) was more than I
could resist. I would have photographs this time. (I didn't,
as a matter of fact. When the moment came, I was too
tongue-tied to ask.)

I was thirty-two years old, about to become a father. I
was behaving like an eight-year-old looking for an
autograph.

I got to Mauritius a day before Kapil arrived. That first
day, I hung around the beach, fretfully kicking at the sand
and looking out over the water at the sailboats bobbing
like a line of heads nodding in assent.

I missed my wife. I felt guilty. I could not wait for Kapil
to show up.

I saw him on the morning of my second day. I was
hanging around the beach again, giving the sand quite a
beating, when, through the window of the hotel's coffee
shop, I saw a face creased in a smile familiar from so many
years and so many pictures. The white, even teeth. The
thick moustache.

This was unusual. In July 2001 Kapil wasn't smiling much.

In 2000, his name had been dredged up in a probe into match-fixing. He was innocent until proven guilty (he never has been; he was named *Wisden* Indian Cricketer of the Century in July 2002, and most people soon forgot that any such charge had been levelled) but he was under a cloud. It was a huge story, on the front page of every newspaper.

In a prime-time interview on Indian television in May 2000, the unexpected happened. As the interviewer kept asking him to put his hand on his heart and say that he had never taken money to underperform, he broke down and cried like a child. He said nothing; he just wept. It made for great television, more riveting than the most compelling of reality TV shows.

Watching the interview, I felt like crying myself.

After that, Kapil went into a sort of self-imposed exile. He wouldn't meet journalists, he wouldn't talk about cricket. He stopped making promotional appearances, he stopped visiting the grounds of the Delhi Cricket Association and talking to young players. He wanted out.

From what we read about him, he seemed not only withdrawn and isolated; he seemed angry and bitter.

I wanted to find out.

By the end of the day, I knew I would have little chance.

That evening, we were taken to another part of the island to watch a sega dance performance. Kapil, who had rarely played second fiddle to anyone during his fifteen-year career, was, along with a gaggle of models and Bollywood actors, the supporting act.

It was hard to reconcile my image of him – arguably the greatest cricketer India has ever had; certainly the most adventurous – with the man who hammered it up on the beach, eliciting laughter that had as much to do with the amount of booze his audience had drunk as with the quality of his stand-up comedy.

'When I went to Australia for the first time in my life as a raw twenty-one-year-old, an Australian cricketer I met asked me, "Have you come here to die?" "No," I said, "I have come here to live, to play, to win." But he insisted, "Didn't you arrive only to die?" '

The third time the line came around, the audience finally got it. Kapil killed the punchline ('And I told him that I had actually arrived yesterday'). There was much clinking of glasses. The spilled Chianti gleamed on the sand.

Perhaps Kapil's Aussie twang was not entirely convincing. Perhaps this lot just took longer than usual to catch the drift.

In the bus, on the way back to the hotel, I asked him about cricket. India was about to play a triangular tournament in Sri Lanka. 'Cricket? I know nothing about cricket,' he said. In the dark, it was hard to tell how wry his smile was. Or how tinged it was with anguish.

He wouldn't talk much; he was wary of journalists. He was friendly enough, though, if I kept off the cricket. 'Nobody wrote about what I did for the country then,' he said once – just once – and I knew when 'then' was.

'One has just one life. Enjoy it,' he kept saying. He travelled a lot these days, he told me. He'd just been to Wimbledon; he'd revelled in Goran Ivanisevic's triumph.

'He is so charged up, so emotional. Emotional people should win,' he smiled and the flashback kicked off again inside my head – runs, wickets, wins, losses, a certain imprudent hoick over midwicket that cost him his place in the side, and the breakdown on TV; the indivisibility of a demigod and his feet of clay.

We were almost back at the hotel now. Fairways stretched off into the distance. The greens shimmered in the sun. I thought of Sydney, Barbados, Perth, Faisalabad – names learnt in geography classes and names which meant nothing till he set their cricket grounds alight. I thought, inevitably, of Lord's. He gave me perhaps the most intense moment of my life. It was unfashionable – unprofessional even – to tell him all this, but I did. He looked out across the green (did it remind him of another green in another place?), squinted at the glare of the afternoon sun (that same gesture, the way he squinted into the glare when he came out to bat), curled his fingers around a cigar ('I don't inhale') and shrugged.

On the last evening, I drank the better part of a couple of bottles of Sauvignon Blanc. Walking towards our rooms, my heavy, slightly unsteady tread made soundless by the hotel corridor's thick carpet, I finally plucked up my courage. I asked to touch the hand that had bowled the best outswinger in the history of Indian cricket.

Kapil smiled and held out his hand. I stared at the splayed fingers and felt, well, disappointed.

It looked like a hand in the end, didn't it? Any hand. But it shouldn't have looked like that. I thought it would be, well, just different. Everything about Kapil, I had reasoned, was different.

It wasn't (how could it be?) And I felt let down. Nobody's fault. Just life.

* * *

Alan Ross, the poet and cricket writer, once wrote: 'I believe that heroes are necessary to children and that as we grow up it becomes more difficult to establish them in the increasingly unresponsive soil of our individual mythology. Occasionally, the adult imagination is caught and sometimes it is held: but the image rarely takes root.'

Sachin Ramesh Tendulkar's magic has been that his image *has* taken root in the adult imagination. He has made men past pimply adolescence rediscover the joys of hero worship. Even the cynics amongst us, those of us ever wary of idolatry, become like awed, star-struck children when he is at the crease. God, on a good day, would be doing well to match his genius, they say.

Forget the figures: seventy-four international centuries by May 2006 and counting; more than sixteen years of international cricket and counting; an average of 55.39 in Tests and 44.20 in one-day internationals. But don't forget that he is only thirty-three – far younger than most people care to remember. As I write, he seems to be in decline. Whether this is permanent, who knows. But this is not how I want to remember him.

To a generation that finds itself on the wrong side of thirty – and beginning to fall into the middle-aged trap of believing that things were always better when we were younger – Tendulkar has shown that a treasured sporting moment need not be culled from the pages of a tattered scrapbook. For those of us to whom arrogance on the pitch meant Vivian Richards lifting Bob Willis over the sight screen, Tendulkar has shown that it is thumping Shoaib Akhtar equally hard over extra cover off the front foot. He has forced us to revisit ideas of sporting glory formed in adolescence. More importantly, he has made us redefine them.

As our lives grow more complicated, and the setbacks and disappointments more painful, Tendulkar – piercing four men on the off side with that breathtaking cover drive – shows us that sudden, heart-lurching delirium still has its place. Tendulkar has destroyed all our pretences to adulthood in the manner that he has destroyed bowlers' averages. When he takes guard, our stomachs churn and our hands begin to get clammy. Even those of us who believe in neither gods nor devils find ourselves praying that he sticks around long enough to offer us an innings (*another* innings) to cherish.

If I were to pick my favourite Tendulkar moments, this book would contain nothing else. I have tried. I have failed. Should I leave out the century at Bloemfontein in 2002 in which he turned the spooned shot over third man into an attacking stroke? Can I afford to omit that innings against Pakistan during the 2003 World Cup? There are just too many. It would be unfair to make a list which does not contain them all.

I remember his centuries in successive one-day games against Australia in Sharjah, one interrupted midway by a dust storm. The fielders buried their heads in the ground as the dust, stinging and sharp, flew into their faces. Tendulkar stood at the wicket, staring into the storm. His face was still. He seemed to occupy a different place from those around him. He did. His focus and his concentration had transported him elsewhere.

I remember his innings, all raw emotion and brutal physicality, against Kenya in the 1999 World Cup when he came back after cremating his father.

I remember a story Navjot Sidhu, his one-time batting partner, told on TV. The story of a sixteen-year-old boy on his maiden tour against Pakistan crumpling in a heap against the Pakistan fast bowlers and, as the stretcher arrived to take him off the field, standing up, his shirt stained with blood, to say that he would not leave. He would play.

I remember... It is useless to continue.

Tendulkar has dominated India's collective consciousness in a way that no other sportsperson (perhaps no other *person*) has done. He has more than bound a nation. He has bridged the generation divide: grandmothers love him; fathers and sons are united, for once, in their devotion. If Sourav Ganguly is Indian cricket's Rolling Stones (iconoclastic, hated by parents but loved by the kids), Tendulkar is our Beatles. Ramachandra Guha tells us that when Tendulkar bats against Pakistan, the television audience in India exceeds the entire population of Europe. One reason for that, of course, is that he has dominated his sport in a way no one else has done in India's history. But that is not all there is to it.

He arrived at just the right time. The country's economy had begun to catch fire, creating a new middle class and a new meritocracy. Tendulkar, more boy than man, prodigiously gifted and incredibly mature for his age, embodied all the qualities that this new class treasured: he was a world-beater, a global citizen, smart, well dressed, a self-made man. (And the money he earned – huge sums, unthinkable sums, more than anyone had made before him . . .) At the same time, he zealously guards his privacy. He is an introvert; that, to a nation and a generation that does not particularly approve of public displays of wealth, affection or anger, is what makes him even more of an icon.

As Mike Marquese has suggested: 'The intensity of the Tendulkar cult is about much more than just cricket. Unwittingly and unwillingly, he has found himself at the epicentre of a rapidly evolving popular culture shaped by the intertwined growth of a consumerist middle class and an increasingly aggressive form of national identity. National aspirations and national frustrations are poured by millions into his every performance.'

Tendulkar was his own man. He was a pioneer. He became Indian cricket's first global brand.

Yet he has remained true to his roots. One key to Sachin's incredible popularity is his loyalty to traditional middle-class Indian values: deference to elders, humility, honesty, hard work. In all his years in international cricket, Tendulkar has never been tainted by scandal. He has never let success go to his head. As a youngster, he was always courteous to those who offered him advice. Now he's a senior player himself (and he became one very early, in his late twenties – he'd played more than a decade of international cricket by then), he has been unfailingly kind and encouraging to the new bloods.

He was, when he started, the son every parent would

love to have. He then became the husband any wife would die for. Now, with two children of his own, he is the father every kid will hold up as a benchmark. And he has become this not by revealing what he is actually *like* in those roles, but by withholding more and more of himself from prying eyes.

Unlike David Beckham – perhaps the one sports star with a similar global media profile – Sachin makes the news only for his cricket. When he got married, only close friends and relatives were invited; the media hardly got a look-in. When he became a father, there were no photocalls of him as New Man, changing nappies in public. When he celebrated his thirtieth birthday, he granted next to no interviews – and reams *still* got written about it. (On his thirty-third birthday in April 2006, he was on the front page of nearly every national newspaper. And this was during an extended form slump and injury.)

What you get from Tendulkar is what you see of him on the pitch. He gives nothing else away.

* * *

I first saw Tendulkar on a cricket pitch when he was sixteen and I was twenty. He was the first hero I'd ever had who was younger than I was. I was completely in awe of him, despite his youth. Since then, I have adored the batting of V. V. S Laxman and gasped at the classical beauty of Rahul Dravid. I have been in thrall to Shane Warne and admired the play of Adam Gilchrist. But none of them makes me feel like I am eight again, and Viswanath is coming in to bat. None of them makes me so vulnerable, so childlike, despite my approaching middle age. It is an uneasy feeling, and I am not altogether sure I like it.

'Heroes,' wrote Ross, 'die with one's youth. They are pinned like butterflies to the setting board of early memories.' Far more effectively than cosmetic surgery, Tendulkar has made us all young again.

5

'In the year in which . . .'

The pillows are puffed up against the bedstead. The TV, a newly acquired black-and-white set with a varnished, wooden body and a long aerial that gets in the way when we negotiate the narrow bit of floor between the bed and the TV, sits on a table with a wobbly leg. I am sitting on the bed between my parents, twitching, barely able to keep still. They shush me as I start up my own running commentary. They're excited too, but they're trying not to let it show. The house is silent. The walls can barely contain the quietness.

25 June 1983, Saturday. Every Indian cricket fan remembers exactly how he watched the Prudential World Cup final between India and the West Indies at Lord's. It is central to the life of anyone who follows cricket in India.

We lose the toss, and are put in to bat. Gavaskar is caught behind off Roberts. 2 for 1. No one thought we would get this far; we'll never get another chance. Now it looks as though reaching the final is as good as it gets.

As Gavaskar walks back, I suppress an urge to stand up and cheer. Since Viswanath's career ended, my antagonism towards Gavaskar has intensified. I swallow a snigger every time he fails. Though that does not happen too often, he's had a poor run this tournament: 19, 4, 0, 9, 25 and now 2. I'm pleased, but this is tantamount to being unpatriotic. (At the Eden Gardens that winter, I barely escape being thumped by a clutch of young men in the stands when I gleefully shout 'Yes!' after Gavaskar is out first ball against the West Indies.) I can't help it. Gavaskar is the establishment personified, dour, safety first, always correct. And yet he is so popular. For a fourteen-year-old, nothing can be more shocking. (With age, I can see that iconoclasm for its own sake is worth nothing. Over the years I have come to recognise Gavaskar's greatness, to understand that without him there would have been no Tendulkar or Dravid. It is a pity that it took me so long to see it. It is too late now. You can be fourteen only once.)

Krishnamachari Srikkanth plays what will become known before long as the shot of the final: on his knees, taking Roberts from well outside the off stump and sending him rocketing to the fence. In 1983, Indian cricket is sufficiently immature – and sufficiently diffident about itself – for a fan to remember a player for just the one shot. Twenty years later, it's hard to see Srikkanth making today's one-day side. (It is a wonder, given his inarticulacy and his tendency to be as irresponsible with his words as he was with his bat, that he has become a television commentator. Or perhaps it is not such a wonder after all, given the state of TV commentary in India.)

We've had to take the bedroom curtains down. A couple of dozen kids from the slum across the way have begged us to. Now they're outside on the street, clambering over each other's shoulders to catch sight of the game.

This is 1983: even many middle-class homes are still without TV sets.

Each time I turn around, I see a new face. These young men have a rota system going, I realise. They perch on their friends' shoulders for a certain number of overs, then swap places. Their cries drown the cheering of the thousands of Indian hopefuls at Lord's. *'Guru, guru, jio jio!'* Come on, come on, you are the kings.

Srikkanth isn't listening. He cracks six more boundaries, then he's trapped in front of the stumps by Marshall. 59 for 2.

Mohinder Amarnath, for long considered India's best – or at least bravest – batsman against genuine pace, puts together a stand with Yashpal Sharma. Amarnath is playing the sheet-anchor role, but he needs to press on. They're plodding. Sharma carries a calculator in his head, they say; it must be on the blink today. Outside, the boys have fallen silent, apart from the odd swear word. My mother gives them dark looks.

I am thinking of the exam I am supposed to sit on Monday. It has been a disastrous summer for studying. For the better part of the past month, I have been glued to the telly, following India's fortunes. At the beginning of the tournament I didn't think we would go far enough to upset my revision schedule. I was able to avoid studying without feeling any guilt about it. 'Enough time, I'll stop watching the cricket after India have been knocked out.'

By the time India came up against England in the semi-final, it was clear that wasn't going to work. Now I argue to myself, with a fair degree of persuasiveness, that if we win, I will do well in my exam despite my evident lack of preparation. If Kapil gets his hands on the World Cup, it has to be a year of miracles.

Michael Holding pegs back Amarnath's stumps to make it 90 for 3. The cavalier Sandeep Patil is in next – he took six fours off a Bob Willis over just a few days ago. And then there is Kapil. When he is out there, really, anything is possible. The atmosphere in the bedroom has picked up again.

Twenty-one runs later, India have lost Kapil, Yashpal and Kirti Azad. Patil does not believe in hanging around. He is nudging singles and twos, going at nearly a run a ball with Roger Binny at the other end. India bat deep, down to their number ten –wicketkeeper Syed Kirmani – but the ebullience of the afternoon has evaporated. The young men at the window are getting wistful: it would have been nice to have put up a decent fight, they murmur.

I am worried about my exam, really worried. Being faced with the prospect of flunking isn't funny. And it seems a certainty now. According to my theory of miracles, if India lose on the pitch, so will I in the examination hall. Because I have not put in a stroke of work.

At 153, Patil is the eighth man out. Kirmani and Madan Lal try to mount a rearguard action, but batting through the allotted sixty overs is beyond them. In the fifty-fifth over, India have folded for 183.

We don't have a whiff of a chance. I spend most of the lunch break playing a percentage game: given the hours I have left tomorrow, what exactly should I try to cram?

When the West Indies innings begins, Balwinder

Sandhu bowls the ball for which he will be remembered for ever. Pitched outside off, it holds its line and then cuts back sharply off the seam. Greenidge *shoulders arms*. He turns around to see his stumps shattered. No one can believe their eyes, least of all Greenidge. (Later, after Sandhu had returned to the obscurity he came from, an uncharitable and probably apocryphal joke did the rounds: the ball hit a worm, a pebble, an umpire's counter; that's why it moved off the pitch. It certainly couldn't have been Sandhu's doing.)

Viv Richards, the Chewing Gum Champion, walks in and finds his rhythm: savage yet languorous, he cuts, drives, pulls the bowling to shreds. It is getting very bloody indeed. I catch my breath despite myself. There is something about this sort of batsmanship, about its sheer imperiousness, that makes you marvel even if you are being hammered. Richards in full flow is all about violence made beautiful, about fearful symmetry.

Haynes is holding up the other end. The West Indies are running away with it.

My mother has not cooked dinner; it is her small way of giving herself a treat. I am asked, considering how things are going, if I will volunteer to fetch naan and a curry from a nearby restaurant.

I am getting terrified about the examination. It was stupid not to revise. One can push one's luck only so far. It is *not* the year of miracles. Unable to bear the torment – and unable to stand the continual reminders of my impending doom – I agree to go out.

That is when it (like *everything*) happens.

The Kwality is a middle of the road sort of place that

serves a decent curry. On a Saturday evening, it's normally full of boisterous, middle-aged men who have told their wives that they are busy in meetings. Tonight there are only a couple of waiters standing next to a radio at the bar. I plonk myself down on one of the sofas and try to catch their eye.

It is no use.

'Score?' I ask, in a voice which at high pitch has begun to crack embarrassingly.

'55 for 2.'

'Really? Who's out?'

'Haynes.'

'Oh. Makes no difference. Will butter naan and mutton do piazi take very long?'

One of the waiters glowers at me and stalks off towards the kitchen, pushing the door that separates it from the dining area so hard that it keeps swinging, to and fro, in large, rapid arcs.

The other waiter slumps on the bar. The radio plays on, not loud enough for me to hear.

Suddenly, the waiter lets out a whoop. He lifts the radio, holds it to his chest with both hands, then puts it back on the counter again and, yelling 'Richards! Richards!', arms outstretched, head steady, body tilting from side to side, he begins to imitate a little boy miming an aeroplane.

Other waiters come running from the kitchen and soon I am in their midst, all of us going round and round in the empty restaurant, each screaming our own crazy yawls.

So there you are. The defining moment of Indian cricket's defining game – and I didn't even *see* it. I was running round in circles with a bunch of waiters, waiting for a takeaway curry.

Later, I will see this moment millions of times – on the news, on videos, on documentaries about Indian cricket and great matches (in this part of the world, there is one every week on some channel or another). Somehow, even after so many viewings, the thrill of the instant, its unexpected, heart-lurching happiness, has not been sucked dry.

Richards pulling Madan Lal, miscuing it a fraction, only a fraction, and the ball tracing a parabola, destined to fall into a region where no fielder can be seen, and then Kapil running backwards, running, running with the sun in his eyes and, I'm sure, his heart in his hands, till he has it in his cupped palms. Had Kapil not hung on, Richards could have told him that he had dropped the World Cup.

The waiters can't wait to be rid of me. Before long, the naan and the mutton come packed in a white plastic bag. Grease runs down its seams. As I walk out, I see the two men slouched over the bar. The radio has got louder.

By the time I have half walked, half run back home, swinging the plastic bag with an expression of triumph that suggests I have taken Kapil's catch myself, it is 66 for 5. Madan Lal has picked up Gomes and Kapil has taken his second crucial catch of the game: Clive Lloyd off Roger Binny. The champions are on the ropes.

My family, like the rest of country, I imagine, is too dazed to speak coherently.

'Richards, Gomes . . . Lloyd!'

'What a catch.'

'Kapil.'

'Madan too.'

'They won't get out of this hole.'

'Don't speak too soon.'

'Here, take the curry,' I say. 'We ought to eat it before it gets cold. Can we have it on the bed?'

We dip our naan into the curry, wiping off the gravy from the tinfoil. Bits of it dribble on to the bed. We're all stuffing our mouths without looking at where the food is going.

Sandhu returns. He snaps up Faoud Bacchus, caught behind. It is 76 for 6.

Jeffrey Dujon and Malcolm Marshall begin to put together a partnership. Knowing them, and knowing how small a target they have to chase, I know it's too early to celebrate.

I keep looking at my watch. It's as though I am sitting in a cinema and it will tell me how much longer there is to go. I cannot bear to keep watching the match. I want it to be over, one way or the other.

Amarnath, trusted, reliable Amarnath, helps me out by bowling Dujon. 119 for 7. The boys at the window have started a chant; fireworks are going off all over town.

The rest of the match is a bit of a haze. Amarnath gets Marshall, Kapil traps Roberts in front of the wicket and I am waiting, we are all waiting for the moment. And then it comes: Holding swivels and turns away and Amarnath is running down the pitch and there is Kapil and Yashpal and Patil all in a mad scramble for the stumps as thousands and thousands pour onto the ground and the players weave in and out, afloat in the sea of people, on their way to the pavilion.

The spray of champagne from the balcony, the droplets catching and refracting the late afternoon June sunlight. A group of men smiling as they have never smiled before. It is hard to make oneself heard at home. Everyone is talking at the same time and the crackers are drowning us out.

On Sunday, I sit with my head between my books and up in the clouds. Scraps of conversation drift in from the adjoining room; my parents, uncles and aunts are discussing last night's game, reading titbits from the day's papers to each other. I plough on with my studies. Even miracles need something to work with. There is too much to revise; there is too little time.

I take the exam on Monday morning. It is as disastrous as I fear. The results appear a fortnight later. I pass. It must have been the cricket, I think. There was simply no other way I could have got through. Who could have expected otherwise in the year of India's World Cup triumph?

*   *   *

How did it happen? I have wondered about this so many times over the past twenty-five years. And why has it never happened again? India was certainly not the most talented side in the 1983 tournament. (And we've had several better teams since.) No one picked it as a dark horse. It did not have a decent track record. It had had far less practice in the abbreviated form of the game than teams like, say, England or Australia.

So how did we do it?

We had great players like Kapil and brave, committed ones like Amarnath. They were lucky. They were plucky.

(Remember, India beat the world champions not once, but twice.) But more than anything else, everything came together for India that summer in a way that things sometimes do in team sport: when all the units in a side weld together, when one player inspires the others, when the cliché of one for all and all for one becomes a demonstrable reality.

The World Cup victory changed Indian cricket. It gave us the confidence to believe that we could compete, that we could actually pull off the improbable.

It also made one-day cricket the more popular – and often the more important – version of the game to fans in India. Previously we'd been hopeless – pathetic – at the one-day game. (The achievements that we could claim were laughable. The slowest innings of all time? S. M. Gavaskar. He batted through sixty overs for thirty-six not out. I love the not out. With victory, we discovered that we'd hated limited-overs cricket not because we were purists but because we had been so bad at it.

Now, everything was turned on its head. All of a sudden, we were the best team in the world. (At least, that was what the record books said.) A few years later, we won the Benson & Hedges Cup. Okay, so it wasn't as impressive as winning a world championship, but the tournament featured all of the game's leading sides. Before we knew it, all these titles – many of them inconsequential in themselves – became crucial to the Indian cricket fan. We never won the Robert Mugabe Cup or the Idi Amin Championship but had we done so, we would have talked about them for years.

As we got better, and the one-day game became ever

more popular, we played it more and more often. Before the mid-1980s, few international tours featured anything but Test matches. As attendance for ODIs skyrocketed, visitors were soon playing one-day series and no Tests at all.

The Prudential Cup triumph arrived at just the right time. Flat, dead pitches and negative captaincy were turning Test matches into a travesty on the subcontinent. When England toured India in the autumn of 1981, they played a six-Test series. India won the first, low-scoring match. The next five were all drawn. Often, less than 200 runs were scored in a day. After that first victory, India took only fifty-eight wickets in the next five Tests. Play was not so much attritional as mind-numbingly boring. It may well have been the most boring Test series in the history of the game.

And this was not a one-off. Nearly every series played on the subcontinent at the time followed the same, dreary, pointless pattern. Spectators began to stay away; they felt cheated. Test matches in India had literally lost the plot; they had been stripped of their most attractive quality: their unfolding narratives.

Under the circumstances, one-day cricket, with its promise of a result, and continuous action in-between, was a godsend. It brought people back into the stadiums. Once satellite TV arrived, it drove viewing figures and advertising. India had become a cricketing nation that was to be taken seriously. And all because of that win at Lord's on 25 June 1983.

But what I remember most about that day, of course, is wheeling around with the waiters at the Kwality.

* * *

My daughter was born the year we beat Australia at the
Eden Gardens after following on. It is one of the greatest
Test matches India has ever played. It is one of the
greatest Test matches anyone has ever played.

It's a nice way to remember the arrival of a child, I
think. Not everybody else agrees.

It's like this. In mid-2002, I am at a bar with a few
friends from university. Most of them have left Kolkata
now. By chance their visits home have coincided. Every
one of them is married; most of them have become
parents. As the evening progresses, we switch from talking
about the way we were to talking about the way we are.
Soon enough, the conversation is about children: why we
choose to have them, how they grow up, how expensive
they are, how they become the centre of your life, only to
leave you with a gaping hole as they begin to make their
own.

One of my friends turns to me and asks, 'Which year
was your daughter born in?'

Now I am not one of those fathers who neglects his
children, who scratches his chin when asked what grade
his daughter is in and mumbles something incoherent. On
the contrary, I pride myself on being a New Man, graceful
with the nappies, efficient with the feeds and as important
an influence on my daughter as her mother is. (It's my
way of making up for having done nothing to bring my
daughter into the world. Nothing, that is, apart from the
impregnation. And that is the nice part.)

But somehow, the question throws me. Perhaps it is
because at the time, I am accustomed to thinking of her
age in terms of months rather than years. (She hadn't had

her first birthday yet.) Perhaps it is just one of those temporary blank periods that hit me once in a while. But the fact is that I can't think of the answer. I scratch my chin, and gaze from the depths of my vodka to the arched eyebrow of my friend. What a prick, the eyebrow seems to suggest, as does the hand that has frozen, its fingers curled around the glass, halfway to his lips. Can't even remember the year his daughter was born in.

'Um, well, she was . . .' And then it strikes me. 'She was born the year India beat Australia after following on. Laxman's epic double, you know. His and Dravid's match. Well, Harbhajan's also.'

My friend looks at me incredulously. 'Are you fucking crazy or what?'

I don't think so. It is just that I tend to think of every major event in my life in terms of something that happened on a cricket pitch. It helps me keep things straight, I find. I think it is a perfectly serviceable way to keep my memory sharp and fresh. (A lot of people use mnemonics, don't they? Are *they* fucking crazy or what?) But the truth is, it is the only way in which I can remember anything at all.

* * *

The 2001 Eden Gardens Test was remarkable, as far as I was concerned, for another reason. I wasn't there. Having watched every international game at the Eden Gardens for the last quarter of a century, having flown all the way from London to catch a final there, I had decided to call it quits. I'd turned my back on the Eden for various reasons. Having made up my mind, I didn't find I regretted my decision. At least, not as Day One ended. (I *did* feel a twinge of bitterness that they had found someone to take my place in the stands. The ground was packed. Clearly, no one in Block L was missing me.)

Australia arrived in India having won fifteen Tests on the trot. They made it sixteen when they breezed through the game in Mumbai in a little over three days. Beating India in India, their captain Steve Waugh was on record as saying, was the final frontier; as the second Test began in Kolkata, there seemed to be little standing in Australia's way.

On 10 March, the evening before the game started, I was discussing India's prospects with a few of my colleagues. (Essentially it was a discussion about whether India could avoid humiliation.) Having had more beers than was strictly necessary for an after-work, camaraderie-fostering trip to the bar, I had a flash of perspicacity.

'It's a game of moments,' I said. 'Remember Tendulkar? Remember him walking back after Ponting took that catch? Remember his face? That could be the image of this series.'

In Mumbai, Ponting had leapt out of nowhere to take what had seemed like an impossible catch. I've seen Tendulkar look disappointed many times after being dismissed but I shall never forget the look of despair on his face as he walked back. Once Tendulkar had gone that day, nothing could prevent Australia's victory. Or India's defeat. Depending on how you chose to look at it. And he knew it better than any of us.

'Yeah, remember how he took them apart in 1997–8?

That was the key then. That will be the key now. Unless Sachin does something . . .' a fellow editor trailed off.

That's when I got my feeling. 'No, it won't be Sachin. It has to be somebody else. It has to be someone they're not expecting.'

It wasn't just the drink talking. History supported my hunch. In 1959–60 against Australia in Kanpur, India's hero had been Jasu Patel. Coming from nowhere, he'd ripped through the Aussies, taking fourteen wickets for 124. Complete unknowns had won us matches against the West Indies on a couple of occasions. Now India had a young spinner called Harbhajan Singh. We didn't know anything about him – except that the captain wanted him and the selectors didn't. That was just the right pedigree for a miracle-worker.

'We need someone to run through the Aussies.'(Former India batsman Sanjay Manjrekar on the eve of the match.) 'We need runs on the board.' (India's coach John Wright.) Simple formula: score enough runs, bowl out the opposition twice, you win the match. You hardly needed an expert to tell you that, do you?

But who was going to do it for us?

For much of the first day, I thought it was going to be Harbhajan. He picked up Mark Waugh, then became the first Indian to get a Test hat-trick. At 269 for 8, we were making a game of it. We may not quite have had a noose round the visitors' necks, but for the moment it was enough that we were not being strangled ourselves.

On the second morning, it was Steve Waugh's turn to play hangman. With support from Jason Gillespie and Glenn McGrath, he completed his twenty-fifth Test hundred. India didn't take the last Australian wicket until the afternoon session.

When India batted, S. S. Das, Rahul Dravid and Sourav Ganguly all got decent starts, but none of them hung on long enough to convert them. At 97 for 7, the series seemed to be over. At least V.V.S. Laxman put up some resistance, stroking the ball beautifully for his fifty-nine. But it didn't make much difference. Before lunch on the third day India had folded for 171, 274 runs behind. Australia enforced the follow-on. There was only one positive sign: Laxman was in such fluent form that when he returned to the pavilion, his captain and coach asked him to keep his pads on. In the second innings, he was promoted to number three, ahead of Dravid.

When Laxman came to the wicket for the second time on Day Three, India's score was only fifty-two. Not one of those present at the Eden Gardens or watching it live on TV had any idea that he was about to make history. I'd have certainly paid more attention myself if I'd known. (But you never know – if you did you'd have been paying attention.) At the end of the day he was 109 not out. India were twenty runs behind.

The Australians couldn't say they had not been warned. Just a few months before in Sydney, Laxman had scored 167. It had been one of the greatest innings an Indian had ever played in Australia. But India had lost that match. Did the stylist from Hyderabad only show us his best form when it was too late to matter?

On the morning of Day Four, we had an appointment with the gynaecologist. I begged my wife to postpone it.

'I really want to watch Laxman bat. Really.'

'You will soon become a father. We have to see the doctor about that. And you want to watch a cricket match in which India will lose.'

'That's not the point.'

'What is the point then? What's the use? Aren't India going to lose anyway? That's what you were saying, weren't you, on the phone last night. The papers say so too.'

'Ah, yes, but you see, the moment there is a glimmer of hope, one shouldn't do anything to encourage it. In fact one should do one's best to *discourage* it. I am superstitious about these things. I only told Ashis that we would lose so that we might have a chance of not losing.'

'Oh, do grow up. You are so infantile, we may as well as not bother about children.'

We cancelled the appointment.

On the fourth morning Laxman came out with Dravid. He went back at lunch with him. Came out after tea with him. And they returned to the pavilion together at stumps, having put on 335 runs in ninety overs. It was something the likes of which I had never seen before.

To find something comparable, at least in terms of figures (probably *only* in terms of figures), you had to go back nearly half a century: Pankaj Roy and Vinoo Mankad's stand of 413 against New Zealand in Madras in 1955–6. Laxman's and Dravid's 376-run stand overhauled the highest fifth-wicket partnership for India (214, Azharuddin and Shastri against England in 1984–5) by some distance, as well as the highest for any wicket against Australia (an unbroken 298 between Vengsarkar and Shastri at Mumbai in 1986–7). Laxman's 281 was also at

the time far and away the highest individual score an
Indian had ever made in the history of Test cricket. In the
Wisden Indian Cricketer of the Century awards of 2002,
Laxman's innings was voted the best Indian Test innings
of all time.

The records are important; but they are not everything.
What was really important was that Laxman's 281 was
against an Australian bowling attack which had been
taking a wicket every nine overs. Laxman had changed
the course of the match, the course of the series and the
course of Steve Waugh's career. The great Aussie's team
had stumbled at the final frontier.

As I write – four years after it happened – I get goose
pimples; at the time, there was merely awe and a sort of
bewildered delight.

Laxman had always been an elegant batsman; but he
had also been one to fritter away a perfect beginning with
a waft outside off stump. He drove you to despair with the
same ease with which his artistry thrilled you. But on 14
March 2001, V. V. S. Laxman lived up to his new nick-
name: very very special. It was an innings of courage,
commitment and stamina. But also of diabolical swishes
and swats. And everything came off. Watching John
McEnroe demolish his opponents, Arthur Ashe once said:
'A nick here, a cut there, pretty soon you've got blood all
over you.' Laxman made things very bloody for Australia.
But not once did he become violent.

In that innings, Laxman gave us the perfect example of
how an athlete can rise above himself; of how a very good
player can, on one day or over a fleeting period of time,
aspire to and attain greatness. It can happen in any

competitive sport. But when it happens in a team game, it is especially exhilarating. Because one individual can carry eleven.

During that fourth day, I felt, for the first time, a wave of remorse for having abandoned the Eden Gardens. I wanted to be there at the ground. What stopped me was that I could not bear to miss the action in the time that it would take me to get to the stadium.

Later, when I read a *Wisden Asia* interview in which Laxman talked about how unbelievable the crowd had been, how it had kept both him and Dravid going, I felt as though my absence had let my side down. I felt as though I had let myself down too, that I had missed the opportunity of a lifetime. Because the opportunity to play a role, however peripheral, in that game may have been the closest shot I will ever have at greatness.

On the final day of the Test, I was in the office. It was one of those days. I pretended I was working; actually I was watching the newsroom TV. ('I'm chasing a story on the phone' or 'I'm writing something which will need a lot of research on the internet' are handy lines when one needs to stay in the office to watch cricket on a work day.) Sourav declared at 657 for 7, the second-highest total a side batting second has ever made. Australia had to last seventy-five overs to force a draw. Or, given that this was Australia, they had seventy-five overs in which to score 384 and win their seventeenth consecutive Test.

For a while Hayden and Slater went at a canter; it seemed as though Laxman and Dravid's heroics had been in vain. Then Harbhajan came on. He picked up one wicket, then two. Suddenly it was 116 for 3. The afternoon

shift on the newsdesk had begun to drift in. We'd all
abandoned work for the day. No one could take their eyes
off the TV. Hayden and Waugh put on fifty gritty runs
but Tendulkar – as he'd done so many times before –
came on to break the partnership. He took two more
wickets; Harbhajan ripped through the rest.

In sixty-eight overs and three balls, the Aussies had
folded for 212. It was only the third time in the history of
Test cricket that a team following on had gone on to win
the game.

At my newspaper's evening news conference, we had a
dilemma – and a huge argument. It looked as though the
BJP's coalition government was in trouble – one of the
smaller parties was threatening to withdraw its support.

'So where do we put the cricket?' asked the News
Editor.

'On top of page one,' I said.

'I mean, it's just a Test match, isn't it? The government
is in crisis,' cut in the Senior Assistant Editor. 'That's got
to be the top priority.'

The City Editor was in favour of playing up the cricket.
The News Editor wanted to stick to the politics.

It was a bitterly fought argument – but it was strangely
without rancour. Whether one thought it was 'just a Test
match' or whether one believed that it was the most
important story to have happened that day (that year, that
decade, in one's life), everyone in the room was
exhilarated, childishly happy, almost light-headed.

Sometimes, it seemed to me that we were arguing only
because we felt we ought to. We were role-playing, being
the combative editors we were supposed to be, each

fighting our own corners. Deep down – perhaps not so deep down, I think now – we all wanted the cricket to win. Like my fixed matches in the courtyard, the heated debate was there only to give the final decision – the cricket, the cricket, the cricket – the seal of authority.

I remember the pictures we ran the next day. Laxman doing a jig; Tendulkar radiant and raucous in celebration; Harbhajan, his face smeared with cream from the victory cake, getting up close to the camera, arms raised in exultation, the index and middle fingers of his right hand splayed in a victory sign. We felt blessed.

My daughter was born five months later. We called her Oishi. In Bengali, that means 'divine'. Is there another way to describe that victory?

6

'And they make millions from endorsements'

'Bastards.'

'They have no shame.'

'No shame at all. No pride in playing for the country.'

'They have sold the country, you see. They have cheated on us. Must have been bribed for them to have played so badly.'

'And they make millions from their fucking endorsements.'

'Then this is what they give us.'

'Bastards.'

17 February 2003. My car has broken down on the way to work and I am at a garage, sitting on an upturned carton and sipping a bottle of water. In front of me, there are a couple of mechanics. One has opened the bonnet and is peering inside; the other is on the ground, beneath the car, fiddling with something I can't see.

Two days ago, India lost to Australia in their first serious fixture of the World Cup. (And just a few days before that, they'd been woeful against the Netherlands. They couldn't even bat through their full quota of overs.

The Dutchmen – given that they're famed more for their dribbles than their drives – found India's 204 too intimidating and were all out for 136.)

'Battery's gone, I reckon,' the mechanic with his head inside the bonnet says.

'Could it be that it has just run out of charge? It's not very old. I don't need to buy a new one, do I?'

'I think we should replace it.'

I keep quiet. The other mechanic emerges from underneath the car.

'Yeah, yeah, replace it. Replace the whole bloody team. Get a new captain. Drop the bowlers. Get rid of the batsmen. Bloody scoundrels.'

'Excuse me…' I say.

Neither man is listening.

The Australia game was a bit of a mess. That's the polite verdict. Going in first, India was unable to bat out fifty overs for the second time in two matches. Worse, they picked up from where they had left off during a disastrous winter tour of New Zealand. (They lost pretty much every game they played – they lost to district sides; they lost games where the weather had made a result almost impossible; they were regularly bowled out in less than fifty overs.) This is the World Cup. We thought the tide was bound to turn. We were wrong.

In the end, we managed 125. It was the lowest total we had ever made in the championship's twenty-eight-year history. Tendulkar fought for his thirty-six but the other batsmen (Sourav, Dravid, Kaif, Yuvraj and Sehwag) did not even reach double figures. Australia overhauled the target in a little over twenty-two overs. They lost Gilchrist while doing so: the wicket seemed like an aberration rather than anything else.

A week into the World Cup. We had played against the Netherlands as though they were Australia. We had played against Australia as though we were Bangladesh. And all this less than a year on from the glorious English summer in which we had chased more than 300 to win the NatWest Trophy; less than six months after we had beaten South Africa and Australia to become joint winners of the ICC Trophy; less than three months after cricket followers across the country had been extolling our brilliant captain and our awesome batting line-up (the best in the world), our team spirit and our fearless youngsters, our spin wizards and killer fielding (the fittest India side ever), dreaming of redemption and glory, of laying the ghosts of the past to rest.

How so much can change in so little time.

'Er, the battery, do you think, then, that charging it will not work?' I ask as if I'm looking for a favour. (It's true, I am. This morning, neither looks eager to work. Both appear to be severely hungover. I suspect most of last week's pay went on the booze over the weekend.)

'No, we'll have to change it. Only way. Cost you a lot more but save you trouble. Or you can take it somewhere else.' One of the mechanics pulls a face.

'Yes, I suppose, that's the only way. A new battery is pretty expensive, you know.' I shrug and go to look for another garage.

'When's the next game?' I can hear one of the guys asking his friend.

'Harare. On Wednesday. Against Zimbabwe.'

I turn around. 'Swear at them as much as you like,' I say on a sudden impulse. 'You won't be talking like that next week.'

I walk out with what I imagine to be a Dirty Harry swagger. I go to the next garage. The battery works fine after it's charged. I save myself money – and trouble.

Over the past four days, the whole of the country has been playing a fiercely competitive game. It's called 'Who Can Think Of The Worst Insult To The Cricketers'. All entries close by 1.30 p.m. on Wednesday. Which is when the India-Zimbabwe game gets underway.

All over Kolkata – in fact, everywhere, if the national papers' photographs are any indication – young men dressed as mourners are staging funeral processions. They walk shoulder to shoulder. Across their shoulders they carry poles on which are strung posters or photographs of each player. As they walk, they chant. '*Bolo Hari, Hari Bol*': the slow rhythmic chant that accompanies Hindus on the way to the crematorium. Once they reach the appointed place (often it's where they have arranged to meet the newspaper photographer), they gingerly lower their poles. Then they set fire to the pictures. (Interesting point: there are no pictures of burials, though presumably Muslim fans are just as upset with the team as Hindus. Is that because the act of burning the photos, of watching the paper curl up at the edges and the faces turn to ash, is a more potent symbol of anger, a more substantial way to *vent* that anger? Or is it just that they make better photo-ops?)

In our neighbourhood, we have what is called a 'local club'. Red Rose Club is not so much a proper club as a dingy room in which underprivileged youths from the neighbourhood gather every evening to watch TV, play board games, drink enormous amounts of dark rum and leer at young women passing by on the road.

To celebrate the World Cup – and India's chances of winning it – the wall outside the club has been covered with a collage of colour photographs of the Indian team. Someone has even got smart with Adobe Photoshop, producing a morphed image in which a triumphant Sourav holds aloft the World Cup. Garlands made of plastic flowers hang around the players' necks. There is a whole gallery for Sachin. Various moods, bat as bludgeon, grinning impishly, tossing a ball, in jeans and T-shirt, cricket whites and coloured gear: the gallery is the centrepiece of the collage. Never has the ugly red brick looked prettier.

On my way home on Monday, I noticed with a start that the wall is looking ghastly again. In fact, ghastlier than in the days of naked brick. All the photographs have been ripped up, evidently in a hurry and with as much viciousness as the vandals could summon. It has not been a clean job (whoever put them up in the first place had not gone easy with the adhesive) and jagged streaks of white indicate the spots from which the pictures have been hacked. The brickwork stares out, like flesh after the skin has been torn away. At the foot of the wall lies a mound of paper – it is what remains of the photos. It has turned squelchy in the evening shower. It is a filthy mass, muddied by hundreds of hurrying feet. In the sickly glow of the street lights, I make out, with a bit of effort, what I think is a bit of stubbly chin. Could be Sachin. Could be anybody. It looks as though someone has defaced the pictures before ripping them off. It's like identifying a body after an accident.

I read in the papers that this is not an isolated incident. Elsewhere in the city, walls which were once covered with cricketers' posters are becoming vacant again. Everyone, it seems, is keen to rid themselves of associations with the national cricket team.

On another wall in another part of the city, someone has spray-painted the sign 'DEATH PENALTY TO THOSE WHO HAVE RAPED INDIAN CRICKET'. In some neighbourhoods, cricketers' photos have been left intact; but the garlands of plastic flowers have been replaced with garlands of worn shoes – a traditional Indian gesture of insult – on the posters.

On the news I hear that someone has painted the wall of Mohammad Kaif's home in Allahabad black. Someone else has pelted Dravid's Bangalore home with stones. His family has received threats. On the southern fringes of Kolkata, at Ganguly's home in Behala, the local authorities are anticipating trouble. On Sunday they posted a posse of policeman to guard the house. By Tuesday morning, the number of policemen has doubled. Scenting a story, journalists have staked out Sourav's place. It is a classic postmodern assignment. They watch the policemen watching other people watching the captain's home. Then they write about it.

The cops, I read, are watching the high walls that run around the imposing building. They are smoking, chatting, playing cards. Photographers take their pictures. The photos are not particularly interesting – pot-bellied policemen hanging around a house – but do show you what it is like to be an Indian cricket player when things are not going too well.

On Monday, the Indian team does a strange thing. Dravid gives the media an audience. Dravid is supposed to be the most articulate member of the side. Besides, his home has been attacked; his family has been living in fear. Dravid says the team is trying. He asks if anyone can tell them what is wrong. He appeals to the fans for patience. Reading the reports, it occurs to me that the story is being treated as though it were election-time politics, a diplomatic incident, even a prelude to war. It does not seem like sport at all. (But then, when has sport ever been only about sport?)

On Tuesday, on the eve of the Zimbabwe game, Sachin addresses journalists in Harare. The story is carried in every paper in India. This is how the *Hindustan Times*, one of the country's best-known broadsheets, describes the moving incident: 'Sitting on a wooden bench outside the practice ground, he made an unexpected call for support from Indian cricket fans. "I am here on behalf of the Indian cricket team," he said. "We ourselves are very disappointed with the kind of performances we have put up and I also understand the disappointments you have gone through. I am just here to assure all of you that we will fight until the last ball is bowled . . . so please continue to support us, as you have in the past. This support will definitely help us." Tendulkar's plea is somewhat extraordinary because it shows the pressure the man – and the team – are under.'

On Wednesday, at half-past one in the afternoon, after Ganguly has won the toss and chosen to bat, Tendulkar walks out with Sehwag to open the innings. They share an opening stand of ninety-nine in only a little more than fifteen overs. It is the kind of start which we had got rather used to over the past year or so. And the team does not look back even once. They bat their full fifty overs – for the first time in many games – and run up 255 for 7. Tendulkar has eighty-one. It is a convincing performance, and Sachin has played with an air of freedom and flamboyance – not to mention menace and mayhem – which we have not seen in recent months.

When Zimbabwe bat, Srinath and Zaheer keep it tight; Harbhajan picks up a couple; Sourav takes two wickets in two balls and celebrates with a fist-pumping jig. As Zaheer pegs back Douglas Hondo's middle stump, the crackers are going off all over the city. The enthusiasm is touching but a little disproportionate, given the quality of the opposition. Prior to this match, Zimbabwe had lost twenty-nine of their last thirty-two one-day internationals against proper opposition.

Late at night, as I lie with my daughter on my chest, trying to get her to abandon her attempts to stay awake, I hear a procession in my neighbourhood. The chant penetrates the thick glass of the closed window. My daughter wriggles and looks up, bewildered. '*Jeetega jeetega, India jeetega*' ('India will win, India must win').

On my way to work on Wednesday morning, I see that the collage is back on the wall of the Red Rose Club. It looks rather fetching. Somebody must have stayed up all night.

* * *

The odd thing is that few here find this sort of behaviour strange. The media reports incidents of fan frenzy (the spiteful and destructive as well as the way over the top, almost idolatrous celebrations) with disconcerting matter-of-factness. Not surprisingly, outsiders don't look at things in quite the same way. The recent outpouring of public grief has even made its way into the London broadsheets.

Reading about it in the *Guardian*, a friend of mine sends me an incredulous email from London. 'You mean they are threatening players' families after they've lost to a side that has beaten just about everyone else in world cricket? What are the papers saying?'

'Well,' I wrote back, 'if you're asking whether anyone's offered a rousing condemnation or if there has been a campaign to remind fans that their response has been a little excessive, there has been nothing.'

'You should send the fuckers to England. No World Cup on terrestrial TV. Not even highlights.' My friend, a freelance writer, has been keeping up with the World Cup on the internet and in the papers. He resolutely refuses to pay Rupert Murdoch his shilling. He is evidently proud of the fact.

'That's why cricket is what it is in England. That's why it is what it is in India too,' I write back.

The typical Indian cricket fan's response to his team's exploits appears even stranger when compared with the way he bears subcontinental life's sundry other cock-ups.

In the national banks, for instance, it takes hours to fill out a form. This is how it works. To get your form, first find the guy whose job it is to tell you who to get the form from. The hierarchy is rigid. You can't just, at random, find the guy who will *actually* give you the form and ask him for it. He will either not be in, or in but not where he is supposed to be. He may be just a couple of paces down the corridor as you hunt for him. He may know you're looking for him. He will do nothing about it. No one else will offer to help. No one else would, in any case. Responsibility is compartmentalised; accountability does not exist. Once your man takes his seat and you shuffle up to the counter, he might decide to be too immersed in some other work (like reading the paper or minutely examining the underside of a coaster for dirt) to give you the time of day. And he may decide to trot off again before you have managed to ask your question. Eventually, when he does divulge his precious information (you must prise this out of him), your quarry will not be in his seat. Then the whole process will start all over again.

I can recall no instance of a bank officer being beaten or abused. I can think of no instance in which his home has been attacked or his family threatened.

Nearly every form of public exchange involving a government employee in this country produces these circuitous, infuriating delays. We have learnt to accept them, to convince ourselves that this is merely how it is and get on with things. Trains are inordinately delayed; the post takes ages to arrive; when phones go out of order, bribery's usually the only way to get them fixed; buses are uncomfortable, irregular and as capable of killing as a trained soldier. But we don't kick up a fuss about it. Of course we have processions and demonstrations and strikes which bring cities to a standstill, but these days they seem more like ritual parodies of protest than displays of anger in any *real*, spontaneous sense.

So what is it that makes us work ourselves into such a genuine rage when we see India fail on the cricket pitch?

For starters, we take cricket seriously because cricket is really serious business now. And because it embraces (or so we believe) all of us: players, officials, journalists, television executives, tobacco pushers, cola giants and fans – especially fans. The British writer Tim Adams, in a discussion of the professionalisation, the commodi-fication, of the game of tennis, turns to the cultural historian Johann Huizinga for an explanation: as players have become serious businessmen, mini-industries, 'A far-reaching contamination of play and serious activity has taken place. The two spheres are getting mixed. In activities of an outwardly serious nature hides an element of play. Recognised play, on the other hand, is no longer able to maintain its true play character as a result of being taken too seriously and being technically over-organised. The indispensable qualities of detachment, artlessness, and gladness are thus lost.'

Cricket has of course become over-organised. And it is definitely taken too seriously. That's because we all think that we are part of it. Indian cricket is like a giant corporation in which every fan believes he has a stake. It's my company too, the logic goes, so I must be concerned about whether its stocks are rising or falling.

Then there is the money. Cricketers in India earn lots of it. They're among the most highly paid men in the country. But here is the thing that infuriates: they don't make their money from match fees, from their performances on the pitch (at least, not directly); they're rich because of all their brand endorsements.

Tendulkar, for instance, would earn about ten times as much from his endorsements – being the face of a car, bike, credit card and cola – than from his match fees. It's the one area where he is not unique. Most top cricketers' earnings from match fees account for only a small fraction of their annual income.

This is where the paradox (along with envy and the resentment and much of the rest of it) arises. When India were performing so poorly in the early stages of the 2003 World Cup, there were widespread calls to boycott products that the players endorsed. It was seen, more or less unanimously, as the most fitting riposte to (and the cruellest punishment for) their failure to live up to the nation's expectations. Hit them where it hurts most: their pockets.

The Indian cricket fan has developed a curious attitude towards these endorsements. When cricketers are not playing well it's not just the fact that they make so much money that provokes his resentment. It's that the money is earned for *off-field* activities. The fan sees the man on the field and the man who earns more in a year than he will earn in ten lifetimes – by peddling a car he can't afford – as two separate entities. And he can't, in his mind, reconcile the two. He adores the one; for the other, he reserves the sort of derision that the underprivileged always have for the privileged. For him Tendulkar is god; Brand Tendulkar on the other hand, is, well, just a brand.

It doesn't help that no other athletes make anything near the kind of money that cricketers make. India's top tennis duo Leander Paes and Mahesh Bhupathi, for instance, have won numerous Grand Slam titles. Their career earnings, from prize money, is substantial. Yet, when they endorsed products (they used to: once the duo split, neither was worth very much as far as the companies were concerned), they made, according to reports, less than middle-ranking cricketers.

At one level, because the fan sees the player as a brand, he tends to expect from him what one would expect from any other brand, a fridge, say, a television, or a car: value for money. (You would be mad, wouldn't you, if your car, for which you have paid good money and which you quite look forward to driving to work every morning, refuses to start three times a week?)

Logically, constant exposure on television should make players more human. But, the fan often asks, how can someone as human as you and me be so ubiquitous, so omnipresent? When a game is on, the companies make sure that ads featuring the players run between every over. Imagine Dravid patting the ball back for a caught and bowled one minute and then cracking impeccable boundaries through the covers in a mobile phone ad in the next; or Tendulkar miscuing a pull and then, in screaming yellow T-shirt and sexy wraparounds, entreating us to drink a cola.

I have always wondered why the average Indian does not carry these feelings over into other walks of life; why, for instance, he does not decide to boycott the banks for the pathetic level of service they provide or advocate hanging corrupt, self-serving politicians. My guess is this: we have little that can be compared favourably to the rest of the world, little to make us proud. Cricket is one of the exceptions.

Indians need cricket to remain an exception. We can't allow the players to slip – it would be too much of a blow to our sense of self-worth.

7

'We won't let them off if they look like winning'

THERE ARE OCCASIONS when people want to pity me – and want me to pity myself – because I am a cricket fan. They think it is not quite, well, *healthy*, for a grown man to stay up half the night watching India play New Zealand away from home, going to work late so that he can catch the play till tea and then staggering home to grab a few hours' sleep before staying up half the night again.

And this, for days on end, for an entire three-month tour.

Sad bastard, they think. (They don't say it – not that often, not in so many words – but I know, because they look at me in the way I would look at someone who hears the word 'cricket' and thinks of insects.) Social life? A blank. Sex life? Doesn't even bear talking about.

I know all this. I don't particularly care.

A fairly typical exchange:

'No, I can't make Thursday evening, There's a World Cup game on, you see.'

'Yeah, I know,' our friend says. She's inviting my wife and me over for drinks. 'It's Pakistan versus Holland.'

'Yes, that's right. So I can't make it. I'm sure Chandrani will manage. Why don't you talk to her?'

'It's Pakistan against Holland, for heaven's sake.'

'Hmm, Pakistan against Holland. Day-night. Half-past five start our time.'

'?!?'

'I'm curious about how Waqar will bowl and I want to see if Anwar is in good nick. We play Pakistan soon, you see.'

'You are a really sad bastard. I feel sorry for you.' She puts down the phone.

I don't, as a rule, feel sorry for myself. I pity those who pity me.

All rules, though, have an exception. Here is the one to mine: the only time I feel ashamed to be a cricket fan is when India play Pakistan.

It's not easy to talk about this. It involves scouring the memory for things that are best left undisturbed. It is like dredging a river for a drowned man. We don't really want to find the body, but we know that we have to.

India-Pakistan games are my worst cricket memories not because, as most of my friends think, India tend to lose. India beat Pakistan fairly regularly at neutral venues – and without fail during the World Cup. But the result is not what makes me embarrassed when I anticipate, watch or remember an India-Pakistan match. It is the baggage the game brings with it: the whole backstory; the tale of two nations sundered at birth and bitter rivals for more than half a century; the manner in which that rivalry has appropriated the contest; the media frenzy that makes these encounters at once more important and less important than a cricket match; the irrationality of fans' expectations; the fangs-bared jingoism. It is, believe me, not pretty.

And *being there* makes it seem worse. I *was there* – at the Eden Gardens in February 1999. I wish I hadn't been. But you can't change the past; all you can do is live with it.

*   *   *

It was the fourth afternoon of an absorbing Test.

This was the first match of the first Asian Test Championship, a triangular tournament of Test matches between India, Pakistan and Sri Lanka to determine the best five-day team on the subcontinent. The tournament had been the ICC's idea. As a means of generating revenue, it was an unquestionable winner. As a means of getting to see India play Pakistan in a Test match, it was a rare treat.

The two teams squared up at the Eden Gardens on 16 February. Saeed Anwar and Shahid Afridi walked out to open the Pakistan innings. A collapse the likes of which had seldom been seen at the Eden Gardens followed almost immediately. Within nine overs, Pakistan were 26 for 6. Afridi, Anwar, Ijaz, Wajahatullah, Youhana and Azhar Mahmood had all gone, prey to a burst of inspired bowling from Srinath and Prasad.

One hundred thousand people kept up a continual roar. Those who had been late getting in were unable to find a place to sit. The Indian cricket fan, a superstitious creature at any time, was not going to take any chances.

'No place here now, go back and return tomorrow

morning. You might ruin the spell,' said the man to my left, his bellow belying his size and his desiccated appearance. The group of young boys he had been addressing – he would never have dared to speak to them like that anywhere outside this stadium (or, come to think of it, anywhere inside this stadium in other circumstances) – smiled and looked sheepishly at the scoreboard.

Someone must have squeezed in somewhere during the drinks break. Or so my meek but menacing neighbour concluded at the end of the day. Because the spell was broken after that first hour. Salim Malik put together a typically gritty thirty-two; Moin Khan made seventy, an innings of patience and guile; and Wasim Akram flailed the bat at whatever came his way to score a cavalier thirty-eight off fifty-two balls. When Pakistan eventually folded for 185, the last four wickets had added 159 runs. The total seemed almost respectable.

It began to seem more than respectable. India made 223 in their first innings. Only Sadagoppan Ramesh made a half-century.

Team games do not, by definition, provide the platform for the sort of who's-quickest-on-the-draw, gun-blazing, kill-or-be-killed showdown that individual sports do. But a particular duel between two individuals within the context of a match provides a mini-theme, a subtext, as it were, at the centre of the larger confrontation. The gladiatorial aspect adds a different texture to the proceedings, an added prickle of excitement and anticipation.

The most memorable Test matches and Test series are always animated by these special encounters. When Australia visited India in 1997–8 it was Shane Warne versus Sachin Tendulkar. During the Asian Test Championship, it was Sachin versus Shoaib Akhtar.

When Shoaib arrived in India in the winter of 1999, he was that rare and fiercely beautiful thing: one of the quickest bowlers of all time, a man capable of inspiring fear in the heart of the batsman. He was not the most reliable; he was not always accurate. But he could, on occasion, send down a blindingly fast delivery, the one which rips through the gate before the batsman has had time to bring his bat down; the one even when we see it broken down into super-slo-mo, still seems frighteningly, unplayably fast.

On the second day of the Eden Test match, Shoaib bowls just such a ball. It is the first ball that Sachin faces – Shoaib bowled Dravid with the previous delivery – and he is back in the pavilion before the crowd, who were applauding him rapturously on his way to the wicket, has had time to quieten down. The mini-theme of the match has been set. In two successive balls, the visitors have ripped the heart out of the Indian first innings.

For a couple of seconds, there is the kind of silence that you find only at sporting grounds when misfortune – unpalatable, unthinkable misfortune – has struck. One hundred thousand people go quiet as suddenly as if someone has flicked a switch. It is dramatic, this silence; it is chastening.

Then the cries erupt.

'Fucking Shoaib, go to hell.'

'I'll screw his sister, bloody bastard. *Saala banchod.*'

'Paki! Paki!' (There is an unfathomable irony here. When Indians call Pakistanis 'Pakis', they have no inkling that for those who invented the term, 'Paki' can mean anyone from the subcontinent. That, in the UK, a Paki can be an Indian.)

No one is blaming Tendulkar. But, and this is the incomprehensible bit, no one acknowledges how good the ball was either. (If it was good enough to have beaten Tendulkar all ends up, it must have been pretty special.) I feel like squirming. But the spectators are packed in so tight that there isn't the space.

When Pakistan come out to bat trailing by thirty-eight, the match has been thrown wide open.

Eager to redeem his first-innings duck, Anwar plays, as he so often has against India, an innings on which the match may turn. His 188 not out is a classic, but it is a lone hand: Youhana gets fifty-six; the other nine batsmen manage eighty-two runs between them. (In an inversion that is so typical of Pakistan cricket, the last four wickets – the saviours in the first innings – fall for merely thirty-two runs.) Srinath takes eight for eighty-five (making it thirteen in the match) but the spectre of Shoaib is looming over the Indian batsmen. No one is quite sure if Srinath's effort has been enough.

India come out needing 279 to win the match.

Ramesh scores well again, though his leaden-footed swishes outside off stump make you wonder how he manages not to get an edge. Laxman plays in his usual limp-wristed manner – if he did not have a bat in his hand, he'd look dreadfully camp. The two put on a century opening stand. Then with the score on 108, Ramesh is out.

'Aren't they going to leave some runs for Tendulkar?'

asks a man in the row in front of me. 'Another 171 to get,' he says with a quick glance at the scoreboard. 'And another wicket to go before he comes in.'

'They should have sent in Tendulkar instead of Dravid,' says my neighbour. 'I want to see him murder Shoaib.'

'Yeah, a duck at the Eden. Can you imagine? No one does that to Sachin in Kolkata. Bloody Pakis.'

As India stride on (125 for 1, 130 for 1) people are beginning to get edgy. No Test between India and Pakistan has ever been decided at the Eden Gardens. The prospect of seeing a winner in a game with so much needle is winding the crowd up. Disconcertingly, it seems to me that a lot of people are spoiling for a fight – whichever way things go.

'Mian doesn't want Tendulkar to get all the glory.' 'Mian' is skipper Mohammad Azharuddin.

Someone else pipes up: 'Mian loves Pakis, na!'

Azharuddin is a Muslim and his religion sometimes makes him vulnerable. The present conversation really doesn't make any sense of course – the new man in, Dravid, is a Hindu just like Sachin. But then, if the sort of people who say these things were rational, they wouldn't be saying them in the first place.

With the score on 134, Laxman falls to Saqlain. There's wild cheering as Laxman trudges back to the pavilion, but it's more to welcome the next man in than to acknowledge the Hyderabad batsman's elegantly crafted innings. With 145 to win and Rahul Dravid at the other end, Sachin Tendulkar emerges from the pavilion, the afternoon sun sliding off his twirling bat.

When Tendulkar walks out to the middle in a home Test, you can almost smell the unnaturally heavy burden of hope that he carries. The clapping and the cheering start from the stands on either side of the pavilion. Then the roar radiates outwards and all around, the ripple of applause swelling to a wave that washes over the ground and then drowns it. Everyone is on their feet; by the time the young man has reached the pitch, looked around, touched his helmet, whirled his bat a couple of times and performed what the Indian writer Mukul Kesavan once referred to as his 'crotch jerk', every pair of hands in the stadium is sore. And he has not yet faced a ball.

As he takes guard, everything goes quiet. You could be inside a cathedral. You can sense the veneration. You can almost hear the prayers. You know that lurking somewhere in the minds of all these people is a sense of fear: that their boundless expectations, just this time, might not be met. When Tendulkar walks in to bat, every spectator feels that anything – and everything – is possible. The silence as he readies to face his first ball is an acknowledgement of that fact.

On the afternoon of 19 February 1999, 100,000 people are waiting for Tendulkar to explode. They're thinking of the golden duck in the first innings. They want vengeance; it is only fair – and only natural.

The first boundary is greeted with the sort of applause you get when a player has reached a hundred. And then, with Sachin not yet in double figures, it happens.

Tendulkar turns away a ball from Shoaib and sets off for a run. From where I am sitting (in the members' stand to the left of the pavilion, beyond the fine-leg fence if the batsman is at the pavilion end), I see the following things in quick succession: Tendulkar approaches the bowler's end; Shoaib is standing in front of the wicket, and they collide; the throw from the substitute fielder hits the stumps; Tendulkar is scrambling. The Pakistanis are celebrating. They think he hasn't made his ground. The umpire gives Tendulkar out. He starts walking back. The scoreboard says 145 for 3. (What has actually happened I cannot say. The Eden Gardens still does not have a giant screen so there are no replays. Even when I see it later on TV, in slow motion and freeze-frames, I am none the wiser.)

By the time Tendulkar has reached the shade of the members' stand, the stirrings have begun to gather momentum. Spectators around me are screaming, an angry, uncontrollable torrent of filth directed at Shoaib and the rest of the Pakistan team.

'Butchers, cheats, Pakistan *murdabad*!'

'Fucking Muslims, go back to your own country.'

'Cheats! Bastards! *Hai Hai!* Go back!'

The first hail of bottles comes from Block J, to my left. They vault over the high fence, over the heads of the policemen ringing the boundary, to land on the edge of the field. Before long, the grass is littered with sharp, squat, pointed, blunt or heavy objects. The players are in a huddle at the centre. The umpires look embarrassed, they're consulting each other and the Pakistan captain.

I'm sitting in the middle tiers of the stand and things are getting dangerous. However hard they fling their ammunition, those in the upper reaches of the stands will never find their target. Bottles – some still full of water –

are falling all around me, like grenades. I cover my head
with my hands, sink to my knees on the gritty concrete
and wait for the worst. The guy next to me (the meek man
with the huge voice) is attacking his concrete seat. A group
of young men have come to lend him a hand. The seat
splinters bits of stone and sand. Carried away on waves of
hatred, they hurl the debris on to the field.

Whenever I look up, I can see faces contorted with
rage. It seems like a riot. It *is* a riot. It is mindless, sense-
less, and after a while it turns in on itself. Small groups of
spectators are beginning to fight among themselves. The
riot police move in, shoving and pushing their way into
the narrow space between the rows of seats, their batons
flailing. Dull thwacks catch anyone who happens to be in
the arcs of their vicious swats.

It takes a while to bring things under control. Even
then, play cannot restart immediately. The Pakistan
players fear, with some justification, for their safety.
They're reluctant to stand close to the boundary. An early
tea is taken. Tendulkar emerges from the pavilion to make
a plea for peace and sanity. He walks the circumference of
the field.

When play finally resumes India have lost their rhythm.
In the evening session they lose the three key wickets of
Dravid, Azharuddin and Mongia. As Sourav and night-
watchman Kumble walk in at stumps, India are on 214.
They need another sixty-five to win. There are four
wickets in hand.

The crowd jeered every time Akram and Shoaib
touched the ball. And they are not done yet. Walking out
of the Eden Gardens, among the thousands trooping

across the maidan outside the stadium and towards the buses and taxis on Chowringhee, I catch snatches of conversation which suggest that the worst is still to come.

'Akram should have called Sachin back.'

'Yes, don't you remember what Viswanath did against England at Mumbai? He called the batsman back.'

'I mean, it was a clear case of cheating. I *saw* it. Shoaib slammed into Sachin. I *saw* it.' The man is shaking his head. Each time he repeats himself he grows more convinced that he is right.

'What do the rules of the game say about it?'

'Aw, forget the rules. It *was* cheating.'

'*Banchod*. Sisterfuckers. We won't let them off if they look like winning tomorrow.'

They don't. And the papers do nothing to help matters. Supporters are waving copies of the Kolkata-based English daily the *Telegraph* as they settle into their seats on the final morning. It reminds me of the Indian parliament, MPs brandishing copies of dailies in the House as sticks to flog the opposition with. 'AKRAM LOSES INDIA, MAY WIN TEST,' says the headline. The *Telegraph* has made no pretence at objective journalism – it has sided with the crowd. So things got out of hand? Come come, the poor guys were given a raw deal. The fault was Akram's. 'He could have called back Sachin Tendulkar and become a hero. But he chose to sour the goodwill generated by him and his team with one gesture he chose not to make.'

Everyone in the ground knows what would have happened to Akram back in Pakistan had he called Sachin back and then lost the Test. They know the Pakistani captain had the rules of the game on his side, that he's a professional cricket player, that he wants to win a tough match by any legal means. Claiming that he should have called Sachin back is like suggesting that a tennis player ask for a key point to be replayed because he has won it on a net call. But that's not what the spectators at the Eden Gardens want to read.

I leave the ground as soon as the first bottle lands on the field. India are nine wickets down, and Akram has bowled beautifully. I am scared; I don't want to repeat the previous afternoon's crouching vigil.

In hindsight, it is a pretty smart decision.

By the time I get back home and switch on the TV (there, that's the masochism at work again), the commentators are talking about the Eden Gardens's hour of shame. Play has been suspended: the barrage of bottles, fruits, stones and slabs of concrete has sent the players off.

It continues for two more hours. Then the crowd seems to calm down. The players are coaxed to return. No sooner have they trooped back than the trouble starts again.

I remember the guy I had met outside the stadium the evening before. 'Sisterfuckers. We won't let them off if they look like winning.' Clearly, he is not alone.

The match referee considers awarding the match to Pakistan, but ICC boss Jagmohan Dalmiya – the man who dreamed up this tournament – is insistent that this charade of a Test match be played out to its grim, sordid end.

Probably bored with the vandalism, thousands of spectators have left the ground. The riot police have moved in again. The truncheons come down, connecting with bone and flesh. The dull thuds are muted on TV. But I was there yesterday, I can imagine what it is like. There are people cowering on the concrete; there are people trying to run; there are children and women. But the police catch them all, flicking out a boot here, bringing down a fist there. The Eden Gardens does not look like a cricket stadium.

In the end, after the stands have been cleared, the players reappear. There's a smattering of spectators in the upper tiers. They make the ground look even more cavernous and desolate. Pakistan take the last wicket before a single run is added. They have won by forty-six runs. The players seem embarrassed, eager to get the game over and done with as soon as they can.

After the match, Akram blames the media more than the crowd. He calls the incident 'the saddest thing ever to have happened in Test cricket'. But he says 'it is all because of you people and your reports. You have held them [the crowd] responsible for the wrongdoings but I will never blame them.'

The Pakistan captain is both right and wrong. The media must bear some responsibility but they didn't start this; they merely fed the frenzy. In the best tradition of tabloid journalism, they gave people what they wanted to read.

The rioters didn't need the press to give them an excuse. They rioted because they wanted to. They revealed the side of them that is best kept hidden. They always do when India play Pakistan.

I was there. And being there is the worst thing.

*　　*　　*

I'm playing a little game with myself now. Join me.

I'm trying to imagine what an India versus Pakistan cricket match would look like to an outsider, to someone who, unlike me, is not steeped in the backstory. Were you living on Mars (or in the United States – as close to Mars as you can get when it comes to talking cricket), what would it look like, this meeting of two Asian neighbours on a cricket field? It should look like a game. It does not.

Here is a selection of extracts I've gathered from around the world. (Okay, that's the cricket-playing world, which, as my football-fan friends never tire of telling me, is not quite a representative sample of the globe.) Go on. Find out what you think. Watch out for the warlike language, the riffs about cross-border tension and terrorism, the chauvinism, the hard-edged nationalistic fervour.

Whenever the two foes play, it is a case of politics, history, rivalry and honour coming together on the cricket field. For Indians and Pakistanis across the rest of the world, today's match is the final and what happens in the rest of the tournament is not important . . . Many temples and mosques have been busy, while some fans have been giving money to charities and homeless people in the hope that their good deeds will secure favour from higher forces for their team.
(*Vivek Chaudhary in the* Guardian, *1 March 2003, on the eve of the India-Pakistan World Cup game in South Africa*)

It was Imran Khan who in his own flamboyant but politically naïve style once declared that if Kashmir were the only issue between India and Pakistan, why not settle it on the cricket field with a match for territory? . . . Such posturing only goes to show why there can never be a lasting peace between the two nations, only tensions made worse by their nuclear capabilities.

There will be words exchanged. There will be skirmishes in the crowd as that great British institution – the brewery – sends its products down the throats of the cricket spectator. There will be flags waved and drums beaten and unique subcontinental bad words will be flying around . . .

This is sport's ultimate derby, greater than the Celtic versus Rangers football match in Scotland where too religious sectarian feelings can run high between Protestants and Catholics.

'This is an encounter that brings into play politics, religion and the foundations of a national identity across a huge swathe of humanity . . .' says the *Nation* newspaper in Pakistan.

India and Pakistan are nations divided by a common culture, much as it is said, humorously of course, that England and the US are divided by a common language. But then, what makes this particular match so significant is it comes in terms of time too close for comfort after the air sorties and the shelling in Kargil and the downing of IAF planes.

(*R. Mohan in the* Indian Express, *6 June 1999, before the India-Pakistan World Cup game in England*)

We know this is just a game . . . But for Pakistani people, we feel this [game] is like a war and our players

are our soldiers and they should not let us down,' said Pakistan cricket board secretary Mohammad Rafiq . . . 'Not disappointing but a crime,' said Mansoor Ahmed, a supporter in Lahore.
(*The* Telegraph, *Kolkata, 10 June 1999, the day after Pakistan lost to India in the World Cup*)

Watching the immense build-up of public excitement, the [Indian] ministry of external affairs was obliged to comment . . . that the game would not affect India-Pakistan relations.
(*The Deccan* Herald, *28 February 2003, on the eve of the India-Pakistan World Cup game in South Africa*)

There is an unsaid sub-text here: we can afford to lose to them at football and table tennis but not at cricket.
(*From* A Corner of a Foreign Field, *Ramachandra Guha*)

When the Pakistan team returned home from the 1999 World Cup, Inzamam ul Haq found his home ransacked by angry fans. Captain Wasim Akram's mother made an appeal, with folded hands, to the fans for tolerance. Most newspapers concluded that the intense anger was not because Pakistan had lost the final (being the second best one-day side in the world can't be that bad, and losing to Australia was no disgrace) but because earlier in the tournament they had been beaten by India.

Now. Go on. What would you think if you knew nothing about India and Pakistan?

* * *

The story goes back to 1947. When India gained its independence it was not as one country but as two. It had seen off the British, but it could not overcome its internal divisions. The result was an imposed Partition and – to oversimplify – one Hindu-majority nation, India, and one Muslim-majority nation, Pakistan. Pakistan's founding father, Muhammad Ali Jinnah, hoped that the creation of an independent Muslim homeland would bring lasting peace to the region. Things did not quite turn out that way.

Nearly one million people were killed in the Hindu–Muslim riots that followed Partition; millions more lost their homes; and the trauma of displacement and exile became encoded in the DNA of both nations. Within months of their births, India and Pakistan were at war. Before Partition, Kashmir's Hindu Maharajah had decided that his state should become part of India. But Kashmir was – and is still – predominantly Muslim. Pakistan believed it was rightfully hers. Kashmir has been a running sore ever since. It was the cause of renewed hostilities in 1965, and low-level border skirmishes have gone on for years. Heavy fighting in Kargil during the 1999 World Cup – just as India and Pakistan took to the field at Old Trafford – almost led to war again. Now that both India and Pakistan possess nuclear weapons, the results would be unthinkable.

The two countries may be at loggerheads politically, but culturally they have much so much in common: heritage, language, food, clothes. And of all that they share, cricket is the most pervasive, the most fervently supported and perhaps the most enduring. Which is why a win – or loss – at cricket is so important. Whenever India and Pakistan meet on a cricket field, it is not simply to play a game. As the social historian Ramachandra Guha says, 'Within India, a loss to Pakistan at cricket is harder to bear than a loss on the battlefield.'

Since the Eden Test of 1999 things have changed for the better – at least on the face of it. In January 2004, India and Pakistan met at the negotiating table in an attempt to sort out their complex, acrimonious relationship. One of the cornerstones of the peace process was what diplomats and politicians like to call 'people to people exchanges'. That March, the Indian cricket team embarked on its first fully fledged tour of Pakistan for fifteen years. It caused a frenzy of excitement. Thousands of Indians followed their team to Pakistan. Perhaps to their surprise, they received a warm welcome. They returned home full of glowing stories about the kindness they'd been shown, the hospitality they'd been offered. For me the most enduring image of that series was not to be found on the pitch, despite Sehwag's triple hundred at Multan. It was of an Indian and a Pakistani flag stitched together and inscribed with a line borrowed from Bollywood: *Pyar to hona hi tha* (Love had to happen between us).

Pakistan returned the compliment at the beginning of 2005. If the atmosphere was not quite as intense this time around, it was filled with a spirit of goodwill that not been seen before. When India disgraced themselves by losing by 168 runs in the final Test at Bangalore, shopkeepers

did not need to barricade their stores against the inevitable rioters. There were no reports of players' houses
being attacked or their families abused. The hysterical
jingoism of previous India-Pakistan games was largely
absent. As indeed it was when India toured Pakistan again
in 2006. It may seem trivial in the scheme of things, but
for many of us it was a benediction. Cricket seemed a little
like cricket again.

Even so, I was edgy throughout these tours. The calm
seemed fragile; I feared it could not last. Somewhere
beneath that deceptive restraint, I thought, the old ugly
emotions still stirred. It would not take much to provoke
an eruption – perhaps just an ill-timed run-out, a bowler
getting in a batsman's way.

*   *   *

I love to watch Pakistan on a cricket field. I love the way
they bring on young talent. I love their audaciousness,
their unpredictability, their guts, their tendency to scale
heights or plumb depths that few other teams are capable
of. Cricket *is* a game of glorious uncertainties, and
Pakistan exemplifies the cliché better than any other side
in the world.

My first memories of watching Pakistan are of the 1978
India-Pakistan Test series. (India and Pakistan did not
play each other between 1961 and 1978.) I fell in love with
Majid Khan's strokeplay; with the murderous elegance of
Zaheer Abbas (another nearly man, like Viswanath,
always in the shadow of Javed Miandad); with the
gentlemanly Asif Iqbal (I almost cried when his rubber

soles slipped and he was run out in his final Test at the Eden Gardens in 1980). And of course there was Imran. The feline grace, the flashing eyes, perpetually narrowed to slits so you wondered how he ever saw through them, the long hair flying behind him in the slipstream as he tore in, the shirt with its three buttons undone, the pre-delivery leap, and the women. Always the women. (A psychiatrist friend once told me that that was why I found Imran so fascinating. I hope it wasn't just that.)

I have often dreamt of the side we would have were Pakistan and India still one country: Sehwag and Afridi to open in the one-days; Sachin and Inzamam in a Test middle order; Wasim Akram and Anil Kumble bowling from either end; Imran the inspirational captain. Occasionally, I have to pinch myself.

For much of my lifetime, I have had to keep this to myself. Voicing my admiration for Pakistan would have been a treasonable offence, especially over recent years. It has not always been this way (and who knows, perhaps things really will be different from now on). It has not been the fault of the players. Flashpoints on the pitch arise not because of any personal antagonism but because of the pressure both sets of fans put their sides under to win. It is the fans' fault, our fault.

I have never burnt an effigy, never threatened a player, never demonstrated outside his home. I was not present at the 1999 World Cup game. But it makes little difference. In a sense one is always there – you don't have to be at the game, or even in the same country, to be implicated, however indirectly. It is our common shame. The fact that I was not one of the rioters at the

Eden Gardens in February 1999 does not make things
any better. As a matter of fact, it makes it worse. I did
not do anything, but my failure to act implicates me
equally.

When India play Pakistan I encounter a doppelgänger
I would rather not acknowledge. It is like meeting an
identical twin who has disgraced himself. I see men like
me – men who on other days and in other circumstances
could be my colleagues, my friends, even my family –
behaving despicably. And I cannot escape the taint of this
brotherhood. We, all of us, have allowed cricket to
become more than a game. As a result, it has also become
less.

I hate India-Pakistan matches not just because of the
chauvinism, the religious bigotry. I hate them because
they are an attack on something deeper, something we
may not care to admit to: our idea of sport itself. In
allowing politics, religion, even war, to hijack our game,
we have given cricket a symbolic value it does not possess.
We have convinced ourselves that the game is important
because it stands for something else. But cricket isn't *like*
anything else; it is only like cricket.

In their introduction to the *Picador Book of Sports Writing*,
editors Nick Coleman and Nick Hornby make this point
eloquently: 'A common misapprehension about sport is
that, in itself, it stands as a metaphor for real life; that we
play, watch and read about sport because we want the rest
of our lives to be illuminated by sport's special allegorical
language, as if sport has something to tell us in the way
that art does. The editors beg to suggest that this is tosh.
Sport is not a metaphor for the rest of life, it is indivisible

from the rest of life. That's its magic. It is not a description of something, it is, simply, what it is.'

And I resent any attempt to take my game away from me.

8

'B for L, J for D'

YOU CAN TELL from their faces. Shining with anticipation, a restlessness revealed by the darting eyes. Above
all else, triumphant. On the buses heading towards the
Eden Gardens on match day you can tell from the faces
who is going to be inside the ground when play begins.
And who is not. They're the ones who look vaguely
resentful, who stare out of the window because they can't
bear to look at their fellow passengers, who are eager to
get off and get on with whatever else that they are
supposed to be doing (because anything else is better than
being on a bus crammed with fans going to the Eden).
They don't fit in; they want out of this celebration.

The conductor, perhaps because he knows that
proximity to the people going to the Eden Gardens is
the closest that he will get to real action, is indulgent.
He's happy to talk about the match. (A rare gesture.
Conductors on Kolkata buses don't talk; unless it's to
ask you for your fare. And sometimes not even that –
they'll shuffle up and merely riffle their sheaf of tickets
under your nose. A sharp, grating sound. Pay for the
privilege of riding on one of the worst transport systems
in the world.)

This is Kolkata's biggest annual picnic. For many, this is the most sought-after prize of the whole year: a plain rectangular stub of glazed paper that tells you your gate and seat numbers. It is a chance to be *there*. It really is. (At the time I first started going to the Eden Gardens in the late 1970s, even on the fourth day of a Test that is dead or dying, 100,000 people would fill the stadium.)

One after another, the buses crawl to a halt at Chowringhee, the busiest intersection in the heart of Kolkata's central business district. I have always wanted to catch the first Chowringhee-bound bus on a match day. (When *do* the first spectators start coming in? *Just when*? I've rolled up two hours before start of play, three hours, and still seen thousands walking up to the stadium.)

Half a step at a time. That's as much of a stride as you can take. The crowd presses in on you from all sides. No traffic is allowed on the roads leading to the ground; the police reroute all the vehicles. They cordon off the pavements; spectators are penned inside rough bamboo partitions. No one is allowed to spill over on to the road.

The first time I walked through this crowd – *along* with this crowd – I was scared. I was nine years old and I had never seen so many people. The tight columns made me feel claustrophobic; I feared a stampede. Over the years, though, I have realised that this is not the danger period. It's too early in the morning for the crowd to be drunk. (Often, it's only seven o'clock.) And since there has been no play we've not yet been disappointed. Tempers have not yet been frayed; no one is actually spoiling for a fight.

These days I get off the bus and plunge right in, taking my place behind the last man in the long queue. It is a good couple of kilometres to the ground. Hard work, when there's no place to put your feet, when all you see in front of you is a sweat-stained shirt and all you can feel is the guy behind you steadying himself in the crush. Just occasionally, to your right you can see the vacant road. There are so many police – on foot, on motorbikes, in jeeps, chattering agitatedly into their walkie-talkies. The emptiness of the road only draws attention to how crushed we are.

Groups – friends, colleagues, family, lovers – try to stick together in the swarm. Some of them carry today's newspapers. They're not for reading. They'll be spread out on the ground's dusty concrete benches. Seats are luxuries.

As I approach the Eden I examine my fellow spectators. The crowd seems so much more, well, *internationalised,* than it used to be. The last time I was here, a year ago, among the shuffling feet, I saw hundreds and hundreds of trainers: Nike, Adidas, Reebok. Shorts, fashionably long for men, and T-shirts, fashionably short for women, covered in swooshes or leaping pumas; jeans (Levi's, Pepe, Wrangler, you name it, you got it); baseball caps turned backwards; shades (Ray-Bans, Gucci); satchels, knapsacks. If you want a snapshot of global sartorial kitsch, here's the place to come.

Unless you look at the faces – these days often emblazoned with the Indian tricolour (a decade-and-a-half-old habit, picked up from watching international football on satellite TV) – you could be in any city in the world. It is a far cry from the days when my mother insisted I wear my darkest pair of shorts and a terry cotton shirt stitched at the local tailors. ('These are best for the Eden Gardens, the grime won't show.')

Like tributaries into a river, the roads finally open out into the green of the maidan at the stadium's edge. Most fans keep on walking when they reach the grass, happy to let their strides lengthen, relieved to find the extra space. Some, though, huddle together in knots. For we've reached the monstrous statue of Goshto Pal (one of Bengal's legendary footballers; his arms are flung out at a painful, almost absurd angle), the most popular prematch meeting ground.

As the crowd pauses for breath and looks up at the upper tiers of the stands, the street vendors approach: chewing gum, chocolates and, in the last few years, Coke, Pepsi, bottled mineral water.

The street vendors are only the first wave. Next come the walking billboards. Big corporations have hired them for the day. They're distributing cardboard sunshades, tacky, pathetic things, with the name of the company in bold letters across the visor. Not many fans have any use for them. It's ironic: the crowd won't take them, even though they're free; but they're happy to shell out for branded baseball caps. They've been educated by the TV spots, the glossy magazines. They know what is *appropriate* to the occasion. Would you rather be seen with a sunshade that says 'ACC Cement' or a cap which says 'Adidas'?

'Extra ticket? Extra? Any price, brother, any price. Which block?' The next tribe has arrived. These are the guys who have not planned in advance, who have left it too late and are prepared to risk the disappointment of

standing by the gates all morning only to leave empty-
handed – back to the sofa at home with a beer because
they have taken the day off work anyway and wouldn't,
for any price, go to the office and admit to not having had
a ticket in the first place. Or else they're really desperate,
crazy enough to have stood in line all night for the day
seats. They're back again this morning: fate is bound to
reward fans as persistent as themselves, they hope. How
could it not?

We're on to the last bunch. Those who want to
exchange tickets. They walk up to you, brandishing their
stubs.

'B for L.'

'J for D.'

'C for K'.

Like all codes, it's simple enough to crack if you know
the key.

'What on earth are they talking about?' an ex-girlfriend
(the only girlfriend I have ever taken to a cricket match)
once asked me.

The way it works is this: say you have a ticket in Block
B, to the right of the pavilion, and your friend has one in
Block L, to the left. You wave your (or your friend's) ticket
above your head and scream, as hard as you can, in the
hope of finding someone who wants to swap; someone
sitting on the left of the pavilion with a friend on the right.

No money changes hands during these encounters. But
sometimes one of the parties will emerge distinctly better
off.

'B for J? Come on, that is no deal.'

Block J is square of the wicket, nowhere near as good a

place to watch the cricket as Block B, which is behind
third man or long on, depending on which end the bowler
is bowling from.

'Well, take it or leave it. I'll find someone else. Thirty
minutes for the toss, brother. Remember.'

The hustling won't make any difference. What matters
is how badly you want to sit with your friend. On
occasion, I have made a bad swap myself. It just depends.

Inside the stadium things look very different these days.
I've been coming here for twenty-seven years now.
Everything changed in 1987, with the World Cup. They
rebuilt the stadium for the final: they added more tiers to
the stands; a fibreglass roof, essential now that they were
playing cricket in what used to be the off-season; a giant
scoreboard square of the wicket. The new scoreboard was
a bit like the Indian batting: it had enormous potential
(more details than anyone could ever want); it was also
scandalously fickle. It still is, after fifteen years. It's
infuriating when it goes on the blink at the death in a one-
day game.

Opposite the pavilion, above the sightscreen, they built
a new stand. It's the only stand in the ground with
individual seats, white plastic bucket chairs that shimmer
in the sun; the rest of us, squeezed on the concrete
benches, look on in envy. The new stand was built for
foreign fans travelling to the World Cup – their pounds
and dollars went further than the humble rupee, justifying
the high ticket prices. These days, the stand's occupants
can spend more on watching a day's cricket than the
average income in Bengal.

There are corporate boxes too, again spin-offs from the

World Cup. For once the Cricket Association of Bengal were a little ahead of the curve. (They must have taken their cue from Sharjah.) In 1987, air-conditioned, glass-fronted boxes were unheard of in India. Their inhabitants, with their televisions and minibars, are insulated from the rest of the ground, deliberately so. (Ironically none of the minibars stock any alcohol. You used to be able to drink at the Eden, but it was a purely nudge-nudge-wink-wink thing. Some spectators spiked their giant bottles of cola with rum, or their soda water with whisky. *Real* men in Kolkata drink only rum or whisky. It stinks. But that's all gone now – you're not allowed to bring bottles of any description into the ground. Water is sold in small, plastic pouches which you tear open with your teeth, water dribbling down your front. The hawkers selling bottles of mineral water outside the stadium have less business these days, although many still buy and down the water in a single gulp before entering the stadium.) The spectators in the insulated boxes sit there in their splendid isolation. The rest of the ground treats them with the kind of scorn that one reserves for rich but stingy relatives who neither bring us nice gifts when they arrive nor leave us generous pocket money when they go.

The stadium has its own class system, which may or may not correspond to the real world. Visitors to the Eden fall into one of three camps: the aristocracy, the bourgeois and the workers. You'll find the aristocracy in the life-members' stands on either side of the pavilion and in the annual and associate-members' stands adjacent to them. For these are reserved for the *members*, those who are here by right (God-given, they assume). Once you are a member there's no more queuing for tickets, no doubt as to whether you'll get in. Just pick up your ticket and go to your seat.

The bucket seats and air-conditioned boxes are the preserve of the bourgeois (nouveau riche usurpers, the members call them): company men enjoying a day at the cricket as compensation for their eighty-hour weeks, businessmen who don't care how much money they spend because the annual turnover will take care of it.

The rest of the ground belongs to the working class: the stands at widish mid-off and mid-on of the pavilion end, and the Ranji stand – perhaps the most raucous and vibrant in the whole ground.

Each of these groups is convinced that it is the only *authentic* presence in the stadium; the others are mere impostors.

Those in the cheap seats claim that they're the true fans – after all, they've queued for hours to buy tickets, they've had to show resolve, determination, indomitable will just to be here, and now they're fighting for space on the bum-numbing concrete benches.

The members know that they are the Eden's real, rightful owners. Those who have bought day tickets (cheap or expensive) are interlopers, here today, gone when the next match is played. They will be here for ever. They and the Eden share a history. They *are* the Eden's history – many of them have been coming here for generations. It's a family thing, and Eden is part of the family.

The monied elite who pack the expensive seats and corporate boxes think that everybody else is shit. Because

they have more money than everybody else. They are
perhaps the least self-conscious and most confident people
in the place. They couldn't care less about being
members; they wouldn't dream of queuing all night.
Money buys privileges and after a while (so long as your
wallet remains comfortably full) those privileges become
rights. Who cares about history, who cares about what
other people think of them? Their wealth inures them to
others' scorn.

At various points in my life, I have watched cricket with
all three sections of the crowd. These rivalries are rubbish,
of course, a joke we can all share. Like all good jokes it
works because there's some truth to it. But only one thing
matters when India's eleven men take to the field: 100,000
people are united in their support.

*   *   *

For some the rhythm of a day's cricket is incomprehensible. Why so slow? Why isn't anything happening?
The game of cricket lends itself to a protracted drawing
out, a suspension of the spectator across a high-voltage
wire of tension and anticipation. Long periods when
ostensibly nothing happens (a new-ball spell, say, when
the bowler beats the outside edge four times in a row and
still does not manage to get a nick – when, for the
uninitiated, the game doesn't seem to be moving *forward*)
can mean plenty is happening. But there comes a time
when nothing really is happening, when play has indeed
stopped. In fact, that time comes at least twice each day –
during lunch and tea.

As Bill Bryson so wryly observes in his book *Down Under*, cricket is the only sport to incorporate meal breaks. They are not there, as Bryson has it, because that's the only way one can be sure that 'activity on the field has gone from very slight to non-existent'. Breaks (for lunch, for tea, even for drinks) are integral to the game. They offer scope for contemplation and reflection, time to review the events of the past couple of hours, time to take stock and to look forward to what is to come. They also have a significance beyond the game itself. You are what you eat, they say. It's a thought that strikes me each time I have my lunch at the Eden Gardens. For every food hamper has its own story. They mirror the people who bring them as much as the ground to which they are brought. In their contents you can sniff the way the game and the ground has changed, and the way their owners have been transformed.

I have never been to a cricket ground with my mother. (This seems strangely inappropriate: it was she who first taught me to be passionate about the game; I have watched and listened to more cricket with her – on the TV and the radio – than with any other single person in my life.) But in a way she has always been by my side. From the day I first went to the Eden until the day that I finally stopped taking lunch, I always sensed her presence. She was there every time I opened my lunch hamper. She always prepared them for me herself – carefully, lovingly, and unfailingly with an eye to the time of the year and the kind of nourishment that would get me through crying myself hoarse for a full day in the sun.

I remember how she fidgeted and fussed over the meal

I took with me that first day. The evening before I set off ('Early, you need to leave very early in the morning or else you will miss the players practising,' she told me), she busied herself with a mound of flour, patting it, sprinkling it with water, rolling it into small, thin, flat circular shapes and then frying them into that most Bengali of delicacies, the *luchi*. I neglected my homework to be near her in the kitchen, leaving her side only to check on my ticket, just to make sure that it had not, for some inexplicable reason, been stolen, flushed down the toilet, or grown wings and flown away.

While she fried the *luchis* and prepared the *alur dam* – peeled potatoes seasoned with green chillies, garlic and onions and smeared in gravy – my mother kept up a constant conversation. Her cricket-ground recipes, she told me, had been handed down to her by her mother, who had ensured that she would not go hungry or thirsty at the field. (That was the edge my mother had over her own: she'd actually been to the Eden herself, many times. She knew what made the best lunch, how parched you felt at the end of the day, which things were best for sharing – as sure a way as any to win friends and influence people at a cricket ground.)

Along with the *luchis* and the potatoes, she loaded my cloth bag (this was before the days of the knapsack or satchel; like most other spectators, I carried an unattractive cloth bag slung across my shoulder) with an astonishingly large number of oranges and lozenges, and a large flask of cold water. ('You're crazy,' I said. 'Who in his right mind would want so many *oranges*?' 'Well, you will and then there will be the people next to you. You have no idea how oranges and lozenges vanish during a day of cricket.' When I left the stadium at the end of the day, the cloth bag had been folded and stuffed in my pocket. It was empty; everything had disappeared, thanks to myself and my neighbours, half an hour after tea.)

I never knew why, but in the days when I first went to the Eden, I was not allowed to drink tea at home. For the tea break, my mother packed me jam tarts and Swiss rolls, and an assortment of my favourite pastries that she had bought from Flury's, my favourite cake shop. On the morning of my big day, frantic the players would take the field without me, I tore from toilet to breakfast table. Then, as I was about to leave, my mother closed my fist over a ten-rupee note and said: 'You won't have tea. Get yourself an ice cream if the water runs out.' It did (run out) and I didn't (buy myself an ice cream). Instead, I put the cash in my piggy bank. Whoever thought that you could actually earn *money* by going to the cricket?

Within a few years, the *luchis* disappeared from my lunch hamper. They gave way to crumb-fried fillets of fish and long, fat chips; immaculately dressed salad in olive oil or vinaigrette dressing; ham and lettuce sandwiches; pasta with tomato and basil. Now that I think about it, these lunches, like the clothes spectators wear to the ground these days, were more appropriate to the Wanderers or the MCG than they were to the Eden.

A decade and a half after my first visit, eating had become a much less messy affair. Plastic cutlery accompanied the meals from home. My lunch no longer rolled around in its box like a corpse too small for its coffin; instead it was packed in shining aluminium foil and greaseproof paper. The flask was replaced by large bottles of mineral water. And the idea of taking so much food that there would be enough to offer strangers I wanted to make friends with had been knocked on the head because there weren't that many (by now, *any*) people with whom I wanted to share my lunch.

On one of my early visits (probably to see Kim Hughes's Australians in 1979), I listened in awe as a thirtysomething gentleman (he must have been as old then as I am now) explained to his small son the implications of dust flying from the pitch before lunch on the second day. I remember the reverential look on the little boy's face (he was scarcely older than my daughter is now) and feeling a twinge of self-pity because my father was not with me. (I have never been to a cricket match with him either.) Perhaps that was why I was so eager to make friends. We shared my lunch; I gave them most of my oranges.

During the India-Pakistan Test in February 1999 I sat next to a thirtysomething father who was teaching his son how best to make a racket with two empty plastic bottles. 'No, you don't beat them against the seat. You hold a bottle in each hand and smash them against each other. Super fast. Like this,' he explained, drumming up a healthy clackety-clack. The son, the reverential look on his face identical to the one I had seen on that little boy's twenty years before, eagerly copied his father.

As the boy got overexcited, the bottles flew out of his hand, hitting a couple in the seats in front of us. The boy cried with frustration. The father said nothing. (I had a bizarre, unsettling vision: had that boy become this man?) I didn't even offer them a stick of gum. (It's silly, I know, but I feared they might stick it on my seat once they were done with it.)

Perhaps I'm being unfair. Perhaps my favourite drink is nostalgia on the rocks. Perhaps it was just bad luck. But it seems as though I was invariably lucky then and am unfailingly unlucky now. All I know for certain is that I do not share my lunch as I used to in the old days.

These days, I often don't take any food with me at all. (My mother has grown old and I want to save her – and myself and my wife – the bother of preparing it; and at my age it seems preposterous to be fussing over a packed lunch.) Instead I eat amid the mini-stampede at one of the many food counters in the bowels of the stadium – a dank, cavernous place which always smells of urine (the food stalls are as close as you can get to the toilets without actually being inside them) and sweat and cheap disinfectant. Here, I get myself an inauthentic biryani or almost inedible noodles (these are noodles you will find nowhere else in the world: pathetic strands swimming in a pool of tomato ketchup and soy sauce) and stand there balancing the plate on one hand as I steady myself against the onslaught of hundreds of people rushing to and from the loo. There's only tap water to wash it down with. Most of my friends say it is about as safe as stuff from a ditch but I have never once fallen ill from drinking it. (It is my ineffectual – and some maintain self-destructive – protest against fizzy drinks.)

Now, as I stand beneath the tiers, in the half-light, trying to finish eating as soon as I can (it is a long, slow walk back to my seat), I feel a stab of longing for the old boyhood lunches. I try to recapture the languid rhythm of those childhood winter afternoons, but it's impossible. Perhaps we always pine for what is lost. Perhaps I miss my mum's cooking. Perhaps I miss being nine.

*   *   *

Ashis Nandy, one of India's leading sociologists, once told me in an interview that you need to be either wealthy or well connected to get into the Eden these days. Only a small fraction of the tickets are for sale. On the eve of the India-Sri Lanka 1996 World Cup semi-final, the Kolkata *Telegraph* put the figure at a mere 4,000, and things haven't got any easier since. (Given how hard these tickets are to get hold of, it's little wonder that the crowd in the day seats feel that they're the only true fans.) The rest are, to use a word popular with the Cricket Association of Bengal, 'distributed'. Which is to say that they go to CAB members and the Association's numerous affiliates. As a rule of thumb, if you're not a member of the CAB your chances of emerging successfully from the 'distribution' process will depend on how much influence you have.

My father was neither wealthy nor well connected. He was, as he often liked to say, a 'self-made man'. The eldest of three brothers, he grew up in a long, narrow two-room flat in north Kolkata. The flat was so small that there was no room for a desk – he studied for medical school sitting on the floor. Once he had qualified he was given a fellow-ship to train abroad. After returning to India, he built up from scratch a practice successful enough to afford me a comfortable childhood and affluent adolescence. He never asked for any favours; he never received any.

My father worked hard to give his family the best of everything (though, he says now, the best that he could give then was not necessarily the best that he wanted for us). As my obsession with cricket grew and grew, it put him in a difficult position. Tickets to the Eden Gardens were hard to come by, even in those days. My uncle had been kind enough to take me to my first game, but that was to see the West Indians. The Australians were due to visit the next year; the Pakistanis, the year after that. It would not be easy.

In the run-up to the Kolkata Test, those who have spare tickets for the Eden (or sources to ensure that they will have tickets) become the most important people in town. You can tell them by their haunted expressions, by the way they'll run away from you on the street. Because anyone with spare tickets to the Test is a marked man. For anyone who has ever done you a favour, for anyone with a claim on you, it is payback time. And if you don't have tickets it's even worse. Even if you can find a benefactor to provide you with what you crave, the debt incurred will not be small. It may take some time to clear. It is a trying time for everyone, one that – even by Indian standards – involves much complicated role playing between the benefactor and the benefited.

My father discovered that getting me a passport to the Eden involved an inversion of roles: as a doctor he was used to being a benefactor; now he had to play the supplicant. He didn't like this one bit. He was forced to remind people of favours he had done them, or swallow his pride, put himself in debt and ask outright. It was contradictory to his nature, it made him awkward and uncertain, but he knew that if there was one thing in life I wanted (*really* wanted, perhaps more than I have ever wanted anything), it was to be inside the Eden Gardens when the Test match was on. Every year he went through with it – the wheedling, the self-abasement – and not once did he let me down.

On a couple of occasions my mother's side of the family, who were nearly all members of the CAB, obliged. Once my father got a ticket for me and then one of my maternal uncles swapped it outside the stadium so that I could sit with him. To my father, it seemed a little less like asking for a favour but it did not entirely assuage his conscience.

One evening in 1984 my father returned home from his clinic and called me in to his bedroom. With a hesitant, shy smile (as though he was embarrassed to witness my reaction), he produced a small piece of glossy card from a plastic jacket and held it out to me.

It took me a while to realise its significance. For in the top left-hand corner of the card was the crest of the CAB; and across the middle, in block capitals, the words 'LIFE MEMBER'. On the reverse, in blue ink, were my name and a number.

If only life allowed more such occasions.

A few months previously, the CAB had advertised for applications for life membership. (You need have no connection with cricket to become a member of the Cricket Association of Bengal, a criterion – or lack of it – that has doubtless contributed to the character and cricket knowledge of the crowd in the members' stands over recent years.) In essence, it was a fund-raising drive. Each selected applicant paid a sum of Rs10,000. In return, whenever there was a match at the Eden Gardens, he was assured of a seat – for as long as he lived. Rs10,000 was not an insignificant sum, but my father had applied. And had been successful.

I didn't drink in those days. If I had, I would have remained in a stupor for months – till the Englishmen came to tour in the winter.

* * *

It is twenty-seven years since I first visited the Eden. In that time I have fallen in and out of love with the place. I have endured some of my worst experiences on a cricket field there; I have been caught in riots, I have heard grown men hurl the vilest insults, I have had my faith in the game itself disturbed. I have vowed never to set foot inside its gates again – after 1999 – and I have returned almost immediately – in 2002.

It is not the look of the place that brings me back. There is nothing remotely pretty about the Eden Gardens these days. Hemmed in by high stands on every side, the suggestion of lurking, suppressed violence in every block, it looks more and more like a football stadium. And the changes have not simply been physical.

Once Kolkatan spectators prided themselves on being courteous and knowledgeable. (Living in a city which has had to accept its marginalisation from the national scene, most Kolkatans pride themselves on being courteous and knowledgeable – it's just about all they had left to cling on to for many years. The new century signalled a resurgence

for Kolkata – better infrastructure, more foreign investment – and perhaps there is a new brashness about the
city now, perhaps the old talk of courtesy and knowledge
is a little muted.) Nowadays there are too many fans who
care too little about cricket – and too much for flag-
waving. Over the past few years they have sometimes
proved a disgrace to the city, the stadium and the game:
they have disrupted matches, even caused them to be
abandoned.

The little things trouble me too. I know I risk sounding
like an old fart, but I miss seeing the ground filled with
radios. These days the mobile phone has taken over – it's
easier to call home and get the verdict from the instant
replays than it is to to use your imagination and work it
out from the expert commentary. The food is different;
the clothes have changed; there are fewer old people in
the stands; the women all look like they want to be on TV;
the Mexican wave (never done too well, always not so
much a wave as a ripple) is inexplicably popular. But there
are as many spectacular performances on the field as
there ever were; and India loses far less often than they
used to.

One thing, though, has not changed a bit since the day
I first passed through the Eden's gates. Every time I go
back, it reaffirms my faith; it shows me how, in very rare
cases, time can appear to stand still.

It happens when I walk into the ground.

I'm past the police and I'm walking through the long,
wide, musty corridor beneath, then between the stands.
And suddenly, in one vivid and unforgettable moment, I
see the field. There it is in front of me, framed by the

stands, beneath a patch of open sky, bathed in a Turneresque light.

It is a delirious moment, an instant when the pulse quickens and the heart thumps. In anticipation. In nostalgia. In that moment, the mind goes into rewind and fast forward at the same time.

I know that I am sounding hopelessly romantic. I should not. I know that the light is not really Turneresque, that that's just how I like to think of it. That considering what I have seen at the Eden in recent years, there is precious little romance left. I should not. But I can't help it. That is the way it is.

There is no other cricket ground in the world which I know will always have a place for me.

9

'?!?'

I HAVE A HOME video, shot on a Sony Handycam, of my daughter's first year. I made it (employing what I thought was my unutilised talent as a film director) with all the tricks that I, and the rather rudimentary machine, were capable of managing. There are clever fade-ins and fade-outs, dinky pans, zooms, crops, freeze-frames, slow-mos, a voiceover in which I tried to be, at various points, objective narrator, tender/long-suffering father and wry humorist, and a host of contrived situation shots with which my daughter largely – and sensibly, I think when I look at the film now – refused to cooperate.

The video captures key moments in my daughter's first twelve months – the first warble, the first toothless grin, the first half-lisp, the first faltering footsteps. Ostensibly it was made so that my daughter could appreciate, when she grew up, how much she means to us.

My daughter rather enjoys watching it these days. 'There's Oishi,' she says, her crooked index finger pointing at the television screen. She seems to enjoy her performance. I don't enjoy mine. I worry that when she grows up, she will sense that the whole video was actually just me showing off. I worry more that she will be right.

It contains, however, one moment that is not disingenuous in any way. It is an instant which sums up life in our family. At the point that this section was shot, Oishi had just begun to learn to walk. She would take a few steps then collapse from the effort. It was as if she was struggling to grasp the significance of this momentous achievement —all she knew was that life would never be the same again. When my wife and I used to watch her in those days, it seemed to us that having walked a few steps, our daughter was pausing to take stock.

The video catches Oishi as she gets up from the floor and begins to do a slow pirouette. Her arms are extended on either side for balance. A smile, half self-congratulatory, half tense (as though she's worried whether she can sustain this effort but is evidently pleased that she is managing well so far) is trembling on her lips. Then she takes a step, treading firmly, carefully, with great resolve and concentration, as though she were walking on slushy ground. The camera pulls away from her and we get a long shot, the entire family sitting in a ring around her, applauding, the brass plant holder in the corner of the room, the lamp, the legs of the sofa and the television propped up on a wooden cabinet. If you watch carefully here, you will be able to catch a glimpse of the TV screen; you will even be able to make out the powder blue shirts of the Indian cricket team. There is a match on.

The camera zooms in again on Oishi, lingers on her bare little feet, then pans up from floor level, pausing to catch her expression. (Presumably I was shooting this scene lying on my stomach, guerrilla-style.) Oishi takes one more step.

At this point, the camera begins to wobble. Horribly. My daughter goes out of focus and we see, in quick and rather jagged succession, glimpses of tiled floor (startling swirls of white mosaic on black), blank expanses of wall, a snatch of a David Hockney print in a gilt-edged frame, a fragment of a lampshade, table legs. Someone's turned up the volume on the television and we can hear the cricket commentary. Tony Greig is talking about Sachin Tendulkar.

Then the recording stops.

I must have been too ashamed to go on, I think now. But I have not doctored the tape in any way. It's there, just as I shot it, to remind me of who I am and what my wife and daughter have had to endure.

It is not a pleasant memento.

It can't be quite *right*, can it? You are filming your daughter's first attempts at walking and you go and fuck it up (*completely* fuck it up) because of a minor landmark in one of Tendulkar's innumerable innings. And that is not the worst of it: I wasn't missing anything; the match wasn't live, it wasn't even a rerun, it wasn't even a re-rerun. It was a re-re-rerun. I had seen it, live. I had watched the repeat telecast. I already had off by heart (I *still* have off by heart) most of the action that was worth remembering. And I still went and messed up a moment that happens only once in a lifetime.

*   *   *

Okay. I am in my mid-thirties. I have a job which I enjoy and which pays me handsomely. I've traded my small car for a larger, more expensive one. I have a wife who happens to be my best friend. We have a daughter who we both love madly, deeply, unconditionally.

I have never been arrested for shoplifting or busted for drugs or questioned for culpable homicide not amounting to murder. I am intelligent enough to make pasta or a curry or do the washing up without any obvious disasters. I enjoy music. I read a fair amount. I take at least one holiday a year. I have sufficient social skills to conduct a reasonable conversation, or so my friends say. I *have* friends.

In short, I have the CV of a middle-class, about-to-be-middle-aged, *average* heterosexual male.

In all – well, nearly all – respects.

So what goes wrong when it comes to cricket? What *is* it?

Over the years, I have discovered something: age *does* make a difference. It does not make me any less stupid or selfish or blinkered. It does not make me any less of a fan. The game is no less central to my life than it was fifteen years ago, when I was an average heterosexual male with no job and no wife and no kid and plenty of time.

What growing older has afforded me is a sense of perspective. Some days I can even step back and try to see myself as others see me. Some days I am even aware that my behaviour may seem strange or embarrassing.

I have realised several other things. I have realised that I *do* cricket the way some *do* drugs. Or drink. Or S & M. Twenty years ago, even ten, cricket was there to fill my time, to fill it in the most interesting and exciting way I knew. Now, I need to make time for cricket. There is just too much going on in the average, soon-to-be-middle-aged, middle-class, well paid, socially active parent's life. Too much clutter. I need to strip away some of that clutter to give cricket its proper place.

No, that is all wrong.

Cricket's proper place is right at the centre of my life. That's where I have to start. Then I can arrange the clutter around it. Luckily this comes naturally to me. But there are occasions – rare occasions, yes, but I can recognise them now and again – when I regret where my choices lead me.

When I make my wife cancel a doctor's appointment, when I refuse to look after my daughter or call off drinks with an old friend I haven't seen for years, afterwards I am miserable, filled with self-loathing. I know that if only I could have torn myself away from the cricket, I might even have enjoyed myself. It is unfair on my friends, my family. It is unfair on me.

But I quickly forget, and when the occasion comes around again, I let the cricket take precedence. If I have a choice between cricket and something else (and every-thing else in life is just 'something else'), cricket will win. The difference is that these days I am aware that there *is* a choice – and that some choices may be the wrong ones.

It is the nature of addiction. All addicts realise afterwards that there is a line they should not have crossed: a last puff, a last drink, a last fix they ought to have resisted. But when the craving returns (it always does, it always does), all the promises go out the window. They forget themselves. They reach for the bottle or the powder or the pipe.

I reach for the remote.

Addicts suffer if they give in to their addiction. They suffer if they don't.

I *do* cricket, didn't I tell you?

* * *

My aunt comes calling one evening during the 2003 World Cup. This aunt is married to my youngest uncle (not the same uncle who took me to the Eden Gardens, and who pretended he was fanatical about cricket just to humour me. He used to spin me tales about how he was friends with Viv Richards and Ian Chappell; I believed every word) and when I was little we all lived in the same house. My aunt watched me grow up; she watched me fall in love with cricket. The two were pretty much the same thing. These days we don't see each other too often and, when we do, I'm accompanied by my wife and my daughter and it's my day off but I'm still fielding phone calls from work (the run-of-the-mill adult encumbrances), and I can see that though I'm familiar, I am also strange, no longer quite the person she once knew. Not surprisingly, my aunt assumes I don't have time for cricket now. She has never said as much – we haven't talked about it – but I know she refuses to believe that a thirtysomething man with a wife and a child can still be crazy about a silly game.

So she comes visiting us one evening during the 2003 World Cup and finds me lying on the living-room floor surrounded by stacks of newspapers, dozens of pens and sheaves of A4. I have a calculator in my hand, and I'm consulting the colour-coded spreadsheets lined up in front of me. My daughter is toddling around the room but I'm ignoring her. The TV is blaring away; occasionally I look up from my work to see how the game's going.

It's probably Namibia versus Holland. (I don't exactly remember, but had it been anyone else, I would have been watching the game properly.)

'Um, hi, tea?' I stand up to greet my aunt, quickly pulling a sheet of paper out of the way of my advancing daughter.

'Well, no, isn't your mother in?'

'Yes, yes, of course. So is Chandrani. Ma has gone for a shower.'

'All right, I'll wait for them. I'm sure they'll want a cup too.'

'*Aami kolom nebo*,' says my daughter. She wants the pens, especially the felt-tips.

'Oishi, come here. Baba is working,' says my aunt. 'What's up? Why are you bringing work home? You should finish all that stuff in the office. I have been telling your uncle for years, he never listens. Do you want to take your work into another room? I shall play with Oishi till Chandrani arrives.'

'No, it's okay. The thing is I am not working and, er, I need the TV too.'

'What? Not work? What *are* you doing then?'

So I tell her.

And as I explain, it begins to sound sillier and more inconsequential than it is (or than I think it is). It comes out all wrong. The bemused expression on my aunt's face does not help.

I tell her that I am filling in my hand-compiled score-sheets for every World Cup game; that I've given each

team its own colour; that there are separate sheets for run
rates; that the pages over there are my Super Six pre-
dictions ('Look, here's the analysis, it's pretty simple really
– if their run rate falls below the figure in the top-left box,
there's no way they can qualify'); that I do this every day,
that it's important to keep it all absolutely up to date.

'?!?'

I spread out my palms and try a shrug.

'But isn't it all in the papers anyway?'

'Yes, but, you know, not *all* of it. And once you start
doing it, if you stick with it you get a more, holistic
picture?' (In my confusion, I turn the statement into a
mild question, using an upward inflection at the end of the
sentence as though I were a teenager.) 'And it is really
thorough. The papers can get things wrong sometimes.
It's fun too, great fun.'

'Fun?'

There's nothing to say in reply.

When my mother emerges from her room, my aunt
tells her that she thought I had 'got over the cricket thing'.
Got over it. As though it was a relationship in which I had
been dumped.

She is amazed, she says, and a little amused, and it's
important that she explains to me that this is not entirely
sensible behaviour. Lying on the floor, I get the gist: she
cannot believe that at my age I still do things like this, isn't
it time I paid more attention to what's important? She is
kindly, my aunt, and her face is indulgent, but I know the
look. It is a look that a lot of people give me.

*   *   *

During my final year at university (when most people
worry about money, jobs, what they're going to do with
the rest of their lives), I wasn't worrying about a career.
My big concern was whether I ought to get a job at all. It
was not that I had an ambition to be a professional
layabout (though, to be fair, studying English Literature
was good practice); it was just that any job was bound to
be time-consuming. And that would have an effect on the
cricket.

Cricket is that sort of game. You can be a football man
in England or Europe and manage. Yes, there's travelling
to away games, yes there are midweek fixtures, but it's
mainly a weekend thing. Besides, a football match lasts
less than two hours (and that's if you're including half-
time). Look at what the cricket fan has to contend with.
Five full days for a Test, one full day (or afternoon and
evening) for a limited-overs international. Between two
and five Tests and lots of one-days in a series. Four, five,
six, seven series in a year. Keeping up with *that* is a full-
time job. Where in my life was there space for another?

Any job I took would have to be flexible, I thought. It
should allow me to determine the hours I worked; it
should offer me the freedom to follow all the cricket I
wanted to (which was *all* the cricket there was). So I decided
to become a writer. I had no idea of what I would write
about, of course.

My father found it scandalous that his newly graduated
son should be frittering away his time on watching cricket
and writing a literary masterpiece he didn't know how to
start. So in the end, I found a job. As a reporter on a
Kolkata paper. I began to enjoy myself. And I began to

see the point of working – not so much for the money, but for the social respectability that comes with having a job in middle-class Bengali society.

The cricket suffered.

I kept track when I could. But when you are out in rural Bengal covering a drought, when the ground is cracking up and the villagers look like they'd kill for a drop of filthy water, you don't ask the nearest guy for the score, do you?

In the years since, I have done my best to achieve a work-cricket balance (or rather a cricket-work balance): I have offered to write about it so that I can watch it (this does not work so well if you're working on the crime beat at the time); I have got myself promoted (so that I can tinker with my work schedule – I've gone to work before the cleaners arrived and left by late afternoon or early evening so that I could catch a match in a different time zone); I have even, to my shame, claimed that my mother was in hospital in order to take the day off.

But the cricket has suffered.

These days, I'm less bothered about the social respectability. I need the money.

*   *   *

One of the problems of being a cricket fan in his mid thirties is that no one takes you seriously. Most people think it's about as mature as wetting the bed. As I get older and more impatient and less inclined to laugh at the world, it grows boring explaining to people that loving a game (okay, loving a game *a lot*) does not necessarily make me maladjusted.

There's a general assumption that sport is a childish, frivolous pursuit. That it is not worthy of the degree of emotional and intellectual engagement that politics, classical music or Estonian films merit. I'm often told that cricket is basically twenty-two grown men meeting in a park to throw things at each other. (Imagine being interested in *that*.) But in these terms Mozart was messing around with doh ray me; Shakespeare was juggling twenty-six letters. Most seven-year-olds manage eight notes and the alphabet. If you can hum piano concertos over your coffee, you are an object of respectful fascination. If you can trot out the Indian batsmen's averages during their 1971 tour of the West Indies, you are a crank. Benign, perhaps, but a crank.

Which is why these days, sometimes, I have to resort to subterfuge.

A couple of years ago I had to go to a funeral which clashed with a Test match India were playing against Australia. So I made a plan. For the period when I would be away from a television set, I asked a friend of mine to text me the score at the end of each over. When I say 'the score' I understate things somewhat; it was more in the nature of a running commentary, like the live reports you get on the internet. My friend must have typed his fingers to the bone. (The logistics of it all still cause me some puzzlement. Amid all this furious texting, when did he actually get a chance to watch the cricket? Anyway, I am grateful to him – I ought to take this chance to let him know.)

At the funeral, I looked suitably sombre, if a little distracted. As I explained to one curious relative, as I

picked up yet another message, things were difficult at
work. My bosses were unsympathetic, my colleagues
recalcitrant. They wouldn't leave me alone, even today of
all days.

Ten, even five years ago, I would not have bothered
with this elaborate charade: I simply would not have
attended the funeral. Now I go – I can't be bothered with
making my excuses. It seems like a waste of time. I find the
explanations I am obliged to put forth irksome. I don't
find the jokes amusing.

Of course, I don't do much to help myself. No fan does.

Not so long ago I went to a dinner party in London
where I didn't know a soul. (The friend I was staying with
brought me along – he felt he shouldn't leave me sitting in
front of the TV with my lager and cigarettes; he really
should have known better.) I was a little nervous, and as a
result, I drank rather more than I should have. While I did
not have a glass in each hand *all* the time, I ended up
rather substantially drunk.

The drink did not help with my nerves. In fact, it made
me edgy, and it gave me the courage to let my edginess be
evident. At one point in the evening, I found myself in
front of a po-faced young woman who, her fingers
wrapped around the stem of a glass of wine she had barely
touched, asked me about right wing Hindu funda-
mentalists in India and the riots in Gujarat. 'Yeah, well,
oh Gujarat. Very embarrassing. I mean, they are, they
just burn buses and kill people. Mmm, complex issue, you
see. I don't have much time for that sort of thing really,' I
said. (This was, I could see, unforgivable.) 'But I do have
time for cricket. India is away in South Africa and . . . um

. . . with the time difference, you know, you wouldn't happen to know the score, would you?'

Po-Face stared at me. I could just as well have made a clumsy grab at her. We did not speak again. I left shortly afterwards, without my friend.

*   *   *

The night India beat the West Indies at Port of Spain in 2002, a close friend of mine lost his mother (a sudden heart attack – she didn't last till the hospital). I remember the phone call; it came in the middle of a whoop-and-whirl I was doing on my own in the living room. I couldn't take the smile off my face even as I drove to the hospital to comfort my friend. There were hundreds of young men out on the streets, celebrating. They thought that I was on a celebratory drive of my own.

I can no longer pretend that how my team performs on a cricket field will determine what happens in the rest of my life. I've left exams behind me; these days there is just too much at stake. As we get older and marry, have children, we become more vulnerable. There is so much more to worry about, so many more people who by being hurt could hurt us too. I don't want to tempt fate.

And yet, sometimes I find myself returning to the old notions, hoping that if things go right on the cricket field, good fortune will be matched elsewhere. It's a comforting illusion – it makes the complexities of adulthood more manageable.

When I first proposed this to book to its publisher, I was convinced (deeply, sincerely and irrationally convinced) that if India won the 2003 World Cup, I would land myself a commission. India did not win. The commission did not come. I went ahead and finished the book. It got taken on by the same publisher. And I heard the news right after India beat Pakistan in a Test series in Pakistan for the first time ever. A coincidence? Or evidence of cricketing karma – the mystical correspondence between cricket and life?

I know, I know. But a small part of me still wants it to be true. If India win, that is.

As I get older it becomes ever more apparent that cricket is a window on to a parallel – perhaps a better – universe. Its disappointments do not have a bearing on my job or my family; its thrills are other-worldly. I need only press a button on my remote, and I will be transported. I will have escaped.

On bad days, I have a fantasy in which I'm much older. I often find myself imagining the worst. (It's not quite a daydream, it's not quite a nightmare – the fear is real but it's also indulgent, even comforting.) My career's over (as the years go by that's something that becomes less and less difficult to envisage); I have arthritis or some other debilitating but not life-threatening illness which leaves me just about housebound; my daughter has left home, my parents are dead, my wife no longer finds me an amusing or interesting companion; and my friends have all died or gone to live in other cities. What will I be left with then? What will prevent me from going over the edge, becoming a slobbering old man drooling into his bowl of soup or plate of boiled vegetables? Should such an eventuality come to pass (and with life, you just never can

tell – life does have a habit of coshing you over the head),
I know I will always have cricket. At the flick of a switch
and the turning of a knob, with the riffle of a newspaper
or the click of a mouse, I will be able to summon those
familiar images, those thrills, that other world. Even when
all else is gone.

So I can't afford not to treat the game with reverence;
to admit, just occasionally, that it may have powers that I
cannot comprehend; to place offerings in front of its altar.
I wouldn't want to offend its gods. That would be stupid,
wouldn't it?

When I was young, I never thought of these things –
one doesn't think of growing old when one is a child. Now
I fear the loneliness that age might bring. And I hug
cricket to myself because one day it may be all that's left
me.

'Today's the day for all this madness'

THIRTY YEARS OF following a team. Three decades of high and lows. Three decades of lows, mostly. Let's face it: if your home ground is the Eden Gardens, if your team is India, it was never going to be easy.

The highs are to be cherished. They are remembered, relived, moment for moment, especially in the bad times. Remember what it was like then? When we won that game? It'll be like that again. We can live with these shocking results. And even if we never win a match again, we have our memories. They are ours. They happened.

Nothing comes close to watching India win a big Test match. Nothing. Partly because it doesn't happen very often.

* * *

On 13 December 2003, I found myself in Catherine Hill Bay, a beautiful little village by the sea some hundred-odd miles from Sydney up the New South Wales coast. We had travelled up by train, my wife, our daughter and I, to attend that most Australian of institutions – a barbecue party – at the beach house of a colleague of mine from the *Sydney Morning Herald*, a paper on which I was spending three months as a visiting journalist thanks to a fellowship from the Australia-India Council.

As the lobsters cooked in the garden and the champagne corks popped, I stepped on to the porch for a cigarette. These days one is made to feel such a prick as a smoker that I was delighted to find I had company. Another guest, Gary, was leaning against his car, a cigarette in his hand, listening to the cricket on the radio. The glare hit me as I walked out, bareheaded, without sunglasses, a little unsteady after too many beers. It was one of those really hot days of Australian summer: the light seemed to have bleached the nearby buildings of colour; everything was so uniformly white (not so much a colour as an absence of tone, shade or texture) that it was hard to tell where the sand ended and the sea began. Feeling a little stunned (the heat, the light, the still air and very definitely the beer) I nodded at Gary and, without a word, leaned against the car as he bent to give me a light.

India were playing Australia in the second Test of the series at Adelaide. The first, a thrilling game at Brisbane in which India had had the upper hand more often than the hosts, had been drawn.

This was the second day of the Adelaide match and Australia, in true Australian fashion, had racked up 556. India, when I took the first pull of my cigarette, were 83 for 3 in reply: Akash Chopra, Virender Sehwag and Sachin Tendulkar were gone. Before I'd flicked the ash for the first time, Ganguly – heroic Ganguly of the century in Brisbane – was run out for two. 85 for 4.

'Your luck's run out, mate. It only lasted till the end of the first Test. Looks like you've dug yourselves a pretty deep hole.'

I agreed. I didn't have a choice.

'But you're used to it, aren't you? It's like this every time you come to Australia. Every time, mate. Must be such a pain.'

Indisputably, I was used to this. We had been here before. As a matter of fact, 'here' was just about the only place we had been for as long as I could remember.

We went back inside to attend to the champagne and the seafood.

By the time play ended that day (by which time, blissfully drunk and spared another encounter with a car radio broadcasting cricket, we had returned to our apartment in Sydney), India had got to 180 for 4 with Rahul Dravid on forty-three not out and V. V. S. Laxman on fifty-five not out.

The following day was a Sunday. In the living room of our Sydney flat, hunkered down on the sofa and repeatedly murmuring, 'Oh fuck, this is fucking unbelievable' (a refrain soon taken up – faithfully if not in its entirety or entirely accurately – by my two-year-old daughter), I watched as Laxman and Dravid, in a reprisal of their famous partnership in Kolkata two years before, put together a stand of 303. At stumps that evening, India were 477 for 7. Laxman had made 148; Dravid was unbeaten on 199. India had run the Aussies ragged, scoring nearly 300 runs in a day's play for the loss of three wickets. When India were finally all out on Day Four, they were only thirty-three runs behind.

Perhaps because they were unused to this sort of thing, Australia seemed a little unnerved in the second innings and were dismissed for 196. India needed 229 to win, to become the first team to take the lead in a Test series against Australia in Australia for ten years.

On the fifth afternoon, as Dravid cut Stuart MacGill to the cover boundary (taking his second-innings score to seventy-two; his average for the match stood at 305), I was standing in front of a television set in the Sport department of the *Herald*. Watching Dravid punch the air, uproot one of the stumps and start running towards the pavilion, I couldn't take the grin off my face. I'd been grinning for half an hour now, and I didn't think I could ever stop.

How long had it been? You had to go back decades to find the last time India had beaten Australia in Australia. Margaret Thatcher was in her first term; the Soviet Union was still a country; Diego Maradona was yet to play a World Cup game; Sachin Tendulkar was seven years old; a couple of the current Indian side had not even been born. *That* was how long ago it was.

On my way home from work that day, with the curved sweep of the harbour to my left and the shopfronts spattered with the gold dust of early evening sunshine, I thought about Melbourne in 1981. My parents had allowed me to bunk off school to listen to the radio. It seemed odd to recall the different person I was then, to realise that, in the years that had elapsed between the two occasions, I had had a child of my own who would be running into my arms in fifteen minutes. Nearly half a life gone between those two wins, half a life swallowed in that interminable wait. Long enough for the world to have changed beyond recognition.

* * *

This Indian team, however, made a habit of triumphant occasions.

India drew the 2003 Australia series 1–1. In the final Test in Sydney, they ground Australia into the dust with their batting. Only Simon Katich and Steve Waugh, in his farewell Test, denied the tourists victory. Soon after, India did what they had never done before: defeat Pakistan in Pakistan in a Test series. Talk about India being the second-best team in the world – this was before England's 2004 renaissance – was swirling in the clear air of the Australian summer and the smoggy Indian winter.

The victories in Australia and Pakistan weren't India's only convincing performances. Since 2001, India had beaten England and the West Indies away (they don't often win away games, no matter how weak the opposition) and if they didn't quite manage to win either of the two series, they came close. In 2004 India beat South Africa at home; and though they lost to the Australians, they were the only team to take a Test off the Aussies that year.

We were watching the best Indian side of all time. Not that we acknowledged that fact very often. One reason for that is that although cricket fans like making comparisons between teams from different eras and arguing about which was the best, they don't really want to come up with an answer. (Because that would put a stop to the discussion.) But there were other reasons too. Our reluctance to admit that we had a terrific cricket side on our hands was partly superstitious. We feared that if we flaunted our beliefs – allowed that yes, we were that good – the spell would be broken. Better to be underwhelmed – and underwhelming – than sorry.

Most importantly, we didn't praise this side enough because we always thought it could do better: because the players had raised our expectations to the point where they were so consistently high, so outrageous, that it was impossible for the team to match them, no matter how well they played. (When Pakistan fought back to draw the first Test of the 2005 series against India, most of us behaved as though we had lost. It never occurred to us that not too many years ago, had we managed to avoid losing to Pakistan, we would have behaved as though we had won.)

Even if the current side shows signs that it is slipping a little, this has been a great century in which to be an Indian cricket fan. From that Test series against Australia in 2003, through one-day tournaments, home Tests, away Tests, we've been given more moments of joy than ever before.

Away wins in Test matches are a fair indicator of how accomplished a team is. In my first twenty-six years as a cricket fan, between the tour of England in 1974 and the Bangladesh series in 2000, India won eight Tests away from home. (During the 1990s, for instance, they won just once: against Sri Lanka in Colombo in 1993.) Between

November 2000 and April 2004, they managed ten Test victories on foreign soil.

Now that scares the hell out of me.

Following Indian cricket, for the thirty-odd years that I have been doing it, has largely been a matter of betrayed hopes. I have endured years of miserable days and nights, when one good bowling performance, one gallant innings in a lost cause – *always* in a lost cause – was all we had to be proud of. Wretchedness was the cornerstone of my life as a cricket fan. And now I have this.

This continuing success is so odd that it is hard to come to terms with. It seems unnatural. (I find it easier to deal with the failures – I've had more practice at that.) For someone like me, even four years of victories can be only a temporary distraction from the real business of Indian cricket: failure. Sometimes I find myself hoping for the bad times to begin again – at least then the worst will have happened, I'll know where I stand. (It's like going to the dentist: the anticipation of the pain is worse than actually being in the chair.) And I can sense their approach: a Test series drawn at home against an indifferent Pakistan; then a series loss to Pakistan in Pakistan; a lost Test to an injury-hit England side; the departures of coach John Wright and captain Sourav Ganguly. In the spring of 2006, despite the team's astonishing one-day record, it is beginning to seem as though the familiar is not very far away.

But I worry far more for the younger generation, kids who are twelve or ten or eight years old, or perhaps not even that. We are all part of the same club, the same family of Indian cricket fans, but the rules are a little different for them. These kids have grown up with success. What must following India seem like to them?

They must believe that if you support a team properly, if you will it to do well with all your heart, you will be rewarded. Happiness will be yours. They think it is bloody cause and effect, see? They do not know; they have yet to find out.

When they do – and they are bound to sooner or later – they will realise that there is nothing so logical about this exercise; they will have to learn to live with random failure and unrequited love. They have been witness only to the vertiginous ascent. And, unlike me, they do not suffer from vertigo.

* * *

On the first four days of the Eden Gardens India-Pakistan Test in March 2005, I go to my club for my daily swim, not in the morning as I usually do, but late in the evening. At this time of day, the place is filled with elderly men who aren't here for the swimming. They treat the pool as a huge, communal bathtub: they wallow in the water, discuss the business of the day, then head upstairs to the bar for a few whiskies.

These men have never had much to do with me. They think I'm too young – and therefore too callow and ignorant – to belong to their club, where you don't count for anything unless you have been a member for at least a couple of decades. Given that you have to be thirty to join, that means you shouldn't really open your mouth until you're well over fifty.

It is instructive to see how a person gets into cold water in winter or early spring; it tells you what sort of a man he is: some dive in, fearless; some walk down the steps gingerly, curling up their toes, letting the water inch up their bodies, and then stand, shivering, their bodies only half submerged; some run down the steps, eager to get the uncomfortable part out of the way, and head off towards the deep end with hurried strokes. Whatever method the old men choose, it's over soon enough. They take their rightful place at the shallow end. On this particular evening, the second of the Test, Pakistan are 273 for 2 at close of play in reply to India's 407. Today's topic of conversation is why we have a really crap cricket side.

'Hopeless lot. In our time, you know . . .'

'They'll lose this Test and then the series.'

'Ganguly should be sacked.'

I am leaning against the wall at the shallow end, panting, my lungs shot after all the cigarettes I've smoked today (well, every day for the last twenty years). I am quiet, listening. I know my place.

'What do you think?' one of them suddenly asks, turning towards me. 'What do you young people think? Should Ganguly be captain or what?'

'Well, yes, I think so. I mean . . .' I start.

But a flurry of voices – 'Rubbish'; 'You have no idea you're talking about'; 'This is the kind of stupidity that lets him off the hook'; 'Drop him now, I say' – stops me finishing my sentence and we are off. I have hardly ever exchanged a word with these guys, there exists a sense of mutual suspicion and distrust between us, but now we are talking, arguing, shouting each other down to make ourselves heard, as though this is what we do every evening after work, as though this is what we come to the pool *for*. I never get my lengths done that day. And I head upstairs with them to the bar soon afterwards.

Three days later, on a warm, spring-almost-summer Sunday afternoon, India complete a memorable victory. I'm watching the game on television; I still can't face India-Pakistan at the Eden. Just after three o'clock, as Harbhajan Singh takes the wicket of Danish Kaneria to put India one up in the series, my phones begin to go crazy – as they always do on such occasions. I know how to handle this: cradle one phone between my left shoulder and my cheek, use the right hand for text messages and the left to take the other phone off the hook and tell the caller that I shall be with him in a moment. This is the first time that India have beaten Pakistan in Kolkata. I know this, but my friends are telling me anyway. I'm not complaining. (How can I? I call several people who don't need telling either and go ahead and tell them too. None of us can get enough of this.)

I feel wound up, restless. I can't sit still even to watch the awards ceremony and the interviews and the post-match analysis. I go out into the still, moist afternoon. The heat hangs like a low cloud over the city.

It is the day after Holi, the Indian festival of colours, and the streets and buildings are still awash with the previous day's revelry. There are victory processions on the streets, garlanded posters of the players held high like standards at the front of a triumphal march. Young men have brought out yesterday's colours, they're dancing, chanting, dipping their hands into paper bags full of pink and red and green and orange and throwing the soft powder heavenwards. The colours dissolve in the after-noon glare like the wispy, blue-grey smoke from the countless cigarettes and crackers all around us.

Every house in the street has its TV set turned up as loud as it will go. It's as though we can't quite take it in, we won't be able to believe it's really happening until the cheering from the stadium is loud enough to drown out the rest of the world. With every roar that goes up, there's a corresponding roar from the people out on the street, until it becomes hard to say where the Eden ends and everywhere else begins.

I park my car on Harish Mukherjee Road – the 'No Parking' sign is so smeared with colours that's its nearly illegible – opposite a hospital that advertises its prosthetics clinic with the sign, 'Legs for the legless'. It is a silence zone, but the 'No Horn' sign has been obliterated too. Everywhere you turn there are cars draped in India flags honking their horns. The passengers are opening the doors, jumping out to join a procession led by residents of the adjoining slum.

'So you must like cricket, eh?' people from England, from Australia, from South Africa, ask me when they find out that I am Indian. You need to see us to really know the answer to that, see us out on the streets in the afternoon heat, radiant faces shining through all the colours on this Sunday afternoon.

'*Cholun dada, aajkei to din*' ('Come on brother, today's the day for all this madness'). One of the guys comes out of the march running towards me as I stand leaning against my car, watching. I ask him what he does for a living. He never finished school, he says. His father died when he was thirteen and he had a mother and three sisters to support, so he found work as a household help. That was five years ago. Now he does odd jobs when he can get them – at a garage, washing cars in the neighbourhood, running errands for the clerks in a government office – but he hasn't had one for a few weeks now. Where did he watch the game? On the tiny set in the local tea shop, packed into a square foot of space with ten of his friends, all of whom are now out with him on the street.

He smears my face with colour. 'Could I borrow a cigarette from you?' he asks. I fish out my packet, give him one, light one for myself and, with awkward dance steps, join their swelling procession.

Acknowledgements

The Calcutta Club swimming pool, where much of this book was written – at least in my head.

Fellow India fans – the true believers.

Tristan Jones, my editor. For *that* e-mail. And everything else thereafter.

Purabi and Dilip Bhattacharjee, my parents. For keeping the faith.

Chandrani, my wife, my best friend. For being there. For being you.

Thank you.

Eat Right, Lose Weight

Pippa Campbell is a Functional Nutrition Practitioner, registered with the Institute for Functional Medicine. She's also a certified Nutrigenomics Practitioner and a certified Metabolic Balance Coach. She is registered with the Complementary Medical Association. Pippa has over 12 years' experience specialising in female heath and weight loss.

PIPPA CAMPBELL

Eat Right, Lose Weight

Your individual blueprint for long-term
weight loss and better health

Lagom

For James, Poppy and Josh. I love you.

First published in the UK by Lagom
An imprint of Bonnier Books UK
4th Floor, Victoria House,
Bloomsbury Square,
London, WC1B 4DA

Owned by Bonnier Books
Sveavägen 56, Stockholm, Sweden

www.bonnierbooks.co.uk

Trade Paperback – 9781788707930
Ebook – 9781788707947
Audio Digital Download – 9781788707954

Designed and typeset by Envy Design
Printed and bound in Great Britain by Clays Ltd, Elcograf S.p.A.
1 3 5 7 9 10 8 6 4 2

Lagom is an imprint of Bonnier Books UK
www.bonnierbooks.co.uk

*The information in this book is not a substitute for medical advice. If you know or suspect you
have a health condition, it is recommended that you seek medical advice from your GP before
embarking on any dietary change. All efforts have been made to ensure the accuracy of the
information contained in this book as of the date of publication. The author and publisher shall
have no liability or for any loss, damage or injury incurred, or alleged to have incurred, directly
or indirectly, by the information or suggestions contained in this book.*

'Pippa Campbell is a fantastic nutritionist and really focuses her attention on women like me who are in the mid-life with all the challenges that brings. She makes things simple and easy to understand and what's more I felt so much better after tweaking a few things with my diet.'
Gabby Logan, Broadcaster and Writer

'Pippa Campbell's book provides an answer to so many people wanting to lose weight the right way. It beautifully describes how to personalise the diet to one of 7 different metabolic types to result in successful, healthy weight loss.'
Jeffrey Bland, Ph.D., Author, **The Disease Delusion, founder, Institute for Functional Medicine**

'Pippa's a genius! I took a DNA test earlier this year and was fascinated by the results. The results enabled me to start taking the right supplements that support my hectic lifestyle as a single mum of two children. I also love sports and exercise – especially strength training – so balancing my nutrition is really important.'
Kirsty Gallacher, TV and Radio Broadcaster and Journalist

CONTENTS

INTRODUCTION

Have you ever lost weight, then put it all back on, and more? Have you ever looked at what a friend eats and thought, 'If I ate the same way as her, I'd be double her size?' Have you ever tried a diet because it worked for someone else, but it didn't work for you? Do you feel more confused about food than ever before?

There is so much advice out there on what to eat and so many diets, and so many promises of quick fixes and amazing results. This plan is different. The Pippa Campbell Method (PCM) does start with a 21-day eating plan to help you lose weight. But by the end of 21 days, you'll be well on your way to finding a way of eating that will suit you for life. Right now, you are likely spending a lot of time and energy deciding what to eat, your head full of all the conflicting advice we hear about food. The idea is that, when you finish the 21-day plan, you'll hardly have to think about how and what to eat, not only to be healthy but to stay a weight you're happy with too.

New clients are often embarrassed to tell me what they eat. They might say: 'I have the worst diet.' Or they are ashamed because they feel out of control around food. Worse, when I ask why they think they're not the weight they want to be, they blame themselves, saying, 'I eat too much' or 'I don't exercise enough', even calling themselves 'greedy' or 'lazy'. If this is you, please don't call yourself 'greedy' or 'lazy' – you're being unkind to yourself and the oversimplified idea of weight and weight loss that's behind all of these statements is plain wrong. We are told we simply need to eat fewer calories and burn more calories, but for many of us it's not that simple. As you'll find out, nutrition and weight is much more nuanced.

Other clients say: 'I have no idea why I can't lose weight – I eat so well.' They are confused because they're eating foods they think will help them lose weight, foods that are labelled as healthy such as porridge, granola or brown rice. The problem is, a diet based on those foods is not right for them.

This book is going to help you unpick the reasons why you are struggling to lose weight. This starts with you understanding why your body isn't functioning at its best right now. In the past, you haven't managed to lose the weight you wanted to because you didn't know your body's specific needs. This book will show you how to work them out, then give you the tools to find a way of eating that suits your body. In the short term you will lose weight, and you will also learn how to maintain that weight.

My training is as a functional nutritionist, metabolic balance coach and nutrigenomics practitioner. I am currently doing a postgraduate training in naturopathy (ND). My functional medicine training taught me about the power of food, that what we put in our mouths every day has a profound impact on our physiological and emotional wellbeing. This has been backed up by my training in naturopathy, which uses food to heal and treats the body and mind as a joined-up system. Metabolic balance trained me in the science of weight management – that it's so much more holistic than simply calories in and out.Nutrigenomics taught me that we each need to work with our personal genetic make-up in order to optimise our metabolism.

As the thousands of women I've helped in my clinic with the Pippa Campbell Method have shown me again and again, what we eat is one of the most important decisions we make every day. Because each time you eat food that suits you, you take one step towards better health and the weight you want. That sounds a little dramatic, but you could think of it as empowering. It means you can make a real difference, right now, one meal at a time.

The purpose behind all my training – and so my purpose too – is to help everyone who comes to see me to feel well, energetic and vibrant, to maximise their health. But that's not what most people come to me for. In the ten plus years I've been in practice, 80 per cent of new clients have told me that their number one goal is to lose weight. So they are often surprised when in our first consultation, we don't talk much about food or calories. I ask questions about how they're eating, sure, but also about their health and how they are sleeping, their energy, their cravings and any other symptoms they are experiencing. Because, as you'll read in the stories of the women who have been kind enough to share them for this book, those who are finding it hard to lose weight always have other symptoms too. Below is a list of the ones that come up consistently. How many of these do you have?

- ☐ Lack of energy
- ☐ Brain fog
- ☐ Cravings for sweet, salty or fatty foods
- ☐ Can't sleep or unrefreshing sleep
- ☐ Mood swings
- ☐ Hungry all the time
- ☐ Anxiety
- ☐ Digestive issues

☐ Constipation and/or diarrhoea
☐ PMS and/or period pain
☐ Bloating
☐ Joint pain

You might be thinking that sleep and digestion are not priorities for you, that you simply want to lose weight. I get it – some of the stories I hear about weight are heart-breaking. Women tell me how it affects their confidence and self-worth, that it takes up so much of their headspace. They say it makes them feel miserable and uncomfortable, prevents them from living a full and fun life. But the symptoms in the list above – and some others that we'll get into later – are in fact clues that help me design the right eating plan for each woman who comes to me for help. I'm going to teach you to become a detective too, to use your symptoms to design your own personalised eating plan.

It might surprise you that, a few weeks after a client's first consultation, when she comes back to see me, she won't usually focus on her weight either. She'll have lost weight, sure, but we'll talk more about how she no longer has any food cravings or doesn't instinctively open the fridge to look for a snack every 20 minutes or has stopped obsessing over and worrying about food. She'll tell me she's feeling more energetic or sleeping better or is having fewer PMS symptoms or mood swings, how she has more energy to work and look after her family and prepare delicious food for herself and move more and have more fun.

Once your body's systems are operating as they should, weight loss will happen. It's a happy side effect of good health; the two go hand in hand. And so, my open secret is that in clinic, I am giving health advice disguised as weight-loss advice: this is really a health book in the guise of a weight-loss book.

I would like this to be your first big mental shift of many: I would like you to move from a weight-loss mindset to a well-you mindset. Yes, if you follow the 21-day eating plan you will lose weight, maybe fitting into clothes from the back of the wardrobe again and feeling more comfortable. But – and this is the exciting part – you'll undoubtedly also experience the positive changes that clients mention most often: more energy, a sharper brain and better mood.

Feeling good in your body and in yourself seems to bring even more benefits too, such as confidence. Women who've done the PCM – both in clinic and on my courses – have told me about applying for bigger jobs or starting new forms of exercise. Some have put on a swimsuit for the first time in ages, or a wetsuit to go boogie boarding with their children. One of my clients even trained to be a trapeze yoga teacher! These are the kinds of things that happen when you learn which foods suit your body and finally feel in control of your eating.

How to use this book

The recommendations in this book are not a substitute for medical advice; if you have a health condition or are concerned about any specific symptoms, speak to your GP before changing your diet. There are three parts to this book. I advise that you start at the beginning and read the whole book before making any dietary changes. I recommend that clients buy a notebook and make notes. Or you could write in this book, treat it like a workbook. The more you write down what's working for you, the better. It's so easy to forget the little things. Your notes will be a brilliant reminder of all your successes, when life is busy or tricky. I would also just like to reiterate here, too, that the information in this book is not a replacement for medical advice. Ask your GP before making any radical changes in your eating. If you have an eating disorder or a cancer diagnosis, please take medical advice before following any of the plans.

At the heart of the PCM lie seven Metabolic Types. Each one involves a body system that's not working well, which is having an impact on your body's ability to lose weight. In chapter 1, there's a quiz to enable you to pinpoint which Metabolic Type you are, based on the symptoms you have.

Once you know this, read the chapter that explains your type, and the way of eating that suits you best, and start the Prep Week for the 21-day plan, in chapter 4. I've seen over and over how the more women prepare for change and learn about their bodies, the better and more lasting their results. Although the eating plan lasts 21 days, it's designed to be a kickstart to a new way of eating for life. I am all about sustainability – keeping the weight off, not just losing it. I chose 21 days because, in my experience of helping thousands of women in my clinic, I've found this is a good time frame to see and feel real results, but also for new changes to bed in; it takes at least 18 days to crack new habits.

However, if you really cannot wait to start getting healthier, I suggest that as you read the rest of the book, you begin by adopting the 5 Foundations in chapter 4. I've called them the 5 Foundations because they are the absolute bedrock of healthy eating and weight loss for everybody. Focusing on these five simple habits alone will result in real and lasting weight loss.

PART 1

The first part of the book explains why you haven't been successful in losing weight in the past and the basis of your new approach to weight and your body.

You'll discover why processed foods are putting you into a cycle of hunger, imbalance and overeating. You'll be relieved to know that your cravings are often biological and not emotional eating, and that fad diets and diets based on calories don't lead to sustainable weight loss.

Then comes a quiz to find your Metabolic Type, which opens the part of the book where you do the detective work about your own body. This will pinpoint the imbalance in your body systems – for example in your hormones, digestion and/or metabolism – and tell you which body system needs the most help in order for you to become well. The beauty of the PCM is that your annoying health symptoms – the ones you ticked previously but also a whole list of others – are the clues that will lead you to your weight-loss transformation and a healthier life.

PART 2

This is where you begin to build your 21-day personalised way of eating. The plan is based on real, whole, natural foods. It's amazing how, when you start eating this way, the body can begin to heal itself and you will find you lose weight. You may not solve a health issue in 21 days, especially if it is long-standing, but you will be going in the right direction and you should feel – and see – the difference.

Everyone starts with the 5 Foundations, a science-based and simple guide to a way of eating that is good for everybody. Next you'll learn the specific foods and lifestyle changes that will suit you.

PART 3

This part of the book sets out what you'll be eating. It begins with a guide to portion size, broken down into protein, carbohydrates and fats. In chapter 14, you will find delicious recipes that you can make while you are doing the 21-day plan and afterwards too. Then, in the following chapter, there's a guide to how to customise your own brilliant recipes, salads and other main meals to suit your type. I've also included answers to the questions I'm most often asked.

Then I'll show you how to adapt the plan after 21 days to make it sustainable for life. There will of course be social occasions and celebrations, days out, holidays and other times when you have less choice over what's on your plate and/or want to eat differently. The PCM will show you how these eating experiences can become both positive and joyful. If, after 21 days, you want to keep losing weight, I'll explain how to do this. If you've lost all the weight you want to by the end of 21 days, I'll give you the tools to stay at the weight you want to be without feeling deprived.

What will your personal journey look like?

Although it's often one of the first questions I'm asked, I can't promise how much weight you'll lose or how fast it will come off during the 21-day plan. It's very common for someone to lose from 1kg to 3kg in the first week, with around 2kg being the average, then 1kg a week after that. The more imbalanced your body is, the longer the weight loss will take. In 21 days, the average weight loss is 4kg, although it's not uncommon for people to lose 6kg.

You can use the 21 days to kickstart weight loss, as the next stage of your weight loss and/or to feel better in yourself. Whatever works for you. My intention is that, by the end of three weeks, you'll have all the tools you need. You'll know how to choose and cook food daily, and for meals out and on holiday. And you'll have a personalised, healthy, varied, natural menu of delicious recipes to fuel your body to function at its very best – and to be the weight that you want to be.

Part 1

How to Eat Right

CHAPTER 1

Why Can't I Lose Weight?

I want to be clear: it is not your fault you can't lose weight or keep regaining weight you lose. If you're like the majority of my clients, goodness knows that you've tried.

The women who come to my clinic typically fall into two categories. There are those who have been eating an extremely restrictive diet for months but the weight isn't shifting. They usually say, 'You probably think I'm not following the diet properly, but I am. People think I'm cheating, but I'm not!'

The other – and this is the larger number – have been on so many diets and gained back the weight so many times that they have given up trying. Or they might have been eating well but something stressful happened or they went through a big life change – such as a new job or baby, or house move or a loss – and all their good eating intentions disappeared.

Trying and not succeeding when it comes to weight loss can be really tough. As our weight goes up and down, our emotions can be on a rollercoaster too. Women often bring an – unjustified – dose of shame along for the emotional ride as well. We live in a world where we are judged on how we look, and it's not our fault if we have internalised some of these pressures. But you deserve to live in a body in which you feel comfortable, healthy and content. And this is what I hope this book will help you to do.

Eat, pray, move

To lose weight, we are often told to eat less, move more. There is some truth in this: movement burns calories, and the more muscle you have, the more calories you burn. If you have a weight-lifting husband, or a sport-obsessed teenaged son, they will need to consume more calories than you. The real picture, though, is much more complex.

When I talk to women about their history with diet and exercise, it's clear that weight isn't just about what we eat or how much we exercise. My client Jasmine is very close in age to her sister, Sophia. They grew up eating the same food, doing the same amount of team sport, with a similarly positive and can-do mindset. She said: 'My sister can eat absolutely any food but if I so much as look at a packet of crisps, I put on a pound. The summer I was doing my GCSEs, Sophia was doing her A-levels. We'd sit and study together and we both ate a lot of junk. At the end of that summer, she was the same size as she had been at the beginning, but I was noticeably bigger.' Maybe you've experienced something similar, with your sister, friends or even your mum? We are not all made the same. What suits one person's body won't be right for all of us. My job is to help you find the eating plan that suits your body.

I take a science-based approach to finding the root cause of weight issues. The question I ask myself about every client in clinic and the one you'll be answering for yourself as you read this book is: why? That might be: why do I put weight on so easily? Or, why am I not losing weight? Or, why am I struggling with my weight?

What is your body trying to tell you?

To dig down into the why, I question women on their signs and symptoms – those I included in the introduction and a whole lot more. I ask them if they are bloated, constipated or not sleeping. I ask what time they wake in the morning. Or whether, for example, they had a weekend of overeating and put on a lot of weight.

I ask these questions because a major reason that weight loss is a struggle or weight rebounds so fast is that most eating plans don't take account of personal biology. Nearly everyone is missing this crucial piece of the puzzle. In order for us to lose weight for good, our bodies need to be working well. Your signs and symptoms will reveal the underlying body imbalance(s) that needs treating for you to lose weight and stay that weight.

Body talking

We usually think of our bodies as a collection of separate organs. We might say we have bad digestion (gut) or anxiety (mind). In fact, each of our body systems communicates to others. There are hormones, neurotransmitters and other chemical messengers flying all over the place. For example, people who have anxiety often have gut issues too; there's a two-way superhighway between the brain and the gut that's key to mood.

So what happens when one body system goes wrong? There are knock-on effects on all the other body systems. When our hormones are out of whack or we have gut issues or we are stressed, our metabolism does not work properly. We get into a vicious cycle of not absorbing crucial nutrients, being hungry all the time, storing more food as fat or not releasing fat stores, so our weight stays stuck or goes up. This is what has happened in your body: one or more body systems being out of balance has caused your signs and symptoms, as well as putting on weight or not being able to lose weight.

Become your own weight-loss detective

People are amazed when I tell them there's a link between their symptoms and not being able to lose weight, but I see this every day in clinic.

Think about when your symptoms started and when you began to put on weight. Maybe you were put on a diet at a very young age? Or the pounds went on at puberty or when you went away to university? You may not have even had to think about your weight until you had children or you hit perimenopause. Then suddenly, you found that, seemingly out of nowhere, you had fat around your middle that wouldn't shift. Our metabolism changes in our forties: there's not a single woman I see in her forties who can eat what she happily ate in her teens or twenties.

Timing isn't the whole story, though, so we need to ask more questions to get to the underlying body system imbalances. Often, signs and symptoms that a body system is going out of balance start before the weight gain. Did yours? Perhaps you began to get bloating or you always had constipation? Or you often felt sluggish and tired? Or suffered from low moods? Or you started to get bad hangovers or reacted to chemicals? Or you had PMT and sore boobs? Or you were tired after eating and craved sugar? Or you felt wired all the time?

And then something happened; it might have been a big stress, as such changing jobs, getting divorced or moving house. Or a long-term stress, such as a bad boss, relationship, having a baby, or perimenopause. Suffering from a virus causes stress to the body too. At some point, your body could no longer cope with its burden and you started to put on weight. And, most likely, your body imbalance symptoms got worse and you gained other symptoms, too.

In my clinic, as well as asking a lot of questions about your history, we also carry out tests. This is a useful way to get 'under the bonnet' of a client's body, to find out more about why they aren't succeeding when it comes to weight loss. Functional tests – usually blood or saliva – of chemical markers in the body reveal the specifics of how well a body system is working. Genetic tests show mutations or variations on genes, called SNPS. These show possible fault lines, the weaknesses in our body systems.

We can't change our genes but we are always changing the way they behave. What and how much we eat, how we exercise, our stress levels and our lifestyle play a huge part too. A bad diet along with stress, environmental toxins and lack of exercise will open those cracks in our genetic make-up.

Every living cell in our body is influenced by what we eat. The wrong foods cause cellular disharmony and metabolic chaos, leading to signs and symptoms as well as weight gain. But the right foods promote metabolic harmony and well-being. *Eat Right, Lose Weight* is a guide to help you hack your genes in that positive direction. After treating thousands of women, I have pinpointed the seven most common body system imbalances that are involved in weight gain, and the signs and symptoms that come with them. I've called these the Metabolic Types, and you'll discover yours in chapter 3. Once you know your Metabolic Type, I'll teach you how to use food and lifestyle to solve it. This will empower you to become your body's own detective, using your symptoms to find the underlying issue behind your weight gain.

In order to start your 21 days with a clean slate (or a clean plate!), let's first tuck into some of the myths and mistaken beliefs, and how they're preventing you from losing weight.

CHAPTER 2
The Truth Behind Body Size

Before we get into the nuts and bolts of losing weight, I want to take a quick detour into our cultural beliefs about weight and food. So often, women who come to see me have become stuck in negative patterns of thinking about themselves. The root is often the common – and mistaken – belief that weight loss depends on having the willpower to cut down on calories and burn more too. If you believe the willpower myth, it means that when you fail, you blame yourself.

But let's look at the latest UK government figures. They show that in the UK, 28 per cent of adults are obese and a further 36 per cent are overweight. That this is the case shows there are fundamental factors at work that are affecting our weight, factors that are more to do with society, not personal willpower.

Seeing this myth for what it is gives you a real chance of escaping from the box of self-blame that I see women stuck in every day. Women are often absolutely miserable by the time they come to see me. They are sick of not being able to get into their clothes, lacking in confidence, sometimes depressed. When I do online consultations, some women don't even feel comfortable turning on their cameras while they're speaking to me. They often think that other people are judging them for failing, for lacking control, for overeating. I've heard so many stories from women whose weight was stopping them living a full life. They won't go on holiday, or they don't feel confident enough to apply for a job they're qualified for. They won't shop for clothes (the changing room, the mirrors), go to parties (nothing to wear), or eat in public (the judgement, again). None tell me they want to be model size – they simply want to feel better in their bodies.

The willpower myth is just one of the stories we have around food, bodies and eating that aren't helping us. It's worth looking at some more, to work out where your attitudes and beliefs have come from.

1. WE PUT LOOKING AFTER OURSELVES LAST

There is so much more to being unhappy with our weight than not being able to fit into our clothes. How we feel we *should* look is bound up with so many influences: cultural expectations, our experience or not of thin privilege, our early life experiences of food and our bodies, our self-confidence.

If you are in your forties and fifties, you hit your teens when Jane Fonda's workout video was a bestseller, and your twenties in the 'heroin chic' era of Kate Moss. This was when diets became a big industry – from Atkins and Dukan to Cabbage Soup (for anyone who is younger, yes, it involved cabbage soup twice a day). Today, younger women have a wider choice of role models and I applaud the body positivity movement that says we deserve to be happy in our body at every size. But a lot of my clients find it impossible to go against years of thin conditioning.

As a nutritionist, I come at this issue from the angle of how your body functions and how you feel, not how you look. I want to know if you have symptoms that are affecting the way you feel and live. When you are in your twenties, you may well feel energetic and vital in a body that is carrying more weight. But most of my clients are 35 plus and by this age, the imbalance in body function that leads to weight gain will likely also involve other issues, such as hormonal issues, low energy and mood, bad sleep, and all the others I have already mentioned.

I want to reiterate that I hope you feel happy and well and that you love your body, whatever size you are. However, it has become clear to me through conversations with countless women that they have often put on weight while they are doing the opposite of loving their body: ignoring it and putting it last. We are conditioned, from the moment we have periods, to look after other people. Some even tell me it feels vain to think about the way they look. Women tend to put on weight during the years they are busy and stressed, very often when they have children or a demanding job, or both.

I meet many different women through my clinic but a story I so often hear is of a woman who, over the years, has kept on buying clothes in bigger and bigger sizes, feeling more and more miserable about it. She might do a quick blast of dieting at New Year or before summer holidays, but otherwise she spends little time looking after her hard-working body. Finally, she reaches a point where she's so stressed about her weight, she doesn't even want to go on holiday because she'll have to bare her arms or lower legs. That is often the point when she comes to see me. Maybe it's where you are now?

Now is the time to think about yourself, to be positively selfish and to start nurturing yourself with lovely, real food. It's not vain to look after yourself. Real, good food is the key to having better health and energy, and feeling positive. Plus, if you're not prioritising yourself, you'll have nothing left for anyone else.

If you're in your twenties or thirties, you may have a different take on weight. Some women your age tell me that they feel shame about wanting to lose weight. They don't want to bow to society's norm, the unspoken rule that women should take up less room. If this is you, let's unpack this. There is undeniable cultural pressure for women to size-conform. And we shouldn't have the way we should look dictated by our culture. But we do, and human nature comes with a pull to stay within society's expectations, wrong or right.

In fact, I think society is playing an even bigger trick on us, beyond telling us the size we should be. As you'll see in the next section, at the same time as we're told to take up less space, we are being sold food that stops our bodies functioning well and makes it almost inevitable that we will gain weight. It's a trap: our culture says we need to be small but in corner shops, cafes and supermarkets, we are surrounded by processed food that has the opposite effect.

2. WE'RE BEING SOLD THE WRONG FOOD FOR OUR BIOLOGY

A caveman goes into a supermarket. No, this isn't the beginning of a joke. This is a deadly serious point, with emphasis on the deadly. We have become accustomed to food that would be unidentifiable to our ancestors. Supermarket aisles are packed with processed food, often full of sugar, fat and additives. It's far from the fuel our bodies evolved to eat.

The trouble is, this food is messing with our minds, and our appetites too. It's designed to be so addictive that we can't help coming back to it time and again. Michael Moss, in his book *Salt Sugar Fat: How the Food Giants Hooked Us*, writes: 'Some of the largest companies are now using brain scans to study how we react neurologically to certain foods, especially to sugar. They've discovered that the brain lights up for sugar the same way it does for cocaine.' Companies have created 'super palatable' foods that contain the perfect amount of fat, salt and sugar. These give us what's been dubbed the 'bliss point' because they fire up our brain's pleasure centres. It's no wonder we keep eating.

These kinds of foods keep selling because of the myth that weight loss is about calories in and calories out, that it doesn't matter where the calories come from. The truth is your body is much more complex than a simple maths problem. For health and also for long-term weight loss, what counts more is the quality, not the quantity, of the calories. And processed foods are low-quality calories.

When you eat, food interacts with your personal biology, which transforms every bite into information telling your cells what to do. Every mouthful affects your hormones, brain chemistry and metabolism. Below are some of the reasons there are no processed foods in the 21-day eating plan:

- **They cause internal inflammation in the body.** I have put this reason first because it's a key and hidden reason that processed foods stop weight loss, and one I've found is most likely to be misunderstood. You'll know the signs of inflammation that occur after injury – heat, pain and swelling – but internal inflammation is much harder to detect. Inflammation is the body's natural defence mechanism against foreign invaders and stresses as well as injury. When the body senses a stress, which can include processed foods containing food additives, artificial sweeteners, sugary foods or processed seed oils, it produces chemicals known as cytokines which are designed to protect you. Keep eating processed foods and these inflammatory cytokines can go out of control, and your whole system can become inflamed. While your body is inflamed, weight loss will be difficult, and you'll gain excess body fat easily.

  On top of that, fat cells themselves produce inflammatory chemicals. And so, this can set up a vicious inflammatory cycle. Internal inflammation can lead to tissue damage and (eventually) inflammatory conditions, including type 2 diabetes, but also high cholesterol and high blood pressure. Long-term inflammation is thought to contribute to the development of heart disease, cancer, Alzheimer's and autoimmune illnesses.

Putting it very simply, we need to put out the 'fire' of inflammation, in order to allow you to lose weight as well as stay healthy. How can we do this? With real food: good-quality ingredients cooked or made from scratch.

- **They are often high in sugar and carbs.** This leads to a rise in blood sugar about 10–15 minutes after eating them, which causes a spike in the fat-storage hormone insulin – and you cannot burn fat while insulin is high. Your body quickly mops up the excess blood sugar, which leads to a blood sugar low. The net result is that very soon after eating, you feel hungry again. Cue more sugar cravings. On the plan, though, you'll be eating the right amount of the right kind of high-quality carbs to ensure your blood sugar stays steady. You might be able to lose weight in the short term when eating sugary and processed food if you are consuming less energy than you are burning. But you'll always be fighting against your insulin swings, always be hungry and craving carbs, and rarely feel full, so, any weight loss won't last.

- **They're low in fibre.** Fibre fills you up and it keeps your bowels regular; regular elimination is necessary to remove toxins and the by-products of your body's metabolism from the body. Fibre is also food for our gut bacteria, which are not only key in the immune system but also have a role in extracting energy and nutrients from food. The 21-day plan prioritises vegetables – nature's brilliant and best source of fibre.

- **They're low in nutrients.** Nutrients are like little keys that make the systems of our body work well. Not absorbing enough zinc? You'll find it harder to burn fat. Not absorbing vitamin B12? You'll feel low in energy. As you'll see when you start the plan, you'll be eating only high-nutrition foods, and in particular the foods that are vital to correct your body imbalance.

- **They're high in the wrong oils.** Processed foods tend to be made with hydrogenated oils and/or processed seed oils, such as processed sunflower, vegetable and corn oil. Your cell membranes are made from the oils you eat and these oils don't make the flexible membranes that allow cells to function properly (see pages 155–6 for more on which oils to use).

For all these reasons, during these 21 days, I'd like you to avoid all packets, if you can help it. Eating real food will allow your body to function better in so many ways, including learning to burn fat again. You might feel deprived at the thought of a life without wine-o-clock crisps or daily milk chocolate. But as a foodie who wants you to feel better, part of my mission is to give you recipes and flavour ideas to make sure your real food is delicious too. You can absolutely shift the way you eat to include more real food instead.

When people choose to eat their former favourites again, whether it's cheesecake or cheesy crisps, as part of their Social Meals (these come at the end of the 21 days – find out more in chapter 16), they often say that they are far too sweet or taste fake and over-flavoured, and that they don't sit well in their stomach. This is how one of my clients described a takeaway pizza: 'It was horrible, too rich and greasy.' Another, who took a week off from following the plan closely while on holiday in Spain (you'll find out how to do this too, in chapter 16), discovered that eating so much fried food made her stomach hurt.

When you eat real food, on the other hand, it begins to taste even more delicious. Clients say that over the weeks of eating good, unprocessed food, their taste buds change. Textures begin to stand out. Flavours pop. After three weeks with no processed sugar, when you have a piece of fruit, it will taste super sweet.

This is not depriving yourself. It's the opposite, like a harvest festival of flavour. There's real freedom in not having what you eat dictated by big food companies too.

3. WE'VE FALLEN FOR FAD DIETS

In the ten-plus years I've been practising, there has been one constant: watching fad diets come and go, then watching them come (again) and go (again). Since fad diets don't work in the long term, they don't last, and so there's always room for a new one.

It's clear why fad diets are appealing. When it comes to weight loss, everyone wants a quick fix. They generally promise great results and are simple to follow (at least for a few days). Maybe you hear of a celebrity who's done one and it's worked for them? Or a friend is doing one and you think she looks incredible? What suits one person, though, may not suit you. My 21-day plan is a way of analysing what your body needs and finding out the foods and portions that suit you and are sustainable for you, in the long term.

Feast, famine, fat storage

The other problem with fad diets is that they are . . . faddy. Following any fad, even with zeal, does not lead to long-term weight loss. The results can run from disappointing to dangerous. If we lose weight too quickly, especially if we do it by eating foods that don't supply enough nutrients, our body thinks there's a shortage, that we're in a time of starvation. Our clever bodies evolved to cope with this by becoming better at extracting more calories from food and slowing down our metabolism so we burn less energy. If a diet is too restrictive, in the long term it can cause weight gain.

Often, clients who've been trying to lose weight by eating low-calorie, processed food, or by doing a juice fast or a weight-loss plan involving soups or salads, say they are hungry all the time and have a lot of cravings. It's because the food they've been eating is far too low in protein. Eating enough protein supports our hormones and helps us maintain our muscle. And the more muscle we have, the more calories we can burn.

When you eat real food that includes enough protein, as you will on the plan, you have fewer spikes in blood sugar and fewer cravings, especially for carbohydrates. You will find you are able to get through from one meal to the next without snacking or feeling hungry.

Food for your brain

There's another downside to fad diets: you don't learn how to prepare real food that suits your body. You follow a plan – perhaps mixing diet powder from a sachet with water for 14 days. I have to admit, this is easier than cooking a piece of chicken or fish, steaming some vegetables and mixing up a dressing. Or similarly, a fad diet that involves five days' worth of juices that you only need to put in the fridge, no prep required, is undeniably much less time-consuming than planning five days' worth of meals, shopping for the food and cooking it. The eating plan may be 21 days, but this is not a quick-fix-three-weeks-and-you're-done kind of situation. It's weight loss at the right speed, backed up by the right nutrients.

So be prepared: this plan will be more work than a fad diet. It will be tough, but not nearly as tough as the constant treadmill of food restriction, then feeling bad about putting weight back on. Time that you invest at the beginning will pay off in the long term because you will gain the tools to find the root cause of your weight gain and, crucially, learn to eat in a way that suits your body, that you can do forever. Imagine how good you will feel knowing that, finally, you understand your body.

CHAPTER 3

Find Your Metabolic Type

Now we've reached the exciting part, where you turn detective to find out more about how your body is functioning.

When I am looking for each client's 'why?' with regards to their weight, my first tool is always their symptoms. Diagnosis is the most critical part of the PCM. DNA tests and functional tests are good to have, but what some clients have called my 'endless' questioning is at the heart of it all. Our bodies are very often trying to tell us what is going wrong with them in a multitude of ways. We just have to learn to speak their language.

How to find your Metabolic Type

In the questionnaire on the following pages, I've recreated the approach I use in clinic, as much as I can without sitting in front of you. You'll see that I've divided the questions into seven sections or Metabolic Types, one for each of the body systems that I've found are most likely to be going wrong in someone who can't lose weight or keeps putting it on. In each section, I've included a list of ten signs and symptoms that, according to my training and experience, are most likely to show up in the people I treat with an imbalance in that body system.

To find your Metabolic Type, simply tick all the signs and symptoms that you have. The section where you have the most ticks, is your type.

Once you've done this, there is a specific chapter for your type, describing what to eat and how to change your lifestyle to suit your body and needs. By addressing the underlying body system that's imbalanced in your Metabolic Type, you will lose weight.

Which signs and symptoms do you have?

METABOLIC TYPE DI

1. Bloating ☑ M

2. Belching or gas ☑ M

3. Heartburn or acid reflux ☐

4. Food intolerances ☐

5. Stomach cramps and/or pain ☐

6. Anaemia unresponsive to iron ☑ M

7. Constipation or diarrhoea, or less than one bowel movement a day, or all three ☑ M

8. Anus itching or thrush ☑

9. Sinus congestion, eczema or asthma ☑ M

10. Brain fog ☑ M

7 TICKS. (M)

If you have the most ticks in this section, you will do the 5 Foundations (chapter 4) + Digestion Type (chapter 5).

METABOLIC TYPE I

1. Fatigue after meals ☑ M
2. General fatigue ☑ M
3. Constant hunger ☐
4. Cravings for sweet foods or any carbs that is not relieved by eating them ☐
5. Must have something sweet after meals ☐
6. Waist girth is equal or larger than hip girth ☐
7. Frequent urination ☑ M
8. Increased appetite and thirst ☐
9. Difficulty losing weight ☑ M
10. Migrating aches and pains ☑ M

5 TICKS — M.

If you have the most ticks in this section, you will do the 5 Foundations (chapter 4) + Insulin Type (chapter 6).

METABOLIC TYPE C

1. Weight gain that's especially around the stomach ☑ M
2. Fatigue ☑ M
3. 'Tired but wired' ☑ M
4. Anxiety ☑ M
5. Poor sleep ☑ M
6. Shaky if meals are missed ☐
7. Cravings for starchy foods or sugars ☐

8. Irritability or 'short fuse' ☑ M
9. Unable to deal with stress ☑ M
10. High blood pressure ☑ M

7 TICKS = M

If you have the most ticks in this section, you will do the 5 Foundations (chapter 4) + Cortisol Type (chapter 7).

METABOLIC TYPE DE

1. Weight goes up and down/inability to lose weight/ unexplained weight gain ☑ M

2. Headaches ☑ M

3. Night sweats ☐

4. Skin problems such as rashes, itchy skin, dermatitis and psoriasis ☑ M

5. Poor cognition, brain fog, memory problems ☑ M

6. Fatigue and lethargy ☑ M

7. Low mood, irritability, anxiety ☑ BIG TIME

8. Strong body odour ☐

9. Bloating or constipation ☑ M

10. Adverse reactions to food and drink (especially additives or processed foods), chemicals, pollution and sensitive to smells ☑ M

M
7 TICKS

If you have the most ticks in this section, you will do the 5 Foundations (chapter 4) + Detox Type (chapter 8).

METABOLIC TYPE T

1. Feeling tired or sluggish ☑ *M*
2. Feeling cold – hands, feet, all over ☑ *M*
3. Require excessive amounts of sleep to function well ☑ *M*
4. Gaining weight easily and/or weight gain despite dieting ☑ *M*
5. Constipation ☑ *M*
6. Low mood and lack of motivation ☑ *M*
7. Morning headaches ☐
8. Loss of outer third of eyebrow ☐
9. Thinning hair or excessive hair loss ☐
10. Mentally sluggish ☑ *M*

M

7 TICKS.

If you have the most ticks in this section, you will do the 5 Foundations (chapter 4) + Thyroid Type (chapter 9).

METABOLIC TYPE O

1. PMS or PMDD ☑ *M*
2. Irregular periods, heavy bleeding ☑ *M*
3. Irritability or rage ☑ *M* 'YES!'
4. Bloating or poor digestion ☑ 'YES!!' *M*
5. Anxiety, panic attacks, low mood, mood swings ☑ "YES!." *M*
6. Insomnia or restlessness but feeling tired ☑ "YES!!!" *M*
7. Fertility issues ☐
8. Endometriosis, fibroids or cysts ☐

9. Headaches more likely to be around ovulation and/or in the run up to your period ☑ *"OH YES!!!!!"*

M 10. Breast tenderness, fibrocystic lumps in breasts ☐

VERY, VERY MUCH SO, BREASTS ARE VERY, VERY TENDER!!!

If you have the most ticks in this section, you will do the 5 Foundations (chapter 4) + Oestrogen Type (chapter 10). *9 M TICKS.*

METABOLIC TYPE S

1. Low mood or depression ☑ *m*

2. Feeling 'flat' and lack of joy from life's pleasures ☑ *M*

3. Feelings of inner rage or anger ☐ *sometimes?)) M*

4. Less resilient to stress ☑ *M*

5. SAD (seasonal affective disorder – feeling down in winter) ☑

6. Carb cravings ☐ *M*

7. Increased appetite ☐ *5-6 TICKS.*

8. Constipation ☐

9. Increased sensitivity to pain ☐

10. Poor sleep or unable to fall into a deep restful sleep ☑ *M*

If you have the most ticks in this section, you will do the 5 Foundations (chapter 4) + Serotonin Type (chapter 11).

Now you know your type, Part 3 sets out your new way of eating. The 5 Foundations in chapter 4 apply to everyone – they are the basis of the 21-day eating plan. From there, you move onto the chapter that gives specific advice for your Metabolic Type.

WHAT IF I HAVE AN EQUAL SCORE IN THE QUIZ?

If you have two sections with the same number of ticks, go with the one where the symptoms are bothering you the most. All body systems that the 21-day plan tackles are interlinked, so changing one will likely affect your other symptoms too, a kind of domino effect. After 21 days, your body will have changed and you can go back and take the quiz again, to see which Metabolic Type is now the most relevant. The plan is about making your whole body healthy, so you won't be doing any harm by concentrating on one area over another.

M 1) METABOLIC TYPO 'O'   9

   2) SEVERAL METABOLIC TYPES.
    a) METABOLIC TYPE DI
    b) METABOLIC TYPE C.   7
    c) METABOLIC TYPE DE.
    d) METABOLIC TYPE T.

   3) METABOLIC TYPE S   5-6.

Part 2

What to Eat on the Plan

Now you are armed with the knowledge of your Metabolic Type, this is where your journey to eating right for your body starts. Whatever the result of the questionnaire in the previous chapter, start with the 5 Foundations over the page. This is for everyone and is the basis of the 21-day plan and the Pippa Campbell Method. Then, head straight to the chapter that deals with your Metabolic Type to learn how to eat right for your body. Within your chapter, you may be referred another type's chapter for a more detailed explanation of what to do. This is because all body systems affect each other.

In Part 3, you'll learn more about following the plan in practice – how to plan, cook, shop, put a breakfast, lunch or dinner together, as well as how to negotiate parties, holidays, office cakes, dinner parties and other tricky moments. You'll also learn what to do after the 21 days, too.

But for now, read on to find out more about how to do the 21-day plan.

CHAPTER 4

The 5 Foundations

These are my five basics, the absolute bedrock of your new way of eating. Whatever type you are, you'll use these as your bible. Because they support all body types, some people will find that doing the foundations is enough to help them lose weight consistently. The secret is that behind these seemingly simple rules, there's a whole range of scientific research, as well as the experiences of the thousands of women we've seen in clinic, who have tried and tested eating like this.

1. START EACH MEAL WITH TWO BITES OF PROTEIN

This is the key to appetite control. Why? As you begin chewing, what's in your mouth sends a message to prime your digestive system for action. When you eat carbohydrates first –including flour, bread, rice, pasta, grains and fruit, but also starchy vegetables, such as potatoes, squash, sweet potato, peas, parsnips and cooked carrots – it prompts the release of insulin, the hormone that tells your body to store fat, into your bloodstream. But protein doesn't work in this way. Eating protein helps you feel full, faster. It is the source of amino acids, the building blocks of your body, including of muscle – which burns fat – and hormones. Eating enough protein can have a profound effect on food satisfaction, preventing cravings, increasing energy levels, building muscle and promoting hormone health. All of this starts with those two bites. And it's why, as you'll see, there is a suggested amount of protein to eat at every meal. It may be more than you're used to.

The first two bites will ideally be poultry, meat, fish, egg, tempeh or tofu. These are classed as high quality proteins, as they have all the amino acids you need. But if you're eating veggie protein such as beans and pulses, still eat those first. With some foods – like smoothies and any recipes containing protein powder – you won't be able to eat protein first, so just do it when you can.

2. LEAVE 4–5 HOURS BETWEEN MEALS

On the plan, you'll have a gap of 4–5 hours between breakfast and lunch, and between lunch and dinner. You also need to finish eating all your food by 7pm. The idea is to have three hours to digest before you go to bed and a 12–14-hour break overnight.

A suggested day's schedule might look something like this. You have a 30-minute eating window for each meal. You'll adapt the timings to suit your day, of course:

7.30am–8am, breakfast

1pm–1.30pm, lunch

6.30pm–7pm, dinner

10pm, bed

And yes, I'm afraid this does mean no snacking. At all. The no snacks rule means no juices, smoothies or other sweetened drinks, including low calorie drinks, and no milk in your tea and coffee – except during your 30-minute eating window. I know this isn't how we've been trained to eat; for most of our lives we've been told that snacking is a good thing! If you are dismayed about this foundation – and people are often happy to tell me that they are! – please know that it's so important for a few reasons:

- It reduces the amount of fat that can be stored. Every time you eat, your insulin goes up for 2–3 hours. And insulin is the fat-storage hormone. While it's high, you cannot burn fat or lose weight. This plan will give you two significant chunks of time during the day when insulin is low and a longer stretch overnight.

- Your body isn't designed to digest food at night. Eating late also affects your sleep and when you're asleep is when you burn most fat.

- It allows your body to go into clean-up mode. That 12–14 hour gap overnight allows your body to enter its clean, clear and renew mode. This is brilliant for getting your detox systems working better.

For the first week or even two, you may find you're hungry. If you are used to eating all the time, you won't be used to these hunger signals. But it's good to feel them; you should be hungry for your next meal.

Clients often say that it's the last hour before a meal that's toughest. It may even feel scary for you to be hungry. The part of your brain that's in charge of survival won't like it; its job is to tell you to eat. Remember, though, being hungry is normal, and it won't be long before you will be able to eat delicious, nutritious food. Your thinking mind is in control.

Your need for snacks will decrease as the days go on. But for the first week or so, if you feel as if you really do need one, have a glass of water, then eat a small portion of protein (a boiled egg, a handful of nuts, quarter of a chicken breast, a slice of smoked salmon).

3. DRINK 2 LITRES OF WATER A DAY

This is such a brilliant habit to get into. Hydration is key to all the body's processes and most of us don't drink enough water. Drinking enough helps weight loss because we often think we're hungry when in fact we're thirsty. It also helps us feel fuller, too. And it helps flush through toxins and waste products, which is important for a well-functioning body. Aim for 2 litres per day, but more if it's hot or you've exercised.

Ways to do this:

- Take a large glass of water to bed. Drink it as soon as you wake up.

- Drink a large glass every time you go into the kitchen, or every time you go to the loo.

- If you don't like the taste of plain water, add a slice of lemon or cucumber (but no cordial, even no-sugar cordial).

- Keep a mug of herbal tea topped up with boiling water.

- Carry a reusable metal bottle with you, so you can refill it on the go.

- Put your glasses of water in your notebook and mark them off each time you drink one.

- You can have two to three cups of caffeine a day, tea or coffee – but between meals, keep it black with no added sugar or milk of any kind. You may prefer to have green tea.

4. CHEW EACH MOUTHFUL (UP TO) 30 TIMES

This may seem such a simple change, but I've seen it have powerful effects on my clients' digestion. Chewing kickstarts your stomach acid and digestive enzymes, as well as manually breaking down the food so it's easier for the rest of your digestion to do its job of extracting the nutrients. If you don't chew well, the food will move more slowly through the digestive tract and can start to ferment, which leads to bloating and wind, as well as constipation. Importantly, chewing thoroughly helps you to eat less and to feel fuller, faster.

How many times do you usually chew? From now on, aim for 30, or stop when your food has turned to mush (for soft foods, it might be before 30). At this point, congratulate yourself. This takes practice to master, so don't worry if you feel the need to swallow at ten bites. Practice is what your Prep Week is for (see page 44).

Focusing on your food while you eat is also better for your digestion. Try not to be on your phone, working at your screen or watching TV. Just eating without doing anything else at the same time will put you in the relaxed mode that's best for digestion and you'll realise you become full much faster too. Make a big deal of each mealtime: make your food look pretty on the plate and enjoy each mouthful.

5. TAKE THE VEGETABLE CHALLENGE

When clients first come to me, the vegetables they're most often eating are tomato and avocado at lunchtime, then spinach and green beans or peas at night. And that is all the vegetables they eat. So, I started my vegetable challenge: every day, try to eat four (or more) different vegetables and then, the next day – and this is key – have four different ones. (If any vegetables from day one of the plan need using up, eat them on day three.)

This is important simply because eating lots of different plant foods supplies us with lots of different antioxidants and helps increase the diversity of the bacteria in our microbiome. These bacteria are key in digestion and the immune system but also affect our metabolism and influence our weight. A study of over 10,000 people for the

American Gut project showed that the more plants you eat, the better your diversity. And more diversity equals better health.

If you don't like vegetables much, start with the ones you do like and keep trying new ones and persevere. One study showed that babies begin to like a food after eight tries. The vegetables may never become your favourite part of your plate, but they are the absolute key to good health.

Veg to love daily

Look at this huge list of vegetables you can eat during the 21 days:

alfalfa sprouts, artichoke, asparagus, aubergine, avocado, bamboo shoots, beetroot, bok choy, broad beans, broccoli, broccoli sprouts, Brussels sprouts, cabbage, carrot (raw), cauliflower, celeriac, celery, chard, chicory, chillies, courgette, cress, cucumber, daikon radish, dandelion greens, edamame, endive, fennel, garlic, Jerusalem artichoke, kale, kohlrabi, leek, lettuce, mangetout, marrow, mushrooms, okra, onion, radish, red cabbage, red onions, peppers, radicchio, rocket, romaine lettuce, runner beans, salsify, samphire, Savoy cabbage, shallots, sorrel, spinach, spring cabbage, spring greens, spring onion, sprouted broccoli, sugar snaps, Swiss chard, tomato, winter squash, white cabbage, watercress, water chestnut, wild garlic.

CARBY VEG

These vegetables are higher in carbs. Most Metabolic Types will eat a portion of these or another carb every evening (NB: with the exception of Insulin Type – see pages 63–4): butternut squash, parsnip, peas, pumpkin, squash, summer squash, swede, sweet potato, turnip.

Foods to exclude

You'll be excluding these foods for the 21 days and there's a good reason for this – when you're trying to get any body system back into balance, you need to omit any foods that may be causing inflammation (see pages 21–22 for more). This may sound restrictive, but I've found that for some people, it can be a weight-loss game changer. You'll be able to add some of these foods back in after three weeks to find out if they suit your body (see chapter 16 for how to do this).

- **Artificial sweeteners.** No diet cola or other diet fizzy drinks, sugar-free cordial, sweetened yoghurts, sweeteners in your tea or coffee. Research suggests artificial sweeteners may stimulate appetite by changing your blood sugar responses.

- **Gluten and dairy.** These are two of the most common inflammation-causing foods. Taking them out for three weeks will allow you to see if they're a problem for you. Switch to an unsweetened non-dairy milk of your choice and coconut, almond or organic unsweetened soy yoghurt. NB: the plan does include ghee and whey protein powder as these are less likely to cause issues than most dairy. Of course, if you already know you're sensitive to dairy, leave them out.

- **Processed foods.** This will help you to avoid sugary and starchy foods, and processed vegetable oils. Wherever possible, cook or prepare foods from their original, whole state.

- **Alcohol.** It's not only high in sugar but can cause gut irritation. And it's always good to give your liver a break. Fizzy water is your new best friend!

- **Limit caffeine.** Stick to to two or three cups a day, as it can irritate the gut. Outside mealtimes, don't add anything, not even non-dairy milk or MCT oil.

CAN I WORK OUT?

Yes, but take it easy, at least for the first seven of the 21 days. You are likely to be tired and have low energy. Aim for gentle movement for 30 minutes every day, such as walking, or doing yoga or Pilates. Stick to your regular exercise schedule if you wish, but a less strenuous version. This is not a time to do any hardcore cardio in particular, as it will make your more tired, raise your levels of stress hormones and make you hungrier.

Do you need a Prep Week?

In the next few weeks, you're going to become very familiar with the 5 Foundations! But they do take some getting used to. I've found that most people benefit from a Prep Week, practising the 5 Foundations before they start the 21-day plan. That will give you time to read the book, order your food, clear your cupboards and start trying out a recipe or two. If you go all in all at once, you're more likely to crash out, too.

During Prep Week, you can also start to work out the times and places that might be harder for you, so you can plan accordingly. This provides a chance to start to cut down on caffeine and/or alcohol, so it's not such a shock when you give it up! Give yourself these seven days to ease in.

Is it the right time?

Don't start the eating plan during a three-week period when your teenager is doing exams, or you're moving house or job, or you're starting a new exercise regime. If at all possible, pick a time when your life isn't crazy (or is as calm as it ever will be!). This is not the time to make major life decisions or changes.

If you tend to eat a lot of processed food, or you drink a lot of caffeine or alcohol, or if your body is very out of balance, you may feel some detox symptoms, for example nausea, headaches and/or tiredness. Doing a Prep Week will help. While you're doing the plan, be gentle with yourself. That means looking after yourself, getting good rest and sleep, and remembering to do gentle movement.

Now turn to your Metabolic Type chapter, to find out more about what to eat for your type.

CHAPTER 5

Digestion Type

Good digestion and a well-functioning gut are not only foundational for your health but absolutely key for lasting weight loss. I find that almost all my clients who ask me about weight loss also have gut symptoms. If this isn't your main Metabolic Type, it's likely to come a close second.

The digestive system has many parts and a breakdown in any one of them can contribute to weight gain or stop you losing weight. The most common symptoms of digestive dysfunction that I see are: bloating, constipation, diarrhoea, gas, burping and reflux. But there are more general problems that you may not link with the gut too: sleep issues, emotional lows, brain fog, poor immunity. While I can't cover all the gut issues that I deal with in clinic, this eating plan will help the majority who have less-than-optimal digestion to get it back into balance, which will then allow your weight loss to happen.

The excellent news is that often simply changing the way you eat can make a difference. I'll address the new habits that will help, along with what can go wrong with your digestion (clue: a lot!) and what you can eat to get it working again.

4 ways bad digestion can stop weight loss

1. INFLAMMATION

In chapter 2, I described why inflammation is such a major block to weight loss. What's important to know is that the gut is the body system that's most prone to inflammation. One reason is what we eat. We didn't evolve to eat processed foods with added colours, preservatives and other chemicals, or high-sugar foods, fried foods and artificial sweeteners. So our digestive system treats them as invaders and this causes inflammation and weight gain or not being able to lose weight. By cutting out the foods that most often lead to inflammatory reactions during the three weeks on the eating plan, you'll stop the cycle of food-inflammation-weight gain.

2. A LACK OF NUTRIENTS

When my new clients have been eating a lot of highly processed foods or following a restrictive low calorie or keto diet, they often have gut issues – and tests often show they're low in nutrients too. There are two reasons for this: they are not taking in enough nutrients and gut inflammation means they aren't absorbing them either. All the parts of this eating plan aim to maximise both your nutrient intake and absorption.

3. AN UNHELPFUL BACTERIAL MIX

You've heard of the microbiome, the trillions of microorganisms that live in the gut. They perform important functions for the immune system and metabolism, including providing essential nutrients and vitamins. The link between weight and gut bacteria is an expanding area of research. We know an ideally healthy gut contains hundreds of bacterial species and that our modern diets and lifestyles – notably stress, antibiotic use, some food additives and eating a limited range of foods – have depleted our gut diversity. Obese people have been shown to have less variety of microorganisms in their guts than non-obese people. More recent research shows your gut microbiome affects how well you respond to trying to lose weight, too. The good news is that, making your gut bacteria more diverse – which you will do by eating a bigger variety of plant foods – is likely to be helpful for losing weight.

4. NOT ELIMINATING TOXINS

You must go to the loo regularly – at least once a day – in order to eliminate all waste materials including toxins. If you don't, toxins can be re-absorbed and circulate around your body. Some toxins can stop you from losing weight by slowing your metabolism. For example, they can affect your liver function, and when the liver doesn't work properly, you're more likely to store fat.

I HAVE A GUT CONDITION: CAN I DO THE PLAN?

GPs tend to lump a lot of different gut issues together under the catch-all term Irritable Bowel Syndrome. Often, clients who've been diagnosed with IBS have been put on a very restrictive diet, which removes a lot of foods that are good for the gut – for example, broccoli and onions. FODMAP stands for fermentable oligosaccharides, disaccharides, monosaccharides and polyols, which are short-chain carbohydrates the small intestine absorbs poorly. This FODMAP diet is supposed to be a short-term intervention, but I see a lot of clients who've been on it for months, even years. If this is you, you may want to reintroduce non FODMAP foods slowly. If you have been diagnosed with Inflammatory Bowel Disease, you can do the plan but it's best to work with a practitioner.

Better digestion, from north to south

The plan will help you optimise digestion at every stage.

IN YOUR MOUTH

Chewing well takes the strain off your digestion further down, reducing your risk of gut inflammation and food intolerances. And if you don't chew well, you're likely to be eating too fast for your fullness hormones to kick in. Cue over-eating!

IN YOUR STOMACH

As food goes into your stomach, the stomach walls stretch, and this prompts the release of stomach acid. This is hydrochloric acid (HCl), which is extremely acidic with an average pH of 0.8–1.5. If we poured HCl on our hands we would get burned, but our stomachs are protected from this by a mucus layer.

HCl continues the process of breaking down food, in particular meat and other proteins into amino acids – the building blocks for all our cells. HCl also triggers the valve at the bottom of your stomach to allow the food into the intestines and the release of digestive secretions in the next part of digestion, too. The high acid environment in the stomach allows for absorption of minerals such as iron, magnesium, calcium, zinc and copper.

Some signs you may not have enough stomach acid are: stomach cramps and pain, diarrhoea after meals or all the time, undigested food in your stool, loss of taste for meat (because it 'sits' in your stomach), strong-smelling sweat or an upset stomach when you take supplements. You may not feel like eating breakfast, notice your fingernails break easily or you have anaemia but taking iron supplements doesn't help.

IN YOUR SMALL INTESTINE

When food enters the small intestine, it triggers a few functions.

Pancreatic enzymes

Once food passes from the stomach into the small intestine, the pancreas secretes enzymes to help digest sugars, fats, proteins and starches.

Some signs you may not be producing enough enzymes are: food intolerances, undigested food in stools, bloating, gas, constipation, diarrhoea.

Gallbladder

The gallbladder contracts and releases a substance called bile to emulsify fats, making them more easily digested and absorbed. If bile isn't flowing properly, undigested fats cause inflammation in the lining of the small intestine. Bile is also needed to help you absorb fat-soluble vitamins such as vitamins A, D, E and K, as well as calcium and iron, and to remove excess hormones and other toxins.

Some signs your gallbladder is not working as well as it should are: stomach upset by fatty foods, greasy/shiny light-coloured stools, bitter taste in the mouth, get drunk easily or have bad hangovers, pain between shoulder blades, constipation and diagnosis of gallbladder stones. In clinic, I find people who've been on the high-fat keto diet and/or consuming a lot of MCT oil can have bile or gallbladder issues. This issue can also be hereditary: did your mother or sister have gallbladder problems?

Intestinal wall

The small intestine is lined with tiny protrusions called microvilli. To absorb nutrients effectively, they must be healthy. The walls are only one cell thick, so can become damaged very easily, in particular by processed foods.

The cells here have junctions that open and close to allow micronutrients into the bloodstream. If they don't function properly, this can cause leaky gut, when undigested food proteins, toxins and pathogens such as viruses and bacteria cross into the bloodstream. This causes inflammation, food allergies and sensitivities and may lead, in some cases, to autoimmune conditions.

Some signs your intestinal wall is not functioning optimally are: food allergies or sensitivities, and bloating 1–2 hours after eating.

THE LARGE INTESTINE

The last stop before elimination is the large intestine, or colon, which absorbs water and electrolytes from what is by now, ex-food. Your large intestine is also home to the microbiome, which powerfully influences all aspects of your health by releasing peptides, hormones and other substances that impact your whole mind and body, not least your brain, cardiovascular system, immune function and insulin response.

Your gut bacteria feed on what you eat. The more diverse your diet and the more plant fibres you consume, the more varied your gut bacteria will become. Good bacteria die when they're fed processed, food-like products. For example, preservatives are put in food to stop bacteria from spoiling it; think what they do to your inner bacteria! If you've taken antibiotics in the past one or two months, that will affect your microbiome too.

Some signs your microbiome in your large intestine is not as healthy as you would like are: you have had thrush, eating sugar makes your symptoms worse, constipation, excessive or foul-smelling gas.

TAKE THE SWEETCORN TEST

This test will show how fast your food is travelling through your system; the ideal is 24–36 hours from mouth to elimination. Simply eat some sweetcorn kernels, either fresh or frozen, and write down the time you do it. Now wait. Most of the fibre of sweetcorn hulls doesn't break down in your gut, so you should see yellow bits in your stool 24–36 hours afterwards. If it takes longer, this shows you really do need to follow the advice in this chapter to get your digestion on track. (NB: don't eat sweetcorn for a week before you do this!)

Digestive Type: what to eat

These foods will help support efficient and comfortable digestion.

VEGETABLES AND FIBRE-RICH FOODS

Fibre comes in two types and we need both. Helpfully, a lot of plants contain both kinds.

Insoluble fibre. This forms the bulk of your food, helping the muscle contractions that move food through the intestines and so keeps us feeling full and going to the loo regularly. It's found in nuts, beans and vegetables.

Soluble fibre. This is key to preventing weight gain. It slows down the rate at which carbohydrates are digested, controlling blood sugar levels and flattening the peaks of insulin, the fat-storage hormone. Soluble fibre has another bonus: it's prebiotic. That is, it feeds your good bacteria. It's found in fruit, beans, flaxseeds, chia seeds, and other nuts and seeds.

Often, clients tell me that they're eating the same breakfast and lunch every day – maybe porridge in the morning and eggs on sourdough with avocado and tomato for lunch. But different plant foods contain different plant fibres and each one will feed different bacteria. To fuel diversity in your gut, your new food mantra is variety. Make sure you are including these in your diet:

- **Raw foods.** These are naturally rich in enzymes that can aid the digestion process. Good sources include raw garlic, raw onion, rocket and watercress.

- **Bitter foods.** These support bile production. They include: chicory, rocket, watercress and dandelion, radishes, mustard greens, artichokes, turnip greens. Cooking with the spices fenugreek and turmeric is good, too.

- **Fermented foods.** Sauerkraut, kimchi and miso add to, support and fuel good gut bacteria.

- **Zinc-rich foods.** Zinc helps with the production of stomach acid. Sources include: broccoli, seafood, beef, pork, chicken, pumpkin seeds, cashew nuts, mushrooms.

- **Good fats.** You'll be eating some fat on the plan, in avocado, nuts and seeds. Extra virgin olive oil is anti-inflammatory and coconut oil is particularly good for gut health as it's both anti-fungal and anti-microbial. See page 155-6 for more.

- **Helpful herbs and spices.** Cloves stimulate digestive enzymes, mint improves the flow of bile and caraway seeds are good for reducing gas and bloating.

Lifestyle advice

- **Breathe before you eat.** As animals, when we breathe shallowly – and most of us do, most of the time – it's a message to our bodies that we are stressed or unsafe. This diverts the oxygen our digestive system needs to the muscles as part of the fight/flight/freeze reaction. Breathing deeply takes us into rest/digest mode. For 2 minutes before eating (and throughout the day, whenever you like), breathe in for four counts, hold for one count, then breathe out for six counts.

- **Change up your cooking methods.** Marinade meat or fish in vinegar or lemon/lime to start the breakdown of protein fibres. Slow cooking methods, such as stewing or braising also do this.

- **Soak nuts, seeds and pulses,** such as beans, peas and lentils, before you cook them. This helps make them more digestible.

IF YOU ONLY DO ONE THING: A DAILY TABLESPOON OF SAUERKRAUT OR KIMCHI

You can add it to your daily salad or to any savoury meal, or eat it separately beforehand. It's full of probiotic good bacteria as well as prebiotics that feed good bacteria. Buy the one that's labelled as live, not pasteurised. Or make your own – see the sauerkraut recipe on page 222.

HOW YOUR GENES AFFECT DIGESTION

A genetic test can reveal your future risk of health pitfalls and, along with signs and symptoms, help you pinpoint the root of your current issues. However, DNA is not destiny; we can turn our genes on and off with how we live and eat.

From the multiple genes we know affect digestion, I've picked out one called FUT2. If you have a variation (called a SNP) on the FUT2 gene, you're likely to have a less diverse microbiome, in particular less of a protective class of bacteria called bifidobacteria. When I see this SNP, I know the client will have to work harder – by eating fermented foods and lots of fibre from vegetables – to improve their gut bacteria diversity.

A NOTE ON FOODS THAT DON'T AGREE WITH YOU

A lot of people ask me about food allergies. True food allergy symptoms are instant and trigger a type of antibody called IgE. What's more common are food sensitivities – around 10–20 per cent of people have these. This is when different antibodies – IgA, IgG and IgM antibodies – are triggered. These responses can take anywhere from a few hours to a few days to show up, then a few days to go away too. This plan won't treat sensitivities but you will be excluding two of the foods that most commonly cause issues: gluten and dairy.

Melissa, 47, was confused about what to eat

'I was certain there was something very wrong with my body. I had a whole list of different symptoms. A few minutes after eating, my stomach would bloat as if I was being blown up by a bicycle pump. I could look five months pregnant.

I've always been prone to constipation but since having my two children, it had become so I hardly ever went to the loo. My bowel would go into painful spasms, so bad it would make me vomit. Twice, I had to call an ambulance and was given intravenous painkillers in my hallway. Investigations showed nothing specific was wrong. The specialist said that it was just how I was made and that as I got older, my bowel would likely stop working before I did, which meant a colostomy bag.

I had been diagnosed with an underactive thyroid, so I was on medication for that, and I had gynae symptoms too – I had to have an operation to have a mass removed from my womb. Every month, I had lot of breakthrough bleeding and PMT where my mood would plummet to the depths of horribleness for a week. My brain fog, lack of energy and constipation would get worse then, too. My doctor offered me a prescription for anti-psychotic drugs for me to take two weeks out of every four. But I didn't want to take them.

On top of all of that, I had horrific night terrors. Most nights, I'd dream about being chased. Once, my husband found me trying to climb out of the window. My daughter woke up to discover me hiding behind the curtains in her bedroom. And I couldn't drink alcohol. If I had two small glasses of wine, I'd get a hangover that you'd think would be worthy of having drunk a magnum of champagne on my own with a straw.

It was hard work to maintain my weight. I have always had to exercise and watch what I eat in order not to be overweight. I used to say, if I even look at a fast food meal, I put on weight. I was size 14/16 and I'm 5ft 11in, but I felt heavy and sluggish, as if I was carrying an excess load. I didn't go to Pippa to lose weight; I went in a last-ditch attempt to get well. But, when my body did start to work better on her plan, I dropped a size, going down to 12/14.

Pippa said my priority was to get my digestion working. Because I felt so bloated, I would eat little and often. Pippa advised me to have 4–5 hour breaks between meals instead, allowing my digestion to work, then rest. She also told me to chew every mouthful properly. That slowed down my eating and got my digestive juices flowing. I found eating less often but eating better had the effect of making me more satiated and I began to give my digestion a bigger break overnight too, fasting until 10.30 in the morning.

I had become very scared of a lot of foods. At one point, I'd stopped eating all yeast, all red meat, kale and other greens, plus starchy vegetables. My friends use to roll their eyes and say, 'What can you not eat now?!' I would eat the same things every day: eggs, soup, fish, salads. I already wasn't eating much dairy – it made me come out in a rash on my face – but Pippa advised me to cut out gluten too and I stopped drinking. Following the plan, I started to eat a wider variety of foods and especially to aim to eat a rainbow of different coloured vegetables every day. I've found that eating seasonally helps me do this.

Keeping a diary of how foods make me feel has allowed me to work out which foods were causing issues. But as my digestion has settled down over the past two years, I've been able to add most of them back in, even red meat. I started feeling better, even in the first week of the plan. First, the night terrors stopped. That allowed me to have better sleep. I started waking up at 6.30am without my alarm clock, feeling refreshed. Next, I found I had more energy. Then I started going to the toilet every day, the feelings of bloating went and along with them, the wind too.

Doing the plan has given me a more of an understanding of how different foods support processes in the body, especially digestion. I hardly ever used to eat cruciferous vegetables but now I eat them daily. I make sure I eat prebiotic foods, like Jerusalem artichokes and leeks. I add sauerkraut to everything: salad, vegetables, scrambled eggs. I always include some bitter foods, such as radishes. For good fats, I add flaxseeds to my smoothie, eat avocado and sprinkle seeds on vegetables and salad too.

Most of my PMS symptoms have pretty much gone. I still have a bit of a mood the day before my period but it's nothing like it was before. My breakthrough bleeding has stopped, as has the period pain. I also look after myself more. I have regular saunas, I take time walking the dog, I go to the gym. I've always done weights and HIIT, but I used to have no energy, so I was like a gorilla dragging my fists on the floor. Now I love it and I can do 45 minutes, six days a week.

This way of eating has become a way of life and my family are along on the journey too. I have faith in my body again and I've stopped worrying about my health. It's both joyful and frustrating, after years of looking for help, that I can feel this good.'

Sample three-day meal planner for Digestion Type

BREAKFAST	LUNCH	DINNER
Miso-glazed Tenderstem broccoli with spinach and poached egg (page 166)	Chicken and shiitake broth (page 173)	Miso cod fillet with Tenderstem broccoli (page 201)
Stewed apples with yoghurt and almonds (page 170)	Bean patties with courgette and preserved lemon salad (page 183)	Red lentil dhal (page 206)
Breakfast smoothie bowl (page 168)	Personalised salad: build a salad (see pages 231–2) with the key foods for your Metabolic Type (see page 54), adding the 'just one thing' (see page 55)	Roasted pork loin with sauerkraut and cauliflower (page 208)

- Stick exactly to the above meal plan, repeating every three days OR
- Create your own meals using The Portion Size Guide (pages 151–8) OR
- Make meals from the recipes in chapter 14 – the ones that suit you will be marked with the initial of your type.
- Do a combination of the above.

CHAPTER 6

Insulin Type

Cravings can be hellish. Women who are the Insulin Type tell me that all they can think about is food and that they feel hungry all day as well as at night. They often need to snack, are drawn to sweets and sugars, have regular energy slumps and never feel satisfied. The Insulin Type is not an easy Metabolic Type to be.

If this is you, you are being ruled by insulin. This hormone is a crucial part of our metabolism but one of its roles is fat storage. And so, when insulin is always high, you'll find it impossible to lose weight. Probably three quarters of the overweight people I see in clinic have issues with insulin. This is especially the case for women in their forties and fifties because as oestrogen levels drop, insulin issues can worsen or crop up for the first time. Women often tell me that they can't eat as many carbohydrates as they could in their twenties and thirties. They'll say, 'I haven't changed what I eat, I've always had toast for breakfast but now I'm gaining fat around my middle.'

How does insulin go wrong?

When we eat carbs, our digestion turns them into glucose, fuel for our cells. The glucose enters the bloodstream via the small intestine. Once there, insulin instructs the body's cells to use the glucose as energy. If there's glucose left over, insulin tells the body to store it in the liver. And then, when the liver stores are full, it will direct the body to store it as fat.

However, when we eat a lot of carbs, we get a spike in blood sugar that then leads to an excess of insulin and a *lot* of fat being stored. The insulin quickly does its job of bringing down blood sugar but this then leads to a blood sugar low. That is when we get energy slumps, hunger when we have already had enough energy and those dreaded cravings.

When we eat the typical high-sugar, high-carb diet every day, we're constantly subjecting our bodies to this insulin-blood sugar rollercoaster. Our bodies weren't designed to function like this. They evolved in an environment of food scarcity. The paradox is, this is why we are drawn to food sources that are high calorie – namely sweet, starchy foods. Our hunter-gatherer ancestors might have found a store of honey once or twice a year; they couldn't go to shops where they could buy honey – or its modern equivalents of: chocolate, biscuits, birthday cake, pastries, breakfast cereal – day and night. Our bodies are not designed to eat sweet foods every day.

Read your body's signs

Because it evolved in scarcity, your body has a mechanism to tell you when blood sugar is low – you feel dizzy, weak, can't think – but you don't have one to tell you when blood sugar is high. We do have warning signs of sorts, though they happen over years, not minutes.

One is putting on weight. Another is insulin resistance. When we keep eating sugary, carb-based foods, the body has to keep pumping out more and more insulin to try to control blood sugar levels. Eventually, the cells can no longer deal with the onslaught of insulin and they stop listening to its message – this is insulin resistance. This can lead to prediabetes and then diabetes.

Insulin issues can be a driver of polycystic ovarian syndrome, (PCOS) too. It's often the reason women with PCOS put on or can't lose weight. Too much insulin can also lead to generalised inflammation in the body, which you read about in chapter 2, and which contributes to Alzheimer's, heart disease and cancer.

There's more: eating sugary foods leads to a health double whammy. The body breaks down sugar (sucrose) into glucose but also into another sweet molecule, fructose. Fructose is digested differently to glucose in that it goes straight to the liver. Too much fructose leads to a fatty, inflamed liver and fat stored around your organs and your mid-section – this fat is called visceral fat. Research shows that visceral fat is the worst kind for your health – and you don't have to be overweight to have this. In clinic, I see a lot of women who are not overweight but who have a high level of visceral fat.

As an Insulin Type, there are two key strategies to focus on in order to keep blood sugar and insulin levels steady, and therefore to stay in fat-burning mode. As a bonus, they will make you feel less hungry, more satisfied and have fewer cravings. They are:

1. Eating less carbohydrate: The eating plan for this type is slightly lower carb than the other types. This means you will cut down on pulses, starchy vegetables and the sweeter fruits, as well as rice, pasta, bread, sugary foods and other more obvious carbs. You'll see that the dinners in chapter 14 give the option of carbohydrate side dishes/additions – sorry, but these are not for you. It may feel tough but this is the best way to get the results you want and there will be plenty of delicious food you can eat, I promise.

However, if you have been eating a lot of carbs, it may be too much of a shock to your system to exclude them straight away. Instead, start the 21 days by including the portion detailed in the dinner recipes and cut down slowly. The same is true if you are very stressed or have thyroid issues. Keep listening to your body and writing in your notebook about how different amounts make you feel until you find an amount that suits you.

2. No snacking: This Foundation is particularly vital for you. Every time we eat, our insulin rises and it stays high for the following 2–3 hours. Remember, while insulin is high, we cannot burn fat.

NEVER FEEL FULL?

One reason you may always be hungry is that your hunger hormones are on the blink. As you become insulin resistant due to high glucose, it has a knock-on effect on leptin, the hormone that is supposed to kick in to tell you when you're full and stimulate the metabolism after eating. Your stomach might be full but your brain doesn't get that message. This leaves ghrelin, the hunger hormone, the one that generates the desire to eat, in charge.

Insulin Type: what to eat

The 5 Foundations will have already got you eating in a way that helps keep your blood sugar even, with plenty of protein. This plan is harder if you're vegan or vegetarian because pulses, although a good source of protein, are too high in carbs for you for these 21 days (though you can have dhal). The best vegan protein for you comes from soy: edamame, tempeh and tofu. It's a good idea to include protein powder too.

Avoiding high levels of fructose, found in fizzy drinks and fruit juice, sweetened yoghurt, sauces and salad dressing, for example, is also key for blood sugar control. And 'eating a rainbow' – the polyphenols found in different colour plant foods have been shown to increase insulin sensitivity. There are more food choices that are especially suitable for you:

Low glycaemic index foods: The glycaemic index or GI refers to the extent to which blood glucose rises after eating a food. Low GI foods don't spike your blood sugar levels. You may also have heard them called low glycaemic load (low GL), which is simply GI combined with the amount of the food you eat, because this makes a difference to blood sugar too (i.e., two bananas will raise your blood sugar more than one banana).

Low GI foods are proteins, fats, greens and non-starchy vegetables, such as cauliflower, broccoli, spinach and tomatoes. By following the eating plan, you're already excluding most high-GI foods, including sugary foods, white carbs, processed foods, fruit juice, dried fruit.

Start the day with a breakfast that doesn't spike your blood sugar. You may find you feel better after eating a savoury breakfast such as eggs. If you haven't got time to cook in the mornings, make a protein shake with 20–30g protein powder (see recipe in chapter 14). If you like cinnamon, it's a great addition as it helps balance blood sugar too.

Eat foods rich in chromium, a mineral that helps with insulin sensitivity. These include: beef, liver, turkey, eggs, broccoli, lettuce, apple, green beans, tomato, carrots, eggs, celery, garlic.

Eat manganese-rich foods. A deficiency of the mineral manganese can lead to poor insulin control, while having enough may help prevent prediabetes. Good sources: fennel, nuts, including hazelnuts, almonds and pecans, mussels, spinach, tofu, garlic.

Pay attention to B vitamins. There are eight key B vitamins – try to include foods that contain them all. One of the richest sources of most of them is liver. Others are: meat, chicken, eggs, fish, seafood, mushrooms, lentils, chickpeas, avocado, leafy greens. (Vegetarians and vegans may need to supplement. See page 257).

Eat gut-friendly foods (see chapter 5 for more). Having the right balance of bacteria in your microbiome has been shown to impact insulin sensitivity.

Cook with spices. Certain spices have been shown to be beneficial for insulin levels, such as garlic, turmeric, fenugreek and ginger. Put a teaspoon of cinnamon daily into a smoothie or on your breakfast – regular intake has been shown to help with blood sugar balance. Research also shows that, 30 minutes after breakfast, people who'd included 6g of cinnamon in their breakfast had a better insulin response, particularly if they were overweight. Finally, there's good research that chillies are good for regulating insulin too; the pepper family includes tabasco, cayenne and paprika, if you don't like very hot food.

Try intermittent fasting. People who have issues with insulin often do well with fasting. That said, you absolutely do not have to fast to get results. Only try it if you don't feel stressed and you haven't been diagnosed with an underactive thyroid. You might have seen people raving about how much they love fasting on social media but it may not necessarily be right for you.

There are various fasting methods but the one I prefer is time restricted feeding. You eat during a window of 8–12 hours, then you fast for the rest of the 24 hours. If you haven't fasted before, start out gently, trying a 12-hour eating window followed by 12 hours fasting.

Stop if you feel weak, shaky, hangry, or it feels too stressful. If a 12-hour eating window feels good, you can try shortening it to 10 hours (14 hours fasting), then to eight (16 hours fasting). Sixteen hours is the longest I recommend going without food.

During the fasting period, take in no calories at all. You can have green or herbal or black tea or black coffee but with nothing added. That includes sugar or any kind of milk as well as the fats that some people add to coffee, such as coconut or MCT oil, butter and ghee. Having zero to digest allows your body to go into repair mode, called autophagy – the ultimate pay-off of fasting. This can only happen when the body isn't digesting, and so has the time and space to clear out old and damaged cells.

There's no reason why you can't do this most days, or even every day for the 21 days (do have a break after that – see chapter 16). You'll feel benefits even if you only shorten your eating window for two days a week – a lot of my clients fast on a Monday and Tuesday, for example. On these days where you have a short eating window, it's best to eat only two meals. To make sure you're eating enough food, add an extra 10g of protein – or half a portion (see page 152) – to each of the two meals as well as an extra side of vegetables.

Some people skip breakfast and have their eight-hour eating window from 11am to 7pm, as this means they can eat with their family in the evening. Some eat only breakfast and lunch. Or they eat at 9am and 4pm. If you choose not to eat in the evening, make sure it isn't affecting your sleep.

Lifestyle advice

The two main lifestyle areas to focus on when this is your Metabolic Type are exercise and sleep.

- **Strength training:** In clinic, I often come across the 'run-weight-off' mentality. Cardio, especially if it's too hard, is a stressor and so will raise cortisol. If you're already stressed (see chapter 7), it will impact your insulin and leave you feeling hungrier after working out. However, the right exercise can reduce cravings and regulate your appetite. Strength training and any exercise where you use your own bodyweight is better suited to your type as it makes your tissues more sensitive to insulin. And the bigger your muscles, the more glucose they burn, even at rest.

- **Put sleep first:** Just a single night of bad sleep can make your body more resistant to insulin. Sleep is also when we burn most fat and it helps optimise leptin too, the hormone that makes us feel full. So prioritise your 7–9 hours. For more, see chapter 11.

Before every meal, do a short burst of exercise, up to 10 minutes. In one study, just three minutes of walking up and down stairs had an impact on both blood glucose and insulin levels.

IF YOU ONLY DO ONE THING: A DAILY TABLESPOON OF APPLE CIDER VINEGAR (ACV)

Use it as salad dressing on any salad by mixing with a tablespoon of extra virgin olive oil and seasoning. Or put the ACV in a large glass of water and drink through a straw (to protect your teeth). ACV has been shown to lower blood-sugar levels after eating and so keeps insulin levels more stable too. One way it does this is by helping more glucose to get into your muscles to use up as fuel. There's also promising evidence ACV may help with weight loss, too.

EMERGENCY CRAVINGS

Following this eating plan should curb cravings. However, sometimes our bodies send us confused signals, especially when our hormones are imbalanced. If you suddenly feel very hungry or you are craving a particular thing, before you reach for something off plan ask yourself these questions to check in with what your body might actually need. If you answer yes to a question below, do the thing suggested, then wait five minutes. If you still have a craving, move on to the next question.

- Am I thirsty? If yes, drink a glass of water.

- Am I stressed? If yes, do something to relieve that: breathing exercise, meditation, call a friend, dance, write a to-do list.

- Am I bored? If yes, think of something fun to do.

- Was my lunch big enough? If you are genuinely hungry, eat a piece of protein: a piece of chicken, some tinned salmon, an egg, a handful of nuts.

HOW YOUR GENES AFFECT INSULIN

A genetic test can reveal your future risk of health pitfalls and, along with your signs and symptoms, help you to pinpoint the root of your current issues. However, DNA is not destiny; we can turn our genes on and off with how we live and eat. From the multiple genes we know affect insulin, I've picked out one called TCF7L2: it gives me great information when I see it come up on someone's DNA test. If you have a variation (an SNP) on this gene, your insulin response to high GI sugary and carby foods is affected, putting you at higher risk of type 2 diabetes and gestational diabetes. The person who has this SNP needs to be extra careful to eat low GI and exercise regularly too.

Ludwika, 43, always felt hungry, no matter how much she ate

'I started on Pippa's plan nearly four years ago, before my fortieth birthday. I was size 18, sometimes 20 and I weighed 106kg. After three months, I went down to size 12/14 and 78–80kg. Since then, I haven't put on a pound. I've never felt in better shape.

I was a chubby toddler who became a big child and then a very overweight teenager. As an adult, I had been a size 16, but it didn't last. I did a low-carb diet once and lost 10kg . . . but then put 15kg back on.

In my mid-thirties, I had two cycles of IVF and one of them ended in miscarriage. That was a very low time and I put on a lot of weight after that, comfort eating. By the age of 39, I felt as if I was 20 years older. I dressed in baggy, shapeless clothes. I felt bloated, had no energy, had to nap a lot. I had terrible mood swings and heavy periods. I had painful knees and joint pain, too. I consider myself to be a naturally happy person but looking in the mirror in the morning would ruin my day. I lost my confidence and I felt as if people were judging me. Because I was unhappy with myself, I became unhappy with everything.

I love to cook but whatever I ate, I never felt full. I'd eat a packet of sweets and be hungry 20 minutes later and then eat some bread and cheese and be hungry again. I'd eat a whole large chocolate bar in an attempt to cheer myself up and get some energy, but I'd just end up feeling guilty. At a restaurant, I'd always have a starter, main course and pudding. And I'd order something fried like calamari with garlic bread or burger and chips, or fish and chips. My favourite pudding was banoffee pie. At night, I'd always have chocolate or ice cream while watching TV.

Then one day, I saw a picture of myself taken when I was out with a friend. The next week, I started Pippa's plan. The first thing I learnt was that I was eating too much food. I began to weigh my food to understand the right portions. For the first week, I had a lot of headaches, and I was always cold and hungry, so I drank a lot of warm water and had a lot of baths. Pippa advised not to exercise in this early stage, only take gentle walks.

Almost immediately, I began to see my body change. In the first week, I lost 3.6kg. I went shopping to buy a dress to celebrate! After six weeks, I'd lost 9.5kg. My mood swings had gone by then too, now my blood sugar was stable. My husband said, 'It's like my Lucy is back.'

I remember I was walking up the hill one day with two bags of heavy shopping that I could barely carry. At home, I put them on the scales and I realised they weighed the same as the weight I'd lost. I thought, oh my goodness, my poor knees!

I'm a foodie, so I enjoyed learning new recipes. And I liked that I could eat some carbs on the plan. I now do an 80:20 version of the original plan. In the winter, I make a lot of broths, with fish and vegetables. Dinner is often soup or salad with roasted vegetables and/or sweet potatoes, and chicken, chicken liver, fish or meat. Some days I fast until lunchtime and then I'll eat a big salad with boiled eggs or prawns, crab meat or chicken.

It took three months to lose all the weight. My parents flew in to visit me for my birthday. I met them at the airport . . . and they walked straight past me! They didn't recognise me. Mum said to Dad, 'Look at our baby, you can see her collarbones!'

It's been worth all the effort. My constipation has gone. I sleep well all night. My knees now work well enough to do a five-mile coastal hike with my dogs. I can get up at five to go to the gym, where I do weights, Pilates and boxing.

Losing weight isn't easy. But keeping it off is harder. People want a quick fix but there is no such thing. I'm not very strict but I don't let myself go, either. For example, last night, we went out to eat because we'd been travelling all day. I had salmon and vegetables with roast potatoes, but I didn't have the bread or dessert. People do ask: how can you not eat chocolate or sweets? But I don't feel deprived, it's my choice not to eat them. I have stopped treating myself with food and I feel happier for it.

I am comfortable at this size. I could go down to size 10 but I'm happy where I am. Of course, I still have some bad days but I deal with them by going for a walk, not to the fridge. My goal was to have a good life, to feel good. And I do. Now, I feel confident getting dressed up and I love my body. I even love myself.'

Sample three-day meal planner for Insulin Type

BREAKFAST	LUNCH	DINNER
Smoked salmon with pear and watercress (page 167)	Spicy tempeh rainbow salad (page 182)	Cottage pie with cauliflower mash (page 194)
Griddled asparagus with lemon and poached egg (page 164)	Smoked mackerel niçoise (page 179)	Fish curry with fenugreek (page 198)
Almond and flaxseed porridge with smashed berries – add extra ½ tsp cinnamon (page 159)	Personalised salad: build a salad (see pages 231–2) with the key foods for your Metabolic Type (pages 64–6), adding the 'just one thing' (see page 68)	Poached salmon with braised fennel or red lentil dhal (well cooked) (page 204 and 206)

- Stick exactly to the above meal plan, repeating every three days OR

- Create your own meals using The Portion Size Guide (pages 151–8) OR

- Make meals from the recipes in chapter 14 – the ones that suit you will be marked with the initial of your type.

- Do a combination of the above.

CHAPTER 7

Cortisol Type

The hormone cortisol is your driving force, in charge of motivation and giving you bursts of energy. Its peak in the morning is what gets you out of bed. From then on, ideally, your cortisol should slowly decrease over the course of the day until it begins to rise again before the next morning wake-up.

But for many of us, this pattern doesn't happen. Our cortisol is erratic. It might be low in the morning and/or high most of the day. This happens because cortisol is also a major player in your fight-flight-freeze stress response, the body's ancient survival mechanism.

How your stress response works

When you go into high alert – you're scared or excited or surprised or put under pressure – your stress response kicks in. This is controlled by three glands, which make up the hypothalamus-pituitary-adrenal or HPA axis. The hypothalamus (at the base of the brain) is in charge. When it senses stress, it tells the pituitary gland (just below it) to tell the adrenal glands (above the kidneys) to release stress hormones, including noradrenaline and cortisol. Together, these give you a burst of energy, with cortisol boosting the amount of blood sugar available to feed your muscles so you can run away or do battle. It does this by releasing glucose stores from the liver but can also turn protein stores into glucose too.

The HPA response is supposed to be a short-term fix, lasting for 20–40 minutes, just until we've escaped the danger. Then a feedback loop should send a message around the system to switch off the production of adrenaline and cortisol. In theory, we should return to our recovery or 'rest or digest' relaxed state. But what I see in clinic is a lot of highly stressed people. During lockdown in particular, I had a ringside seat to this via Zoom. I saw women who didn't leave their screen all day, were eating at their desk because they felt they needed to be logged on and available, who were trying to home school and cook – and whose eating fell off a cliff.

Constant stress leads to a dysregulated HPA axis and cortisol that is high when it should be low, so you're tired and wired, or low when it should be high, so you might struggle to get out of bed. The HPA axis also controls digestion, mood, emotions, sex hormones, sleep, memory, immune function and, crucially here, blood sugar and appetite. Dysregulation can lead to faster ageing, chronic disease, exhaustion, a weakened immune system and, of course, weight gain.

4 ways cortisol can inhibit weight loss

In the short term, stress will shut down your appetite. But when cortisol stays high, it can lead to weight gain and make losing weight much harder, for a number of reasons.

1. IT AFFECTS YOUR INSULIN RESPONSE

While cortisol stimulates our metabolism to give us a surge of energy in a situation of stress, it always increases appetite. It boosts blood sugar in your bloodstream, which then increases insulin, the fat-storage hormone. When cortisol is high, the body also turns protein stores into glucose, a process called gluconeogenesis.

2. IT MAKES YOU CRAVE CARBS

When you're stressed, you rarely feel like eating a salad. Instead, it's been shown that high levels of cortisol make it more likely you will reach for sweet foods and carbs. These 'comfort foods' increase levels of the feel-good hormones serotonin and dopamine, which give temporary relief.

3. IT AFFECTS OTHER HORMONES

As cortisol is a hormone of survival, when you're stressed the body will manufacture it as a priority, over other, essential – but not urgent – hormones, such as thyroid hormones, which control your metabolism, and the sex hormones oestrogen and progesterone. Stress reduces levels of testosterone too, which can lead to a decrease in muscle mass. Because lean muscle burns more energy, over time, having less muscle mass means you'll expend less energy.

4. IT PROMOTES VISCERAL FAT

Visceral fat is the fat around the middle that sits around the organs, the kind that has the worst effect on health. Research suggests that if you eat a high-sugar diet and you have high cortisol, the knock-on effect is that you create more visceral fat.

What provokes your stress response?

I'm not going to tell you that you need to relax more – that would be annoying! Ideally, I'd like you to assess and think of ways to reduce all your sources of stress, so you're not constantly triggering your HPA axis. You can make any changes slowly; the object is to feel less stressed, not overwhelmed!

Life ups and downs. We can't control the big shocks: accidents, illness, income loss, death, divorce and Covid. But we can reduce stress from the more everyday stuff by asking for help, advice and support with relationships, finances, life admin and work; children, schooling and exams; moving house and renovations; perimenopause and menopause. We can also ask people to talk through situations and help us to pinpoint our sources of stress, and brainstorm ways to reduce them, whether it's the school run or an insurance claim. Bigger things, such as difficult relationships or money issues, may require professional help to navigate.

Eating carbs. Stressed clients often start the day with a carb-based breakfast such as sourdough toast with butter, porridge or granola and eat a sandwich for lunch. Mid-morning and mid-afternoon, their blood sugar levels, which have spiked due to all the carbs, come crashing down and so does their energy and mood. And then the body releases cortisol to bring their blood sugar back up, and so the insulin and cortisol rollercoaster carries on all day.

Not eating. Stressed people sometimes skip breakfast or lunch. Intermittent fasting can be good for some people (see chapter 6). But if you're stressed, not eating acts as a further stressor.

Uppers and downers. Stressed people use caffeine or a mid-afternoon sugar kick to keep going, or drink wine or even smoke a cigarette in the evening to relax. Instead, look after your body when it needs it most.

Exercising too hard for too long. You've probably experienced hunger after a hard session of cardio (such as a long run); this is because it not only uses up your energy stores but also spikes cortisol. Stick to more gentle exercise.

Cortisol Type: what to eat

This is how and what to eat to help support your nervous system.

MORE PROTEIN AND VITAMIN B FOODS.

Protein at every meal is even more important for this type than for all the other types. It will help keep blood sugar steady, reducing cravings (see chapter 6 for more on this). It will keep you full, so you don't overeat. And it is a source of tryptophan, which helps support mood (see chapter 11 for more on this). If you don't have time to cook eggs at breakfast, protein powder can be your saviour, as the base for a protein shake (see pages 163 and 165).

The stress response, including making key brain chemicals, uses up B vitamins. And that also makes eating protein foods – meat, poultry and fish – key, as they are good sources of Bs. Vegans may need to supplement (see page 257). You also need foods containing the amino acid tyrosine, used to make adrenaline. Good sources: sunflower, sesame and pumpkin seeds, chicken and turkey, eggs, fish, tofu.

EAT REGULARLY

If you say you're 'too busy' to eat, you probably need to eat. Stressed women should not be fasting. Try to eat breakfast within an hour of waking. Overnight, try to not to leave more than 12–13 hours without eating. If you have dinner by 7pm, have breakfast by 8am.

ANTIOXIDANT-RICH FOODS

Stress leads to an excess of chemicals in the body called free radicals. These cause inflammation and the kind of cellular damage that leads to cancer, cardiovascular disease and neurodegenerative conditions. To mop up free radicals, you need plenty of antioxidants, which you can get from varying your veg. I've found stressed people often stick to the same two or three vegetables every day.

These are key antioxidants and their sources:

- **Vitamin C-rich foods.** Vitamin C is depleted by the stress response. And in some studies, consuming high levels was shown to decrease stress hormones. It's found in vegetables and fruit, particularly green, leafy vegetables, peppers, lemon juice, tomatoes, strawberries, broccoli, Brussels sprouts and sprouts (e.g., broccoli sprouts and alfalfa).

- **Quercetin-rich foods.** These are important to counter brain inflammation caused by stress. Good sources: capers, red onions, onions, shallots, spring onions, kale, peppers, asparagus, parsley, sage and berries. Also, tea and olive oil.

- **Vitamin D-rich foods.** Having enough vitamin D can block the action of an enzyme that's needed to make cortisol. Ideally you'd get 20 minutes of sunlight on your limbs every day, but it's also in oily fish and liver (also see supplement appendix).

- **Vitamin B5-rich foods.** You need vitamin B5 to make adrenal hormones. Good sources: poultry, meat, liver and kidney, salmon, seafood, beans and pulses, mushrooms, avocado, broccoli, cauliflower, kale and tomatoes.

- **Vegetables.** All vegetables contain antioxidants, but some that are particularly rich are: artichoke, kale, cauliflower,

red cabbage, peppers, Brussels sprouts. Also, cruciferous
and leafy greens (see page 95), and sulphur vegetables
(see page 95).

- **Dried herbs and spices.** Incredibly antioxidant-rich, they are
  all worth using despite the fact you only use a little.
  In particular: turmeric, peppermint, cinnamon, clove,
  oregano, rosemary, sage, saffron, tarragon.

- **Berries.** The chemicals that give them their purple and
  blue colour are powerful antioxidants. Eat: blackberries,
  blackcurrants, blueberries, raspberries and strawberries,
  plus pomegranate.

- **Green tea.** Replace coffee and tea with this. If you leave
  in the bag for just 30 seconds, you'll be drinking more of
  a calming chemical in tea called L-Theanine and only
  minimal caffeine.

- **Cacao.** Packed with antioxidant polyphenols, cacao also
  contains a calming chemical called anandamide, which is
  the brain's own version of the THC in cannabis. Don't worry,
  it helps you feel calm without altering your mind.

MINERAL-RICH FOODS

The HPA axis needs the minerals magnesium, iodine and iron in
particular to function properly. Good sources: leafy greens, seaweed,
seafood, eggs, liver, red meat.

LOW GI FOODS (SEE PAGE 65)

As high blood sugar is also a stressor, eating low GI foods will
help keep blood sugar levels balanced, which in turn helps balance
cortisol levels.

GUT-FRIENDLY FOODS

It's been shown in animal studies that there is a lot of communication between the gut and the HPA axis. Poor gut health has been linked to mental health conditions including anxiety and depression. Fermented foods encourage the right bacterial mix in the gut. Eat: kimchi, sauerkraut, miso.

Lifestyle advice

When you are a Cortisol Type, the main area to focus on aside from what you eat is to find ways to reduce your stress levels, in whatever way that suits you. Ideally, that will include:

- **Moving slowly:** Exercise increases your brain's production of feel-good neurotransmitters, endorphins. And regular exercise means the positive benefits keep on building, including bigger muscles and better sleep. However, hard cardio is not your friend and neither is HIIT. Even moderate exercise has been shown to raise cortisol. The way to recovery is by doing slower workouts: walking, swimming, yoga, QiGong and Pilates.

- **Spending time outside:** In one Japanese study, hiking in a forest was shown to lower cortisol levels by more than 10 per cent. Try to walk outside for 45–60 minutes a day if you can. Even just being in nature, surrounded by green or next to the sea or water has been shown to lower it too.

- **Breathing better:** Breathing shallowly, as most of us do most of the time, is a physical signal to your body that you're in danger. This kicks off the stress response and raises cortisol. Find something to help you breathe more slowly and deeply, whether it's meditation, hypnotherapy or breathing exercises.

- **Drink holy basil tea:** I often speak to stressed people who are drinking eight or more cups of tea and coffee a day. If you are this type, one is enough! Cut down slowly, over a week or so, or you may feel dreadful. Drink a cup of holy basil tea (also called tulsi in Ayurvedic medicine) after dinner. This herb has been shown to work on the stress pathways to the brain.

- **Cut out alcohol:** You've already cut out alcohol on the 21-day plan. Although you might think alcohol calms you, in fact it raises cortisol levels.

- **More pleasure and people:** What makes you feel good? Fun and connection with other people are both potent antidotes to stress.

IS STRESS STOPPING YOU SLEEPING DEEPLY?

Your cortisol is supposed to be high in the morning, then go down during the day until a low point at midnight, when it begins slowly to rise again. The low in the evening is what allows the sleep hormone melatonin to rise. But when your HPA axis is dysregulated, cortisol stays high and suppresses melatonin. This both disrupts the quality of sleep and shortens it, leaving you feeling tired-but-wired, as well as hungrier.

What are your evenings like? Are you still on work calls or emails? Doing hardcore exercise? Ideally, after your evening meal should be your relaxation and wind-down time.

Cortisol affects sleep in another way, too. If you have a very high-carb meal or a few glasses of wine in the evening, it will lead to a drop in insulin in the middle of the night. This then prompts a spike of cortisol, which could wake you up in the early hours – even if it doesn't, you won't be sleeping as deeply.

THE CALMING BREATH

Breathe in for a count of four, hold for a count of one, breathe out for a count of six. Repeat for a minute. Slow, deep breathing has been shown to get you out of fight-flight-freeze state into a slower, steady, relaxed one, while improving emotional control and mood too.

IF YOU ONLY DO ONE THING: EAT A TABLESPOON OF PUMPKIN SEEDS ONE DAY, AND ONE OF WALNUTS THE NEXT.

Sprinkle them onto your salad or breakfast, or add to your morning smoothie. Pumpkin seeds are a good source of the calming mineral magnesium, which helps to regulate cortisol. Research shows that eating a diet high in walnuts can improve your physical reaction to stress, due to their high content of a type of fat called ALA, one of the omega-3 fatty acids.

HOW YOUR GENES AFFECT CORTISOL

A genetic test can reveal your future risk of health pitfalls and, along with your signs and symptoms, help you to pinpoint the root of your current issues. However, DNA is not destiny; we can turn our genes on and off by how we live and eat.

From the multiple genes we know affect cortisol, I've picked out one called FKBP5 because it's part of cortisol regulation, signalling to the brain to lower levels. If a test shows you have a variation (called a SNP) on this gene, your cortisol levels are likely to stay higher for longer after stress and so you'll have to work harder at keeping cortisol low.

Belinda, 60, *has weathered some hard times with the help of the PCM*

'Sticking to Pippa's plan has seen me through some of my toughest years. I first went to see her four years ago, mainly because I wasn't sleeping. I was getting night sweats and I hadn't had a proper night's sleep since I'd lost my husband, David, 18 months earlier. I wasn't eating well. David had always done the cooking and I was too exhausted to make proper meals for myself. Pippa showed me how to eat and what to cook, and she got me sleeping. As a bonus, I lost 10kg, going from 73kg down to 63kg.

Once I was sleeping, I had a clear mind to make some life changes, including going part-time at my high-stress job in finance. But in reality, I was still doing a five-day job but in three days. I was still stressed all the time. Even so, I kept to eating and living well, and I think that's what got me through and what gave me the confidence to leave my job a year later, with no job to go to.

By this time, I'd been going to hot yoga classes for four years and trapeze yoga classes for 18 months. So, when I saw an ad for yoga trapeze teacher training in Kuala Lumpur, I decided to go for it! I was going do something I really loved. As soon as I came home, I started to teach.

At the beginning of 2020, the pain from an old injury, a prolapsed disc, came back but far worse than it had ever been. I was bent double, unable to stand for any period of time. It was bad timing as a couple of months later, Covid hit. I ended up having to wait over a year for an operation. In that time, I kept to everything Pippa taught me. I couldn't exercise but I wanted to stay healthy enough to have the operation, and to recover faster.

I had the operation at the end of January 2021. Unfortunately, during the operation, I had nerve damage that particularly affected one side. I had to lie flat for three days and my hospital stay, which was supposed to be two days, ended up being three weeks. Feeling really down, still in pain and unable to walk, I started to eat the carb-heavy hospital food.

I came home on crutches, unable to do even the most basic tasks. But I was determined: I started eating well again and, slowly, my mobility improved. Then, that November, my eating went on a downward spiral. I live by myself, and although not all Covid restrictions were back in place, people weren't going out pre-Christmas, so I wasn't seeing anybody. I was still eating well, but in the evenings I started to drink wine. And as soon I had a glass of wine, I'd think: what can I eat with this? Of course, it was chocolate and crisps. After dinner, I'd pop to a nearby shop and stock up. Then I'd eat it all in one evening.

I began to have night sweats again. I was only sleeping two or three hours a night and my skin looked dehydrated. My memory was terrible and my mind was foggy; I'd read a sentence and not know what it meant. I couldn't exercise because one foot was still numb. I was anxious that I'd never be mobile, let alone be able to cycle or do trapeze yoga again, or work on my beloved allotment. Over November and December, I put on a load of weight, going up to 82kg.

At the beginning of January 2022, I decided to give up wine – and snacks too. By this time, my foot was a little less numb so, slowly, I started teaching trapeze yoga again. I decided to join Pippa's Female Food Club. I knew I'd be in safe hands.

I began to plan, going through my cupboards and stocking up on the foods I needed. Then, at the beginning of February, I started the club properly. For the first few weeks, I gave up gluten, dairy, alcohol and caffeine. Instead of fasting in the mornings, I began to have breakfast, a protein smoothie, which I discovered that I love. I photographed exactly what I was eating and shared it every day in the Facebook group – having that accountability really worked for me.

In a few weeks, I stopped having night sweats and my sleep improved. And once I was confident the plan was working, I could relax a little.

Now, nearly four months later, I'm down to 65kg. I keep to the plan 80:20, which means I can go out at the weekend, I can have a gin and tonic, wine or cocktails. The difference between this and any other plan I've done is that the next day, I get straight back on it and I'm confident I won't put on weight.'

Sample three-day meal planner for Cortisol Type

BREAKFAST	LUNCH	DINNER
Matcha tea, spinach and kiwi smoothie (page 165)	Leek and watercress soup with balsamic onions (page 177)	Chicken tagine or chickpea tagine (page 191)
Griddled asparagus with lemon and poached egg (page 164)	Smoked mackerel niçoise (see page 179)	Lemon and garlic salmon traybake (page 199)
Smoked salmon with pear and watercress (page 167)	Personalised salad: build a salad (see pages 231–2) with the key foods for your Metabolic Type (pages 79-82), adding the 'just one thing' (see page 85)	Turkey, bok choy and shiitake mushroom sweet and sour broth (page 216)

- Stick exactly to the above meal plan, repeating every three days OR

- Create your own meals using The Portion Size Guide (pages 151–8) OR

- Make meals from the recipes in chapter 14 – the ones that suit you will be marked with the initial of your type.

- Do a combination of the above.

CHAPTER 8

Detox Type

'But I don't drink too much.' Giving up alcohol is often the first thing clients assume I mean, when I suggest detox. But detoxing is not just about eliminating alcohol. Your body's detox process is a finely tuned rubbish removal system. Not only does it detoxify alcohol, but everything that you eat, breathe, touch and smell. It also has the job of processing the products of all the chemical reactions inside you, including the hormones that you've used and now need to excrete. All of this work happens mainly in your liver, but also in your kidneys, large intestine, lymphatic system and via the sweat glands.

The second thing people assume when I say 'detox' is that I'm suggesting a liquid diet of fruit and vegetable juices, or lemon juice and maple syrup. The word has been co-opted to describe a short, sharp, extreme deprivation diet. But this kind of diet isn't advisable or helpful.

The third assumption is that detoxing is only for January. The reality is, we need to support the body's detox pathways day and night, because they are working 24/7 too. In particular, we need to support our liver, the major detox organ.

What's your toxic burden?

People often display a variety of different symptoms that show their body is struggling at some point in the detox process. The detox system is like dominoes – one overload, malfunction, blockage or inefficiency in one part can lead to problems and symptoms in a whole range of others, too.

An effective detox is so much more than a quick fix. Stopping drinking alcohol is part of it, yes, but only part. Our bodies weren't designed for the chemicals we now encounter every day. But most of us happily eat artificial sweeteners and food additives, without giving a thought to how these chemicals have to be eliminated. Some chemicals, such as BPA in plastic, act as hormone disruptors and our liver needs to detox those too. It also has to process the by-products of all our bodily processes, for example our used up oestrogen.

If you are the Detox Type, your signs and symptoms are telling you it's time to start eating and living in a way that helps your body detox. And so, during these 21 days, you're going to learn to give those systems some extra support.

Detox and weight loss

I often find that when people start to support their body to detox, it's the key to lasting weight loss. There are several reasons for this. For example, there's increasing evidence that if you have a high toxic load, you are more likely to be obese and even to develop diabetes.

The liver is the body's transport hub – nearly everything has to pass through it. Its job includes breaking down fats and helping balance blood sugar levels; it has to work extra hard to break down refined carbohydrates and sugars. The other main liver stressors are hydrogenated oils, or oils damaged by high heat and rancid oils (see pages 156–7 for a guide to oils).

The liver also makes bile, which helps digest fats. The liver dumps your toxins and waste products into the bile and sends it to the gallbladder. During digestion, the gallbladder contracts and releases bile into the small intestines. Here, bile helps you to absorb the fat-soluble vitamins A, D, E and K. Some bile goes into the stool to make it soft, where it's safely expelled along with the toxins. Some is reabsorbed and recirculated.

Or, this is how it should work. However, when bile is overloaded with toxins (including used oestrogen; see chapter 10), it becomes sticky and doesn't flow well.

This has a few knock-on effects. Sticky bile can inflame the gallbladder and potentially lead to gallstones. It means you'll have trouble absorbing vital fat-soluble vitamins (a blood test might show that someone who is taking vitamin D supplements still has low levels). You will struggle to break down fats in foods, which can lead to weight gain. You may become constipated and won't be getting toxins out of your body efficiently, which also can lead to weight gain.

How your liver detoxes

The breakdown of toxins in your liver happens in three phases. On this plan, you'll be supporting all three.

PHASE 1

The structure of the substance to be detoxed is changed to make it water soluble. At this stage, the liver is often creating a compound that's even more toxic to the body. This is one more reason why you need all three phases to go smoothly – you don't want to get stuck with the intermediate chemicals.

How to support this: Reduce the toxic load going in. We can't avoid all toxins but we can take care to reduce what we're exposed to – what we are breathing, eating and drinking, and putting on our skin (see pages 97–8 for more).

PHASE 2

This will depend on the compound but the basic process is that the liver attaches molecules to the compound to prepare for the next stage. To do this, it needs a whole variety of different nutrients from your food.

How to support this: Eat a rainbow of different-coloured vegetables as well as good-quality fats and protein.

PHASE 3

Excretion. It's now bile's job to carry the toxins into poo. Good detoxing here depends on having a well-functioning gallbladder and a bowel that moves regularly.

How to support this: Eat bitter foods to stimulate the gallbladder, make sure you get lots of fibre from vegetables and stay well hydrated.

Detox Type: what to eat

You can really rev up the efficiency of your body's detox machine with what you eat. By following the 5 Foundations, you're already supporting your liver in key ways: plenty of water and vegetables; no alcohol or processed foods. Getting enough protein is particularly important because the amino acids in protein are needed to bind to the toxins in the liver in order that they can be excreted. This is what else you can do:

- **Switch to organic or wild foods where possible.** This will help minimise your exposure to pesticides, herbicides and antibiotics used in farming.

- **Cut down on saturated fat.** You're already doing this on this eating plan. Too much can cause bile production issues which makes it harder for the body to get rid of toxins. Choose chicken, fish, seafood and vegetarian proteins over red meat.

- **Eat more cruciferous vegetables.** I don't use the word superfood lightly but these really are superfoods for supporting your liver. Eat two a day, choosing from: broccoli, cabbage, cauliflower, kale, Brussels sprouts, red cabbage, bok choy, collard greens, watercress, sauerkraut, Romanesco, mustard greens, turnips, kale, rocket and radishes.

- **Include sulphur-rich vegetables.** Sulphur compounds increase levels of an antioxidant called glutathione, the powerhouse that keeps the liver ticking over. Cruciferous vegetables are a good source, but it is also in garlic, onion, spring onions, shallots, beetroot, asparagus.

- **Eat bitter foods.** These support bile production. They include: chicory, rocket, watercress and dandelion, radishes, mustard greens, artichokes and turnip greens. Cooking with the spices fenugreek and turmeric is good too.

- **Focus on antioxidant foods.** Plants contain antioxidants which support multiple detox processes. These ones are particularly rich in antioxidants:

  Spices: turmeric, ginger, cinnamon, saffron.
  Herbs: dill, parsley, rosemary, mint, oregano, sage.
  Berries and/or pomegranate seeds: eat a handful of

each daily, as their purple and blue colouring is a powerful antioxidant.

Beetroot: rich in liver helpers called betalaines.

Lemon zest (from an unwaxed lemon): high in limonene, which studies suggest may help reduce fat in the liver.

Cacao: not only rich in antioxidant polyphenols but also a calming chemical called anandamide.

- **Don't forget gut supporting foods.** These include: fermented foods that are rich in good bacteria, such as sauerkraut, kimchi and miso, and foods containing prebiotic fibre, which feeds good bacteria in your gut. Eat: Jerusalem artichokes, asparagus, leeks, onions, garlic, chicory, beans, flaxseeds and chia seeds.

- **Consume iron-rich foods.** Iron deficiency can affect phase 1 function. Good sources: lean meat, liver, eggs, oily fish, game and the darker meat from poultry. If you're vegetarian or vegan, you can get iron from beans, pulses and green leafy vegetables.

HOW TO SUPER POWER YOUR BROCCOLI

To get the maximum sulforaphane, the beneficial detox compound in broccoli, it's best to eat it raw. Research shows that boiling and microwaving reduce the sulforaphane. Don't like your broccoli raw? Scientists have shown the next best thing is to cut it into small florets, wait up to 90 minutes before cooking, then stir-fry it lightly.

WHAT'S REALLY WORTH BUYING ORGANIC?

Ideally, we'd only eat organic food but that's not always possible. The Dirty Dozen and the Clean 15 lists come from yearly US research that tells us about the types of produce that are subjected to the highest amount of pesticide and the produce that tends to be farmed using the least, so you can see where it makes the most impact to buy organic. These are the most recent lists:

DIRTY DOZEN: *Strawberries, spinach, kale, nectarines, apples, grapes, peppers and chillies, cherries, peaches, pears, celery, tomatoes.*

CLEAN 15: *Avocados, sweetcorn, pineapple, onions, papaya, peas, asparagus, honeydew melon, kiwi, cabbage, mushrooms, cantaloupe melon, mangoes, watermelon, sweet potatoes.*

Lifestyle advice

You can do a lot to reduce the amount of toxins going into your body, such as:

- Wash all non-organic fruit and vegetables to get rid of some pesticides and herbicide residues. Rinse in a weak solution of vinegar or Veggi Wash.

- Filter your drinking and cooking water. Avoid water that's been bottled in plastic, as it can leach out small amounts of hormone-disrupting chemicals.

- Don't store food in plastic or aluminium foil when you can avoid it. In the fridge, use glass, enamel or ceramic containers. Instead of plastic boxes, use glass or stainless steel.

- Replace old non-stick and aluminium pans when you can. Switch to stainless steel, cast iron, ceramic and glass cookware.

- Don't take till receipts. The thermal paper they're printed on is coated in BPA, a chemical that's been shown to act as a hormone disruptor.

- Use make-up and scent based on natural essential oils rather than artificial perfumes. In particular, swap to nail polish that doesn't contain formaldehyde.

- Get a good amount of quality sleep. A lot of the body's detox processes happen overnight (see chapter 11 for more).

- Reduce stress if you can. Find a way to relax daily: clients often say nature, meditation and simply resting helps them (see chapter 7 for more).

- Exercise regularly. Even 20 minutes per day is beneficial for the body and mind. It stimulates the circulation and gets you sweating, which helps you detox via the skin.

- Do daily body brushing or body gua sha, which is massage using a specially shaped tool. Both help the lymph system, another system that's key to detoxification.

- If you like to have a bath, add two cups of Epsom salts and soak for long enough to start sweating.

SIMPLE WAYS TO IMPROVE YOUR AIR QUALITY

Did you know that inside air can often be more polluted than outside air? It can be full of harmful particles and toxic gases, including ozone, carbon monoxide and volatile organic compounds (VOCs). If you can open the windows, do. These changes will also help:

- *To reduce dry cleaning, try to buy washable clothes. If you do dry clean, air the clothes outside for a few days.*

- *Don't use scented candles or air fresheners. Instead, use a diffuser and use organic essential oils.*

- *If you use a printer, make sure the room it's in is well ventilated.*

- *Fill your house with plants they absorb pollutants from the air.*

- *Switch to chemical-free cleaning products and beauty products, particularly nail polish.*

- *Don't vape or smoke, and ask smokers and vapers to go outside.*

IF YOU ONLY DO ONE THING: EAT (AT LEAST) TWO CUPS OF GREEN, LEAFY VEGETABLES

Greens contain so much of the good stuff you need for your liver to work well, including glutathione, that powerful antioxidant. As well putting them in your salads, you can steam them, add them to soups, curries, and stews, or chop and add to pasta sauce, or make pesto. Vary them so you have a different mix every day. There's lots to choose from: broccoli, spring greens, spring cabbage, kale, spinach, rocket, bok choy, Brussels sprouts, mizuna, watercress.

HOW YOUR GENES AFFECT YOUR ABILITY TO DETOX

A genetic test can reveal your future risk of health pitfalls and, along with your signs and symptoms, help you to pinpoint the root of your current issues. However, DNA is not destiny; we can turn our genes on and off by how we live and eat.

From the multiple genes we know affect detoxification, I often find one called GSTM1 comes up for Detox Types. It's common to have variation (SNP) or even a deletion of the GSTM1 gene. This means you have poor activity of the key antioxidant glutathione that helps to prevent damage from pollutants, medication, heavy metals, alcohol and other toxins. This wouldn't have mattered thousands of years ago before we were exposed to so many, but it does now. If this is you, you have to work harder – sulphur foods and cruciferous vegetables (see page 95) well as eggs and meat – to get good levels of antioxidants.

Puja, 43, *discovered she wasn't detoxing effectively*

'As a young teenager, I was size 16 but I could never understand why. I really didn't eat that badly. And I didn't eat that differently from my friends, but they were all smaller than me. I used to think: What am I doing wrong? Is there something wrong with me? Throughout my twenties and early thirties, I'd go on diets but it would be hard to lose weight, or I'd lose the weight and regain it straight away.

When I went to see Pippa, aged 39, I had a lot of other symptoms too: brain fog, low mood, fatigue, bloating, PMS and constipation. I was 86kg. She said she thought my detox systems weren't working well, that I had a backlog of toxins including oestrogen. I booked in for some DNA tests and they showed my issue was exactly what my symptoms had suggested: I tend not to be good at detoxing.

I started the plan and I started to lose weight. It took me 18 months to lose 2st 7lbs, going down to 11st, but I've now kept it off for three years.

I make sure I'm eating protein and fats at every meal. For breakfast, I used to eat cereal. Now, I might have boiled eggs or smoked salmon with avocado on gluten-free bread. Or a protein shake with greens, a handful of blueberries and a tablespoon of flaxseeds. The flaxseeds help with oestrogen detox. I also have a handful of broccoli sprouts with each meal and I eat broccoli every day too. When I eat enough protein, I notice I can last the five hours that's recommended between meals. I have three meals a day and I only snack if I'm really hungry, although that's very rare. I know I feel better when I drink my full two litres of water a day.

After I'd lost the weight, I carried on eating the same way but just loosened the rules. I like that no food is now banned. Sometimes when I'm out with friends, I do eat too much, but I know I can stay this weight when I stick to the plan 80:20.

I know I need to vary what I eat for my gut health. And so I try to eat different vegetables each day, although I do have my favourites: broccoli and cauliflower, as well as leeks, artichoke, ginger, garlic, onions, red onions.

It does take some effort to keep finding new recipes using new foods. I use a lot of the recipes on Pippa's website. She taught me to experiment with food, to try different things, to find out what suits my body. I like to grill or stir-fry meat. I try to be creative with eggs, so I might make an omelette or little egg muffins with chopped vegetables and herbs.

Last year, I joined her Female Food Club so I could try more new recipes. It was so interesting to meet so many women in the club who have similar symptoms to the ones I used to have.

I like that it's up to me to work out what foods suit me. I found doing a food diary very useful in this. At the beginning, it helped me stay on track. When I started reintroducing foods, it helped me realise when any symptoms came back. For example, I thought I could get away with eating foods like pizza or fried food or gluten, but I now know I can't! They make me feel tired afterwards. If I do have bread, I have sourdough and rye bread as I know they suit me better. And I stay away from processed foods because if I do eat something processed, like chorizo, for example, it tends to give me indigestion, bloating and repeats on me. And I'd rather feel great the next day than eat a food that doesn't suit me.

I used to live off caffeine and the buzz it gave me but I have realised it was also making me anxious and stressed. Now I have a single coffee a day, which I really enjoy. I have also realised I have to be very careful with alcohol or I get a terrible hangover. When I do drink, which is not every week, I can have two small glasses of wine.

At home, I looked at all the cleaning and beauty products I was using. And, over time, I have slowly switched to versions with no chemicals. If I'm stressed or anxious, I do breath exercises. And at night, I'll have a bath with Epsom salts, which contains relaxing magnesium and helps detox through the skin.

When I was overweight, I felt tired all the time. Now, I don't get nearly as many PMS symptoms, or bloating or constipation, and I hardly ever feel lethargic. I feel more positive, too. On my fortieth birthday, at a bar in London, I wore a knee-length flowery dress. I would never have worn something so short or so fitted before. It felt so good not to be self-conscious in the photos.

I feel much more confident now I know the food that works for me. If there's something not right with your body, you can find out what it is and do something about it. I am proof that you don't have to give up.'

Sample three-day meal planner for Detox Type

BREAKFAST	LUNCH	DINNER
Chia yoghurt breakfast bowl (page 161)	Spicy green beans and broccoli with charred spring onions (page 181)	Bombay cauliflower steak with roasted onion bhaji (page 187)
Detox smoothie (page 163)	Raw vegetable salad (page 178)	Fish curry with fenugreek (page 198)
Spicy beans on cumin aubergine (page 169)	Personalised salad: build a salad (see pages 231–2) with the key foods for your Metabolic Type (pages 94–6), adding the 'just one thing' (see page 100)	Chargrilled chicken with pumpkin seed pesto (page 189)

- Stick exactly to the below meal plan, repeating every three days OR

- Create your own meals using The Portion Size Guide (pages 151–8) OR

- Make meals from the recipes in chapter 14 – the ones that suit you will be marked with the initial of your type.

- Do a combination of the above.

CHAPTER 9

Thyroid Type

Have you ever been away for a weekend, eaten a bit more than you usually would and come home to find you've gained half a stone? Or perhaps you tried a diet that was working for a friend but it didn't seem to have any impact on your own weight? Or your weight loss was super slow, even though you were exercising hard? Or you tried fasting but found you put on weight? These are all real-life stories I've heard from clients who are the Thyroid Type.

The thyroid issue I'm referring to here is low thyroid function or hypothyroidism, when not enough thyroid hormone is getting into your cells. It's not only more common than overactive thyroid, it's the thyroid issue that can lead to weight gain.

Low mood, low energy

The thyroid gland, at the front of the neck, is tiny but mighty. It's in charge of the speed of our metabolism, i.e., how all our cells use energy. If it's not working well, it can not only make you feel low in energy but low in mood too. Typical symptoms include feeling the cold more than other people, puffiness around the face and eyes and sometimes a low sex drive. The symptom that almost everyone experiences is extreme tiredness.

Like all body systems, your thyroid function is a complex balancing act of hormonal and chemical interactions that can go wrong at any stage. When thyroid hormones are low, the pituitary gland in the brain sends thyroid stimulating hormone (TSH) to tell the thyroid gland to release more. The thyroid makes two types of hormone: a little of the active, fat-burning type T3, and a lot of inactive T4. You need to convert T4 to fat-burning T3, which happens in the liver but also in the gut.

If you have thyroid symptoms, your GP may send you for a blood test, usually to measure levels of TSH. If results are outside of a 'normal' range, you'll be prescribed medication. However, what's considered normal under NHS guidelines is not optimal. I do see clients who've been told their TSH is 'normal' but who have thyroid symptoms.

In clinic, we test for a whole series of markers that look at the different parts of the thyroid system: TSH but also T3 and T4, among others. We measure thyroid antibodies to find out if your body is seeing your thyroid as foreign and attacking it. We assess if you are converting T4 to T3 well. And if T3 is able to get into cells to work. We also look at the liver, digestion and stress levels, as these all affect your thyroid function too. The good news is, getting the right nutrition will have a positive impact on balancing thyroid function.

Thyroid Type: what to eat

Both fasting and very low-calorie diets are too much of a burden on a metabolism that's already struggling, so you need to focus on eating well and eating regularly. Having enough protein is very important, as it is for all Metabolic Types, but you should also include the suggested carb portion in the evenings (see page 154), for example of butternut squash, parsnip, pumpkin, swede or sweet potato.

- **Selenium and iodine:** These are the two most important nutrients for the thyroid. Iodine is a crucial part of T3 and T4, while selenium is necessary to convert T4 to T3 – and needed to make glutathione, a key antioxidant in the thyroid. Fish and seafood are high in iodine but seaweed is the best source. Make sure you eat the whole egg not just the white, as the yolk is rich in iodine and selenium. All meats and poultry provide good levels of selenium. Mushrooms are a good vegan source, as are sunflower seeds, chia seeds, flaxseeds and Brazil nuts.

- **Vegetables:** Eat a variety of vegetables, as explained in the 5 Foundations. However, when you eat cruciferous vegetables – bok choy, broccoli, Brussels sprouts, cabbage, cauliflower and kale – it's best to lightly steam them.

- **Organic liver:** Apologies to vegans and vegetarians, as well as liver-haters, but, as you'll see below, liver is a brilliant food for the thyroid.

- **Vitamin D:** This is essential for the activation of thyroid hormone in the cells. Found in liver as well as oily fish, egg yolks and some mushrooms. But the best way to get vitamin D – besides a supplement – is from 20 minutes of sunshine a day on your limbs, with no sunscreen. (NB: in summer months, avoid 12pm to 3pm.)

- **Zinc:** This is needed for T3 production. It's found in meat, seafood, pumpkin seeds and other seeds, pulses and beans, eggs and, yes, liver again!

-

- **Vitamin B12:** Half of people with thyroid issues have low levels of B12. It's found in meat but also organ meat, including liver. If you're veggie or vegan, you may need a supplement (see page 257).

- **Vitamin A:** Having low thyroid function can also affect the usual conversion of the carotenoids found in plant sources, such as apricots, carrots and other red, yellow, and orange coloured fruit and vegetables, to the active form of vitamin A, retinol. You can get retinol directly from eggs, oily fish and liver.

- **Choline:** This nutrient is essential to make flexible cell membranes, needed for T3 to get into the cells. Eat eggs, fish, meat, soy, fish roe, nuts, beans and, again, liver.

- **Omega-3:** This is key to making flexible cell membranes too. Eat fatty fish, such as salmon, sardines, mackerel, trout, herring. Veggie sources include chia seeds, pumpkin seeds and walnuts.

- **Helpful herbs and spices:** Ginger, turmeric, parsley, lemon balm (drink as a tea).

Lifestyle advice

You might be surprised at the number and range of things that can affect the thyroid. It's worth looking at the following areas of your life:

- **Limit mobile phone use.** One recent area of research is the effect of the radiation emitted by mobile phones. Due to the thyroid's position at the front of the neck, it's directly in the line of fire. Studies have shown high mobile phone usage changes levels of thyroid hormones.

- **Clean up your water:** Fluoride and chlorine both affect thyroid function, so filter drinking water and switch to a fluoride-free toothpaste.

- **Clean up your cookware:** There are some chemicals in non-stick cookware that have also been shown to impact thyroid function. Ideally, cook in stainless steel, cast iron, ceramic or glass (see chapter 8 for more on reducing your exposure to toxins).

- **Take a break from cardio:** Cardio is not the answer. Long, high energy consumption sends danger signals to the body, which then switches into survival mode, lowering the metabolism in order to save energy. Research has shown that hard cardio training can turn off the production of T3 in women. When this happens, instead of burning body fat, you're more likely to store it. Stick to slower exercise, such as strength training, Pilates, yoga, walking, swimming.

- **Heal the gut:** Twenty per cent of the conversion of T4 to T3 happens in the gut. It's worth giving your digestive health some attention (see chapter 5 for more).

- **Reduce stress levels:** The thyroid system is very responsive to stress. And stress comes in many forms: it might be mental, emotional or physical stress (such as overexercising) but not eating the right food and not getting enough sleep will also impact stress levels. (For more, see chapter 7.)

WHAT ELSE CAN AFFECT MY THYROID?

The thyroid has been called the 'canary in the coalmine' for health. Because it's such a delicate system, it's often the one that goes wrong first. Women have times in their life when they are most susceptible to thyroid conditions. In postpartum thyroiditis, the thyroid gland becomes inflamed after having a baby. Another is during the menopause, because taking HRT can have an impact on thyroid receptors, as high oestrogen directly affects thyroid function by reducing the liver's conversion of T4 to active T3.

Thyroid issues have also been linked to: being intolerant to gluten, being infected with the virus that causes glandular fever (Epstein Barr) and the bacteria that cause stomach ulcers (H pylori).

IF YOU ONLY DO ONE THING: EAT A DAILY TEASPOON OF SEAWEED

Seaweed is rich in iodine and many women – particularly young women, pregnant women and the over 55s – are deficient in iodine, a mineral that's crucial for thyroid function. You can buy seaweed seasoning in the herb section of bigger supermarkets to sprinkle on salads or you can do the same with crushed nori (the seaweed sheets used to wrap sushi). You can also use nori sheets as a wrap (see page 202) or snack on them.

HOW YOUR GENES AFFECT THYROID FUNCTION

A genetic test can reveal your future risk of health pitfalls and, along with your signs and symptoms, help you to pinpoint the root of your current issues. However, DNA is not destiny; we can turn our genes on and off with how we live and eat.

From the multiple genes we know affect digestion, I've picked out one called DIO2. This gene is in charge of converting T4 to T3, the active form of the thyroid hormone. If you have this variation, it's even more crucial that you eat foods that are rich in iodine and selenium – because if you don't, you'll likely end up low in T3 and have symptoms of low thyroid function.

Lisa, 48, has struggled with her slow metabolism

'During lockdown, I was on gardening leave for six months between jobs. I decided to take this pause in life to concentrate on my health, for the first time in years. My weight had gone up to 107kg. I have two children, aged six and ten, and I've always had a full-time, demanding job. I bought a Peloton and I started eating healthily, counting calories. In six months, I lost 9kg.

But after that, the weight loss slowed right down, no matter how few calories I ate or much exercise I did. I couldn't work out why, when I was being so disciplined. I was eating around 1,500 healthy calories a day and, including exercise, burning around 2,800–3,000 a day. On that basis, I should have been losing two to three pounds a week but I was only losing a pound.

Being overweight made me feel a kind of shame. I'm in a senior job and I thought that people would judge me for being overweight, for lacking control or not having discipline.

I started working with Pippa. She noted that I was puffy around the eyes and felt sluggish, as well as being very slow to lose weight. She said this pointed towards thyroid issues. I wasn't surprised. There are thyroid issues in my family. And since my teenage years, I've always gained weight easily and found it hard to lose. In the past, at slimming groups, people of a similar size to me, who started at the same time, would lose three or four pounds a week, while I'd lose just one.

I had my DNA tested. It showed my genetics are against me: I have a few genes that make me more likely to have a slow metabolism, including a slow thyroid. I don't metabolise fats and sugars very well, and I don't detoxify oestrogen very well either. The upshot is, if I want to stay healthy and slim, I need to be extremely disciplined. I'm not being a victim when I say that – I've accepted it's the cards I have been dealt. There are worse things.

Pippa advised me to up my protein and to focus on eating more vegetables. When I ate like this and started on thyroid support supplements, I found that I could keep losing a pound a week but without having to be quite as strict.

Pippa also advised me to cut down on cardio and do more strength training. She said my body was treating so much cardio as a stress, so my thyroid was slowing down my metabolism. At the time, I was doing the round the world challenge on my Peloton – 250 miles a week, which took around 12 hours. Pippa was right; the weeks I did more cardio, I didn't lose more weight. In fact, while I was training for the London Marathon last year, I put on weight.

By the end of 12 months, I'd lost 26kg. Now, 18 months later, I have put some of the weight back on. At first, I thought it was down to my new job and working away three days a week. It's been hard to keep to the same level of discipline, to organise myself and the household. I have found myself eating biscuits in long meetings and a having a glass of wine and pasta and bread at my regular work dinners.

Then recently, I found out that it's likely down to me starting the perimenopause. It makes sense: my hormonal symptoms have ramped right up. I used to have a couple of days of my cycle where I felt negative and unmotivated, now it's up to seven or eight.

But now I've got all the tools and I understand my body. I'm easing back into the plan because it works. I've started having a protein shake for breakfast and I'm making sure I eat enough protein through the rest of the day. Next, I'll add a second good habit: carrying seeds and protein with me. After that, I'll keep adding more good habits on top. I know what to do.'

Sample three-day meal planner for Thyroid Type

BREAKFAST	LUNCH	DINNER
Baked portobello mushroom and poached egg (page 160)	Bean patties with courgette and preserved lemon salad (page 183)	Beef and mushroom stew and 'cheesy' cauliflower mash (page 185)
Smoked salmon with pear and watercress (page 167)	Cauliflower and rosemary soup (page 172)	Pan-fried liver with crispy sage and celeriac mash (page 200)
Detox smoothie (page 163)	Personalised salad: build a salad (see pages 231–2) with the key foods for your Metabolic Type (page 107–8), adding the 'just one thing' (see page 110)	Nori wrap (page 202)

- Stick exactly to the above meal plan, repeating every three days OR

- Create your own meals using The Portion Size Guide (pages 151–8) OR

- Make meals from the recipes in chapter 14 – the ones that suit you will be marked with the initial of your type.

- Do a combination of the above.

CHAPTER 10

Oestrogen Type

We almost always talk about oestrogen as A Good Thing, that it's better to have more. It's true that oestrogen does a lot of great work for women. It's a feel-good hormone that's not only key in sex and fertility, but is also a multi-tasking powerhouse. It modifies the production of endorphins (happy chemicals) in our brains, especially mid-cycle. It controls body temperature, protects our nerves from damage, protects our memory and supports heart and liver function. It helps keep the collagen in our skin firm and healthy, our tissues moisturised and our bones strong. When it comes to weight loss, oestrogen helps keep our metabolic rate high so we burn more energy and it regulates the metabolism of glucose and fats, so we store less energy as fat.

During our fertile years, we make our own oestrogen. Our ovaries produce most of it but our fat cells and adrenal glands produce some too. We may add some from taking the Pill or other hormonal contraception. Then, as levels drop with perimenopause, we may do the same with HRT.

However, you can have too much of this good thing. Excessive levels of oestrogen can send your body into chaos – a condition called oestrogen dominance. This is the hormone imbalance I'll be focusing on in this chapter as it's the one I see most often in clinic and is a major reason as to why some women struggle to lose weight. Women with oestrogen dominance often find that if they're trying to lose weight, their weight loss plateaus in the second half of their cycle.

Oestrogen dominance is also the underlying cause of so many hormonal issues for women: PMS, irregular periods, bloating, anxiety, mood swings, fibroids and cysts, lumpy breasts. The usual medical line is that these things are common and normal, and so we have to live with them. However, what you eat can make a real difference to your symptoms as well help with weight loss.

How does oestrogen dominance stop you losing weight?

Oestrogen dominance means the level of oestrogen in the body is too high in relation to the other key female hormone, progesterone. It's this imbalance that causes problems.

It can be due to excessive oestrogen levels, but also to poor clearance of used oestrogen. You can suffer from oestrogen dominance during your fertile years, when you're making oestrogen. But it can also start or continue during the perimenopause and menopause, if your progesterone levels drop faster than your oestrogen levels. In clinic, I often see this pattern in women who are taking HRT.

Because it has so many actions in the body, excess oestrogen stops you losing weight in several ways:

1. **It blocks oestrogen receptors.** When oestrogen has been used, it needs to be cleared out of the body. If this doesn't happen,

the old oestrogen hangs around and can block your oestrogen receptors, which stops all the fresh oestrogen being able to do its job regulating your metabolism. And when it's recirculating, your body will treat it as a toxin. My motto for oestrogen is: use it, then lose it. Which is what the eating advice in this chapter will help you do.

2. **It impacts your thyroid.** Oestrogen and thyroid hormones have a close relationship. Too much oestrogen can trigger your thyroid to behave as if it's underactive. This then leads to fatigue and weight gain (for more on this, go to chapter 9).

3. **It affects insulin.** Oestrogen dominance affects your body's response to insulin, the fat storage hormone. That leaves you less able to use blood glucose efficiently as energy, and so your liver is more likely to convert the excess glucose into fat (for more on how, see chapter 6).

Why does oestrogen dominance happen?

Your eating and lifestyle may be contributing. For example, you may not be going to the loo regularly, the final stage of clearing used-up oestrogen out of your body. Or you may have a genetic tendency to be less efficient at detoxing used-up oestrogen. Your ability to do this can also be affected by alcohol, other toxins, stress and being low in certain nutrients.

If you are or become overweight, you can get into a vicious cycle: the extra fat cells make more oestrogen, it's not cleared away quickly enough and you become even more oestrogen dominant, and you gain more weight. We are also exposed to fake oestrogens in our environment, called xenoestrogens, that mimic oestrogen. They include chemicals such as bisphenol A (BPA) and phthalates in plastic bottles, phthalates and parabens in skincare, some pesticides and herbicides in food.

GETTING RID OF OESTROGENS

The body detoxes oestrogens (our used-up oestrogen as well as xenoestrogens) in three phases. We inherit genes that make us better or worse at each of these phases, but their effectiveness is also heavily influenced by diet and lifestyle.

Phases 1 and 2 take place in the liver. In phase 1, the used oestrogen is transformed into a compound that's more toxic than the original oestrogen. This leads to phase 2, when the toxic compound is made water soluble, so it can then leave the liver. It's carried out of the liver in the bile salts. These go into storage in the gall bladder, ready to be released to help digest fats.

However, when the bile salts are overloaded with excess oestrogen, they become sticky and sludgy, so they can't be released as needed. This is why women are more likely to develop gall bladder problems, including gall stones, particularly when they start HRT.

Phase 3 takes place in the gut. Here, it's important to have the right balance of gut bacteria. For example, if you have too much certain unhelpful bacteria, they make an enzyme called beta glucuronidase that binds to oestrogen and takes it back into circulation again.

Eventually, the oestrogen is eliminated safely from the body via stools. This is why it's so important to have a bowel movement at least once a day. If you don't, the used-up oestrogen can be reabsorbed back into the body.

It's important to make sure that what you eat is supporting all three phases, including elimination – in other words, there's no point in getting oestrogen out of the liver if it's left swilling around in the gut. The 5 Foundations will help by keeping you hydrated and making sure you eat plenty of fibre. The more specialist eating advice below will also ensure you're eating to support healthy bile production too.

Oestrogen Type: what to eat

These foods will help clear out used oestrogen and reduce your oestrogen levels.

- **Cruciferous vegetables:** These are a daily essential in your vegetable quota because they are oestrogen super balancers. All vegetables in the cabbage family are excellent at supporting your body's detox of oestrogen. Common ones are: Broccoli, cabbage, cauliflower, kale, Brussels sprouts and red cabbage. You can also include: bok choy, collard greens, watercress, sauerkraut, Romanesco, mustard greens, turnips, kale, rocket and radishes. Best of all are broccoli sprouts.

- **Sulphur rich vegetables:** Sulphur compounds increase levels of an antioxidant called glutathione, key to liver function. They're in cruciferous vegetables but also garlic, onion, spring onions, shallots, beetroot and asparagus.

- **Bitter foods:** These support healthy bile production (for more, see chapter 5). These include: chicory, rocket, watercress and dandelion, radishes, mustard greens, artichokes and turnip greens.

- **Phytoestrogen foods:** Phytoestrogens are compounds that occur naturally in a wide range of plant foods. Like xenoestrogens, they mimic your body's own oestrogens but in a positive way, helping to regulate levels of oestrogen in the body. Flaxseeds are a great source and, because they're full of soluble fibre, they can also help regulate blood sugar and insulin levels (see chapter 7). Other good sources are fermented soy foods, such as miso, tempeh and tofu, and also edamame.

- **Good fats:** Eating good fats is key to keeping your hormones balanced. On the plan, you'll be getting these from extra virgin olive oil but also avocados, nuts and seeds and oily fish such as salmon, sardines or mackerel.

- **Proteins:** You already know from the 5 Foundations that you're going to be eating protein at every meal. This is particularly important for hormones because the building blocks of protein – amino acids – are needed to make all our hormones.

- **Helpful herbs and spices:** Turmeric and rosemary both help detoxify oestrogen.

IF YOU JUST DO ONE THING: EAT TWO TABLESPOONS OF BROCCOLI SPROUTS PER DAY

Broccoli sprouts are the very richest source of sulforaphane, the chemical in cruciferous vegetables that helps you detox the used oestrogen from your body. Two tablespoons contain the nutritional power of two whole heads of broccoli. Whizz them in a smoothie, add to salads or chop and sprinkle like a herb. You can get them in most supermarkets or you can buy seeds and sprout them yourself. (NB: if you don't blend them, chew well to release more of the sulforaphane.)

TRY SEED CYCLING

Seed cycling is a naturopathic remedy that's used to help balance women's hormones. It sounds a bit bonkers but it does have its roots in science. The idea is that eating different seeds will regulate oestrogen in the first half of your menstrual cycle and progesterone in the second half. I have used it with clients as part of a programme to balance hormones and I think there are some benefits as part of an eating plan – although it's not the whole answer.

Days 1–13/14, the follicular phase (from the first day of your period): *Eat one teaspoon each of freshly ground flax and pumpkin seeds per day.*

Days 14/15, the luteal phase (to the first day of your next period, the first day of bleeding, enough to wear a tampon): *Eat one teaspoon each of ground sunflower and sesame seeds per day.*

You can increase these amounts to 1 tablespoon after the 21-day plan.

How does it work? Flaxseeds regulate oestrogen levels, while zinc from pumpkin seeds may promote progesterone production in preparation for the next phase of the cycle. The lignans in sesame may help prevent oestrogen levels from increasing too much. Meanwhile, the vitamin E in sunflower seeds is thought to help boost progesterone levels.

HOW YOUR GENES AFFECT YOUR LEVELS OF OESTROGEN

A genetic test can reveal your future risk of health pitfalls and, along with your signs and symptoms, help you to pinpoint the root of your current issues. However, DNA is not destiny; we can turn our genes on and off with how we live and eat.

From the multiple genes we know affect oestrogen, one called CYP1B1 is particularly revealing, when I see it come up on someone's DNA test. If your test says you have an SNP (variation) on this gene, it means that when you break down oestrogen you're more likely to produce chemicals that have been linked with PMS, fibroids and other hormonal imbalances. Having this gene shows me you need extra support with detoxing so this doesn't happen.

Caroline, 48, lived with hormonal havoc

'I have had PMS since my very first period. But over the years, my symptoms have got a lot worse. By my early forties, the emotional symptoms were almost impossible to live with. I'd develop terrible anxiety for the week leading up to my period. My moods were so erratic, I'd suddenly feel an irrational hatred of my (lovely!) husband. It was awful, not being able to stop my mood swinging up and down and up again. My breasts would become painful, then then my period would come along with stabbing pains. Those lasted a couple of days, then I'd be back to normal. I also felt generally low in energy too.

I went to see my GP, who offered me antidepressants, but I didn't think that was the answer. People told me I just had to accept feeling hormonal, that it was part of being a woman. I hoped changing what I ate might help me feel better, so I went to see Pippa. I didn't go with the intention of losing weight, although I have since lost over 3kg, going from a size 12 to a size 10.

I have always been interested in food and cooked a lot, so I assumed I was eating quite well. For breakfast, I'd have home-made granola and compote with yoghurt. By 10.30, I'd be looking in the cupboard for a biscuit to have with coffee or some dark chocolate from the fridge. I'd eat a sandwich at lunchtime and by 3pm, I'd be hungry and grazing from the cupboard yet again, or even eating my daughter's sweets.

Pippa explained that my need to snack and cravings for sugar were due to the sugary foods and carbs I was eating, which were making my blood sugar and insulin go up and down. Even though the granola and compote were home-made, they weren't right for me.

For the first few days on Pippa's plan, I really missed coffee, wine and dairy, and I felt irritated by having to follow a set structure. It put me in a pretty grumpy mood.

Pippa told me to eat more protein, so I switched my sugary breakfast to either a protein shake or eggs. And within the first week, I felt the difference. I didn't have hunger pangs and I didn't feel so stressed, either. I started to like the fact that I had a set menu, which meant I knew what I had to buy meal-wise. I enjoyed trying new recipes and we found some new favourites. My daughter, who is ten, loves the lettuce wraps that you can make with beef or turkey mince.

I have stopped craving sugar and carbs completely. In fact, I don't really enjoy sugar. I used to pinch a few sweets from my daughter. Now I can't believe how sweet they taste. And when we go out for dinner, I no longer fancy having a dessert.

Recently, my husband gave me a lovely compliment – he rarely comments on my looks but he said I was looking great. It's now been ten months. I've got the energy to play tennis and exercise, and they make me feel good. I know that when I'm eating properly, I feel calmer and I'm more relaxed (although I can't profess to be a saint as I don't always stick to the plan). My hormones have improved a lot. Sometimes I do still get PMS and period pain but it's not as bad. But I now have the confidence that I understand my body, and things are going in the right direction.'

READ PAGE 43
ONE WEEK

Sample three-day meal planner for Oestrogen Type

BREAKFAST	LUNCH	DINNER
Almond and flaxseed porridge with smashed berries (page 159)	Chinese cabbage salad with edamame and ginger (page 174)	Falafel with spiced slaw (page 197)
Miso-glazed Tenderstem broccoli with spinach and poached egg (page 166)	Spicy tempeh rainbow salad (page 182)	Prawn hot and sour broth (page 205)
Detox smoothie	Personalised salad: build a salad (see pages 231–2) with the key foods for your Metabolic Type (pages 119–20), adding the 'just one thing' (see page 121)	Orange and balsamic chicken traybake (page 203)

- Stick exactly to the above meal plan, repeating every three days OR
- Create your own meals using The Portion Size Guide (pages 151–8) OR
- Make meals from the recipes in chapter 14 – the ones that suit you will be marked with the initial of your type.
- Do a combination of the above.

CHAPTER 11

Serotonin Type

If you ticked lots of boxes for the Serotonin Type, well done for getting far enough to open this book and even considering trying to lose weight. Because if you're low in serotonin, you may struggle with feeling low. Clients who are this type often tell me all they want to do is curl up in bed. But bear with me – if you can implement food and lifestyle change, you should start to feel brighter and be able to lose weight too.

You've probably heard of serotonin as the brain chemical or neurotransmitter that regulates our mood. There's a class of antidepressants including Prozac that work on this system, called selective serotonin reuptake inhibitors, or SSRIs. Serotonin's job is to make us feel emotionally stable, more focused and energetic, as well as less anxious and more relaxed. And, crucially, if you're trying to lose weight, serotonin is also our natural appetite suppressant, curbing cravings. When you have enough serotonin in your brain, you can feel satisfied even when your stomach isn't full.

However, right now, it appears that you don't have enough

serotonin. What does low serotonin feel like? Not only will you experience low mood, feel anxious or stressed and be low in energy, but you are also likely to want to eat more, especially carbohydrates. The reason for this goes back to how we make serotonin in the brain.

The key building block of serotonin is an amino acid called tryptophan, that comes from eating protein. Chicken and turkey, in particular, are excellent sources. Once you've digested your protein, the tryptophan will reach the bloodstream. Then, for you to make serotonin, tryptophan needs to travel from the blood through the blood–brain barrier, into the brain. You could think of it as crossing a bridge. But there's a problem: tryptophan must compete with some of the other amino acids found in proteins too, which are faster and better equipped to cross the bridge; if tryptophan were travelling on foot, it would be as if the other amino acids were travelling in cars. So tryptophan is at a disadvantage.

For tryptophan to get over the bridge, it needs help. It needs you to have the right amount of the hormone insulin in your blood – not too high or low. That will come from eating carbs, but it must be the right amount and the right kind of carbs. Without those carbs, you won't produce serotonin.

If you go on a very low-carb diet, no matter how much protein you eat, your brain won't get the tryptophan it needs to manufacture enough serotonin. I see this often. Quite a lot of new clients are either on or have tried very low-carb plans, such as the ketogenic diet. Some have spent weeks, even months, avoiding any and all carbs. Some have even stopped eating vegetables because, officially, they are classed as carbs (if there's one life-changing piece of advice I'd like you to take from this book, it's to eat more vegetables!).

That's why when you cut out carbs, your mood can suffer. You may feel 'blue', irritable or less resilient to stress. These symptoms will be worse if you're one of the people who have a genetic tendency either to not make serotonin well, to be less sensitive to it or to metabolise it too quickly.

That explains my carb cravings!

The tryptophan-carb-serotonin connection is also one reason we crave carbs when we're feeling low or stressed. It's your brain telling you what you need to feel better. Really, this is self-medication: carbs give you relief from feeling low. Clients who used to restrict carbs in the past often tell me that when they went back to eating them, they ended up overeating them.

If you tend to be a comfort eater, the good feeling you get from your carb-induced serotonin surge will reinforce this. Some people will binge on carbs, eating a whole load of sugary or starchy foods all in one go. A typical time for this is after drinking alcohol, when you get that don't-care-any-more feeling. Others stick to whole foods but eat far too much of them – you might eat three bowls of granola in a row, or constantly snack on nuts and dates.

While you need some carbs to make serotonin, overeating carbs can have the opposite effect. The resulting surge in insulin can lead to too much tryptophan crossing the blood-brain barrier, then you make more serotonin than you need. This can lead to drowsiness after you eat, the so-called 'food coma'.

If you consistently eat too many carbs and overload the brain with serotonin, this uses up the nutrients needed to make serotonin, such as B vitamins. Your brain can also become overwhelmed by the high levels of serotonin, so it stops responding to them. It seems counterintuitive but the upshot of this is also symptoms of low serotonin, such as loss of interest in life and depression.

What's taking your tryptophan?

Stress can be a major contributing factor to low serotonin too. I'm referring here to stress in its widest definition, including inflammation from illness and eating processed foods, fluctuating blood sugar as well as blood pressure. Under stress, the brain experiences something called the 'tryptophan steal'. Instead of the tryptophan from your food being used to make feel-good serotonin and melatonin, it's diverted to making more essential compounds that are needed to keep your under-stress metabolism functioning.

The 5 Foundations will help with preventing the tryptophan steal, as it is an anti-inflammatory way of eating. But you will also benefit from addressing life stresses too (see chapter 8 for more on this). And following the food advice below will help you find your sweet spot, so you get enough – but not too many – of the right carbohydrates.

Serotonin Type: what to eat

Follow these eating rules to get your serotonin system working better.

- **Plan meals around high-tryptophan foods.** Tryptophan is an amino acid that you must get from your food – the best sources are turkey and chicken. Eat either one of these at least once a day. Other good sources are salmon and eggs. The best vegan source is tofu, but you can also get some tryptophan from edamame, pumpkin seeds, peanuts and peanut butter, almonds and almond butter, sesame seeds and tahini. Vegetarians may need to supplement with protein powder (see page 257).

- **Have a portion of carbohydrate in your evening meal.**
  You are one type who really does need some carbs daily.
  But the right amount will vary from person to person, so
  it's a matter of experimenting. It may take a few days or
  even weeks to find your sweet spot. Try having a portion
  of starchy vegetables at dinner such as peas, pumpkin,
  beetroot, squash or turnip (see full list of carby vegetables
  in chapter 4). That might be enough to ensure an even
  mood, sleeping well and not waking up hungry. If you don't
  notice a change within a few days, try having some other
  good-quality carbs, including wild or basmati rice, quinoa,
  buckwheat noodles, new potatoes, fruit and pulses as well
  as carby vegetables (see full list of carbs in chapter 13).

- **Seek out pro-tryptophan foods.** You can eat to prevent the
  tryptophan steal too. Foods that help are the cruciferous
  family (for more, see page 119) and other anti-inflammatory
  foods, such as oily fish and turmeric. Green tea is also good.
  You can buy decaffeinated green tea or dip the teabag for
  just 30 seconds to minimise the caffeine.

- **Eat gut-friendly foods.** Another reason why your serotonin
  might be low is poor gut health. Although 80 per cent of
  serotonin is synthesised in the brain, the remaining 20 per
  cent is made in the gut. The new field of psychobiotics
  looks at how gut bacteria affect mood. For example, studies
  have shown that probiotic bacteria can alter tryptophan and
  serotonin levels in the brain. Eat fermented foods such as
  sauerkraut (see recipe on page 222), kimchi and miso. For
  more gut-friendly foods, see chapter 5.

- **Make sure you get enough vitamin D.** The synthesis of serotonin from tryptophan needs to be activated by vitamin D. The best way to get enough is 20 minutes of sunlight on your limbs (avoid 12pm to 3pm in summer), but it's also in oily fish and liver (see page 257 for advice on supplementing vitamin D).

- **Try these other helpful foods.** There are some other key nutrients needed in the chemical reactions that help change tryptophan into serotonin:

    Magnesium: found in green leafy vegetables, beans and
        pulses, nuts, cacao.
    Zinc: found in liver, meat, seafood, pumpkin seeds, eggs.
    Vitamin B6: found in turkey, chicken, salmon, beef,
        sunflower seeds, spinach.
    Quercetin: found in capers, red onions, onions, shallots,
        spring onions, kale, peppers, asparagus, parsley, sage and
        berries. Also, tea and olive oil.

Serotonin, sleep and melatonin

Getting enough sleep is not only essential for health, reducing your risk of diabetes, heart attack and stroke, it's also a great weight-loss habit. I advise everyone to aim for 7.5–9 hours a night. Some women tell me they don't prioritise sleep because they prefer to do other things. If that's you, go to bed earlier! Your body repairs itself while you sleep, releasing hormones that stimulate muscle and protein synthesis, as well as a fat breakdown process called lipolysis. You're practically burning fat in your sleep.

Lack of sleep also makes you more likely to put on weight by increasing inflammation and negatively affecting your blood sugar control. And it ruins your concentration, coordination, creativity and cognitive function, sapping your patience and making you prone to mood swings. You are likely to be more impulsive on less sleep and more likely to snack, as it affects leptin, your satiety hormone (for more on this, see chapter 6).

However, if you have a serotonin issue, you're likely to have disrupted sleep patterns because serotonin is a key hormone in our day-to-night cycle. To make serotonin, you need exposure to daylight, preferably morning light. Ideally, as the sun goes down, we are supposed to have less light exposure, which prompts melatonin (the sleep hormone) to slowly rise, peaking around bedtime. Of course, most of us don't have lifestyles that fit with this: we switch on the lights and sit staring at light-emitting screens in the evening. However, our bodies evolved to be active in the daylight and sleep when it gets dark. The closer you can stick to this natural schedule, the better you'll feel and the better you'll sleep.

If you don't have enough serotonin, you won't have enough melatonin. A lack of melatonin can reduce sleep quality, cause sleeplessness and even insomnia (there's another key hormone in the sleep-wake cycle, cortisol; more on this in chapter 7).

These are some steps you can take to ensure you get a good night's sleep:

- **Make a sleep schedule:** Your body loves to sleep and wake at the same times each day.

- **Exposure to daylight first thing:** The best kind of light to trigger serotonin is daylight. So taking a walk first thing is ideal, as this helps to establish a regular sleep-wake cycle – and exercise is important too. If you can't fit this into your day then walk at lunchtime or eat your lunch outside.

- **Try a morning light box:** If you suffer from low mood in winter, when there's less daylight and we go outside less, it may be because your serotonin isn't being triggered. A light box is a good way to get enough light in these darker months.

- **Turn off the light:** After dark, turn the lights down to allow sleepy melatonin to rise. Keep the rooms you're using only as light as you need in order to see. That means reducing screen use, too. Turn screens off at least an hour before bed.

- **Time your eating and sleeping:** Ideally go to sleep before 11pm. Most people sleep best if they don't have any caffeine in the 6-10 hours before bed and stop eating three hours before bed. This allows you finish most of your digesting before you go to sleep. However, if your sleep is still bad after you've increased carbs at dinner, eat a small portion of carbs before bed.

- **Sleep hygiene:** You likely already know all the usual sleep hygiene advice: cosy bed; cool, dark, quiet room. Some people use apps that help them meditate, do hypnotherapy, listen to sleep stories or practise yoga nidra.

PERIMENOPAUSE SUPER LOWS

There's a close link between oestrogen and serotonin. In fact, one of oestrogen's functions is to make serotonin receptors in the brain more sensitive. That's one reason why, when oestrogen levels drop in perimenopause and menopause, you might experience symptoms of low serotonin. You can feel low, less resilient to stress and overwhelmed as well as anxious, irritable, panicky and less able to concentrate. Because these symptoms look like depression, GPs often prescribe antidepressants when HRT might be more beneficial.

IF YOU ONLY DO ONE THING: EAT 110G TO 150G OF CHICKEN OR TURKEY PER DAY

You need tryptophan to make serotonin and melatonin to help with both mood and sleep. Combine it with a small amount of carbs, such as pulses or starchy vegetables, to help the tryptophan get to the brain. It can be trial and error to find the amount you need: it might be anything from a tablespoon to a cupful of butternut squash, parsnip, sweet potato or potato to a cupful.

HOW YOUR GENES AFFECT SEROTONIN

A genetic test can reveal your future risk of health pitfalls and, along with your signs and symptoms, help you to pinpoint the root of your current issues. However, DNA is not destiny; we can turn our genes on and off with how we live and eat.

From the genes we know affect serotonin, there are two that are relevant here, TPH1 and TPH2, because food can have a significant impact on them. When you have an SNP (variation) on TPH1 and/or TPH2, you are not good at converting tryptophan to serotonin. If this is you, up your intake of tryptophan – good sources are chicken and turkey.

Sharon, 54, used food and alcohol to change her mood

'Eight years ago, I was self-medicating with alcohol. I was going through a complicated divorce and I'd lost my best friend, who was like a brother to me. I'd been on and off antidepressants most of my life but I didn't want to take them again as I found they made all my emotions flatline, including the good ones.

Despite meeting a lovely new man, I was in a bad place. I would start thinking about my first drink of the day at 4.30pm. I'd drink a bottle of wine, closely followed by spirits just to block my emotions. In truth, I didn't even like drinking. But it numbed me. I felt suicidal and I couldn't see any way out. I wrote a letter to my son and two daughters to say goodbye. I wrote that I was sorry for being the worst mum, that I was a drunken mess and no good to them.

I thought that my symptoms might be down to perimenopause, as my periods had stopped. But my GP wouldn't give me HRT. Then, five years ago, I read about a private doctor who specialises in menopause. As soon as I could get an appointment, my husband drove me to the clinic. In the consulting room, I could barely hold my head up, I felt so full of shame.

The doctor said I was right in the middle of my menopause and prescribed me HRT. In just three weeks, I felt transformed. I started to hate myself less – but I didn't stop drinking. At this point, I'm not sure how my husband stayed with me.

Then in 2018, my son made a comment about my drinking. At that moment, I knew I wanted to give up. I didn't want to go to AA, so I decided to quit on my own. I began quietly researching, starting with a book, *Glorious Rock Bottom* by Bryony Gordon. I didn't tell anyone I was quitting in case I failed. I started with a few days, then just kept going.

I've always eaten a lot of sugar; I used to have cola cubes for breakfast on the school run. But as soon as I stopped drinking, I got extreme cravings for it. I found myself raiding my daughters' sweets at 4am, anything I could get in my mouth. All my adult life, I'd been a size 6 as I have a tiny frame. By this time, I'd put on nearly 19kg and was up to a size 12/14.

I read up about sugar addiction and discovered that it's more addictive even than cocaine. I realised it was time to stop eating it. It took me three weeks to get it out of my system. I had a dull headache and I lost all my energy. But I still wasn't eating well: I loved crisp sandwiches on white bread and I was addicted to salad cream on everything.

I began to learn about nutrition and hormones, and that's when I came across Pippa on Instagram. She explained that I was still eating some sugar in processed foods like salad cream, albeit hidden under other names. I started Pippa's three-week programme. My Christmas present to myself was a DNA test that showed me the right foods to eat for my brain to function properly.

Now, I love salmon, eggs and avocado for breakfast. I eat fish three to four times a week and make lovely curries in the slow cooker, which we have with lots of vegetables, or chicken with sweet potato fries. I do eat sweet foods, but stick to wholefoods such as dates and 85 per cent dark chocolate and a cake I make with sweet potatoes. I have swapped vegetable oils for olive oil and coconut oil. If I eat foods containing vegetable oil now, my stomach bloats.

Over time, the weight I'd put on came off, a pound a week. Now, I'm back to size 6. But the changes I made were always about feeling better mentally, rather than weight. I'm still learning about food and how to feel better. It's my new addiction along with Wim Hof cold showers, saunas and Pilates. What matters most to me is the lovely relationships I now have with my children and my husband. It must have been so hard, watching me going through the highs and lows of self-sabotaging with alcohol and food. A couple of months ago, I went to my daughter's twenty-first and danced all night without feeling the need to have even one alcoholic drink. I love my new life.'

Sample three-day meal planner for Serotonin Type

BREAKFAST	LUNCH	DINNER
Chocolate tofu bowl with cherries and coconut (page 162)	Courgette and kale pakora with minted yoghurt (page 176)	Cauliflower, kale and red pepper dhal (page 188)
Matcha tea, spinach and kiwi smoothie (page 165)	Cauliflower and rosemary soup (page 172)	Orange and balsamic chicken traybake with roasted onion bhaji (page 203)
Miso-glazed Tenderstem broccoli with spinach and poached egg (page 166)	Personalised salad: build a salad (see pages 231–2) with the key foods for your Metabolic Type (pages 130–2), adding the 'just one thing' (see page 135)	Turkey mince wraps with Brussels sprouts slaw and avocado dressing (page 215)

- Stick exactly to the above meal plan, repeating every three days OR

- Create your own meals using The Portion Size Guide (pages 151–8) OR

- Make meals from the recipes in chapter 14 – the ones that suit you will be marked with the initial of your type.

- Do a combination of the above.

Part 3

The Plan in Practice

Now you know what suits your type, this section is all about what and how to eat.

Chapter 13 explains portion size, the proportions of the macro-nutrients – protein, fat and carbohydrates – you'll be eating on the plan. There is portion control because even though you'll be eating nutrient-packed fresh food, it's still possible to eat too much of it (don't worry, it will be satisfying!). You'll be weighing your food while you're doing the 21-day plan but by the end, you will have learnt to judge the right amounts for you by eye.

You've already seen the suggested three-day meal plan for your Metabolic Type, which will have given you an idea of the food that you'll be making. The recipes themselves are in chapter 14. The ones most suited to you are marked with the Metabolic Type initial:

DI   I   C   DE   T   O   S

But all the recipes fit with the 5 Foundations, so feel free to pick any you like the look of. Once you start to cook them, you'll see how easy it is to make delicious food that is good for you!

You can also build your own meals following the guidelines in chapter 15. This allows you to adapt recipes you already use, or to find new ones that fit with the plan.

At the end of 21 days, you may be at the weight you want to maintain or you may still have weight you feel you want to lose, and so chapter 16 is about adapting the plan to suit your life.

First, let's think about what will help you get the most out of the next 21 days. We'll do some trouble shooting in advance, so that you won't get stuck when you hit a tricky moment.

CHAPTER 12

How to Set Yourself Up for Success

This chapter is a moment to pause, to assess how you feel and where you are with the idea of making this – pretty radical – life change. I've seen how everyone needs to take it at their own pace and this is a chance to work out what you need to do first, in order to succeed.

In chapter 4, I wrote about the Prep Week. A lot of clients find easing into the 21 day plan in this way is really useful. It gives them the chance to get to know how it feels to live by the 5 Foundations (and perhaps start to lose a little weight too).

Meet your Food and Mood diary

This will be your most useful tool. Writing down your food and feelings in certain situations as you go will help you to become a detective of the foods that work for you. It will also give you clues as to what might take you off plan, so you'll be aware of potential issues when certain situations arise.

WEEKLY CHECK-IN

Rate yourself out of ten (ten being the most positive) for how you feel about each of these areas each week:

Energy levels
Skin health
Hair condition
Sleep quality
Diet
Appetite
Mood
Anxiety/stress levels
Bloating
Weight-loss progress

WHAT TO WRITE IN YOUR DIARY EVERY DAY

Each time you eat, write down:

1. Time and place.

2. What you ate. Ingredients and portion sizes.

3. How you felt before you ate. This will tell you how hungry you were.

4. How you felt afterwards. This will help you work out which foods do and don't suit you. Did any of your signs and symptoms come back? Did that breakfast or lunch fill you up? For how long? Did you sleep well after that dinner? If not, experiment with different foods.

5. What could you have done differently? This will help you the next time you're in a similar situation. See chapter 15 for more on adapting your food as you go along.

Clearing out your cupboards

Are you someone who can ignore food in the house that's not included in the plan? Or do you need to clear your cupboards and fridge of those foods? Most of us are the latter. It's not a personality flaw, it's just being human. We're wired by our survival biology to eat fatty and sugary foods.

Once you've completed your 21 days, you will become less likely to want to go back to your old way of eating. But it may take a week or two to adapt and until then, you don't want to have to rely on willpower.

Having a clear out is a good way to set yourself up for success and a chance to do a food label check, to work out which foods contain ingredients that aren't good for you. Empty each cupboard and the fridge in turn. Take everything out and look at the label. Are there any of these ingredients on there?

- Sugars. If it ends in an -ol, it's a disguised sugar

- Artificial sweeteners and colours

- Palm oil, hydrogenated fats, sunflower oil

- Flavourings, preservatives, emulsifiers

If you are confused about ingredients, a simple guide is to stick to choosing foods that are as close to their natural state as possible, and don't eat ingredients you don't recognise.

To avoid throwing food away, can you give it to a food bank? And if you can't clear out the foods you want to avoid because your family or housemates eat them, can you put them together in a drawer or cupboard where you don't see them as you walk into the kitchen?

Where's your head at?

Before we get into the food and recipes and how to put a meal together, it's worth checking in with yourself to ensure you are mentally prepared to start the plan. These are some common patterns I see in clinic.

AM I A STARTING-TOMORROW PERSON?

You're not the only one! My advice, if this is you, is to find a start date that will work for you, where you have three weeks without too many social occasions, family commitments or unusual work stresses. It doesn't have to be now, it can be in a few months. Put it in your diary so it's there in writing and you can build up to it.

But right now, why not start with the 5 Foundations? And cooking some of the recipes? What about trying out the 'If you only do one thing' from each chapter and writing down how that makes you feel? Some of my clients start by doing just one new thing a week. If it feels too much to make all the changes at once, if slow and steady works better for you, that is how you will win the race.

DO I FIND IT HARD TO KEEP GOING?

Have you tried to change what you eat before but found it hard to keep going? If this is you, be kind and don't judge yourself. You are like almost every client I see, which is why this plan has sustainability for the long term at its heart.

Ask yourself: what might hold me back from keeping going? Be honest with yourself and write down any reasons that come up. Now, think about how you can address these reasons in a way that will support you. For example, you might think: 'I'm too busy in the mornings to even think about breakfast'. The solution for a lot of women, is to make a protein smoothie. Or you might think, 'my family won't like the food'. Can you look through the portion size ideas and see if the meals you already make can be tweaked to suit the plan? If the block is because you do best with more accountability, think about joining my online Female Food Club; a lot of women find the group support and hearing how other women do on the PCM really empowering (see pages 254–5 for more).

That said, if you don't want to do or keep doing the 21-day plan, but simply want to use this book to tweak how and what you eat and/or find new recipes, that is fine too!

WHEN AND WHERE ARE MY WEAK SPOTS?

Everyone has moments when they find themselves eating unwanted foods or drinking alcohol before they've consciously realised they're doing it. Those challenges will come. On day five, you might be at a friend's house and she opens a bottle of wine. On day seven, you might walk past the shop that sells your favourites sweets or on day 15, there's cake at work for someone's birthday. Those times when you are likely to give in are important to think about in advance, so you can either plan not to go into the situation, or to go into it consciously, knowing what you will do instead of eating. That said, if you do eat something off plan, don't worry. Just make a note of it, so you can be prepared next time. And the good news is, after the 21 days you'll be able to plan in the things you're really missing.

Some people tell me a common trigger is when they fill up with petrol, go to pay . . . and find themselves with a bar of chocolate in their mouths before they've even left the forecourt. Your moment might be leaving the gym after exercise or walking home after work when you are hungry and you feel you need something. What can you do to pre-empt these situations so you're ready with a plan of action when they inevitably occur?

It is hard to avoid drinking because it's so bound up with having fun. You will have to be very clear with yourself that for these 21 days, you have decided not to drink. Some clients say it's helpful to be the designated driver – not only to stop them drinking but so they can leave when they want to. And think about what you're going to drink before someone gives you a glass of wine – for example, fizzy water or soda water with a squeeze of lime and lots of ice. There's a doubly good reason to turn down alcohol: clients most often report that they eat off plan after a drink.

Eating is inextricably linked with mood for so many people, too. When you're down, you want those salt and vinegar crisps to cheer yourself up. For these 21 days, can you think about the bigger picture? You are in charge of what goes in your mouth. Break your usual pattern and do something to distract yourself at the point you would usually reach for the crisps: go for a walk, watch a funny video, make a call.

Maybe when you're told you *can't* eat something, you want to eat it more? Can you turn this into a positive and think about what you can eat more of? Real food, fresh vegetables, lovely sauces. Look at the recipes in chapter 14: which ones include your favourite foods?

Balancing your body systems will, over time, reduce the cravings as well as the hormone and mood swings that most often lead to eating sugary and processed foods. But in the meantime, you'll also have to consciously be aware of and intercept some unwanted eating habits before they happen, too.

What can I do when life doesn't go to plan?

The most common reason to stop following an eating plan is to deviate from it, then never get back on it. For example, the story people tell me most often is that they caved into having a glass of wine when out for dinner, then said yes to pudding. The next morning, they thought, 'Oh, I've blown it anyway,' and went back to their old way of eating.

The PCM is more realistic, so it can carry you through these kinds of difficult days or weeks. When life is stressful or busy, you simply decide to step off the plan for a short time. You accept this is a time when you might not lose weight. The result is, you won't feel as if you're blowing it, so you won't become disheartened. And you'll know the plan is right there to pick up as soon as you have the capacity.

The key is, it can still be a time that you don't gain weight. If you can't do the plan, can you keep to the 5 Foundations as a minimum, even if you may not be able to do them perfectly or all the time?

Ideally, you'll do this consciously. But if you fall off the plan by accident (that glass of wine! That pudding!), you won't be the first person (or, indeed the last). Don't think of it as a failure, just a small blip. As soon as you realise, come back to the 5 Foundations. Which of these can you manage?

- **Two litres of water a day.** Take two big glasses of water to bed and drink them first thing, before you swing your legs out of bed.

- **No snacking.** If you have no choice because you've missed a meal, snack on protein; take an emergency pack of nuts in your bag.

- **Two bites of protein to start each meal.** If this isn't possible, take a bottle with a scoop of protein powder so you can add water and drink it before you eat.

- **Varied vegetables.** Any time you can, add in more vegetables, even if it's just a bag of carrot sticks or a bag of rocket.

- **Chew your food up to 30 times.** You can do this even if you're eating on the go or in the office.

If you can keep (mainly!) to the 5 Foundations, you'll find that when you're ready to get back on track properly, you'll be in the best possible place to try again. Don't feel bad, get busy! Plan your next week's meals, aiming to make them as delicious as possible.

What do I do if someone's trying to pressure me into eating or drinking something that's not on the plan?

It is not rude to say no to pudding. Clients often tell me they feel real peer pressure to join in with their friends and colleagues. Particular sticking points are often cakes on a Friday in the office, drinks after work and dinner at other people's houses.

If they are good friends, perhaps you can be honest? One client told a friend how she felt. She said, 'If you want to be a good friend, please stop asking me to eat foods I don't want to eat.' You could even ask to bring your own food.

If that doesn't feel comfortable, Mumsnet has a great saying: 'No is a complete sentence.' You don't have to explain yourself. Or you can say just a little: 'No thank you, I'm on a meal plan for my health.' Or 'No, thank you, I'm on a meal plan for my thyroid/hormones/blood sugar control.' Or 'No thank you, I don't feel like it right now.'

Please don't feel bad. It's better to say no thank you than to accept food you don't want that isn't going to make you feel good. Alternatively, for the 21 days, take some of the pressure off yourself having to say no by suggesting social get-togethers that don't focus on food or alcohol. That might be walks, runs, fitness classes or swims, exhibitions, gardens or museums, talks, trips to the theatre or the cinema, book clubs or crafting or whatever you love doing.

In the following chapter, you'll learn about finding the right amount of food to feed your body, because quantity is as important as quality.

CHAPTER 13

The Portion Size Guide

The ideal lunch or dinner is made up from specific proportions of macronutrients – protein, fat and carbohydrates. In this section, you'll see exactly what your plate is going to look like.

Clients are often surprised at the portion sizes I suggest. Sometimes they say they're eating more than they have for years. They're not used to eating the quantity of vegetables, in particular. Or they're used to eating little and often, having smaller meals and then snacking throughout the day – especially into the evening. But as you now know, the body prefers a bigger, filling meal, then a gap to digest, which allows it to go into fat-burning mode.

Other clients tell me the portion sizes feel small compared to what they are used to. If you were eating carb-based meals, you may have had to eat a lot of volume in order to feel satisfied. But when you eat high-quality, nutrient-dense food, you'll find you don't need that amount of bulk. Your new way of eating – with a good portion of protein and lots of fibre – will leave you feeling full.

Getting portions right

To begin with, until you get used to what your new plate looks like, weigh your ingredients. This is important: the weights are worked out from what helps people to lose weight, consistently. After doing this for a few weeks, you'll be able to judge it by eye. You won't have to weigh your food for very long, I promise!

1. PROTEIN

As you know, eating enough protein is the key to feeling full. It helps to regulate your blood sugar, which will reduce cravings. It also helps to keep your hunger hormones on your side. Eating enough protein means you can make muscle, and the more muscle you have, the more energy you burn.

Protein portion size: 110g–150g protein, measured raw, per lunch and dinner.

If you are smaller, you'll tend towards the lower end and if you are bigger, towards the upper end. Some people simply feel better with a protein portion that's on the larger side. This may be you if you don't feel satisfied after eating. Try it out for a few days. Do you feel better when you eat more protein? Does your weight loss improve? If so, then stick to the bigger portions.

One protein portion will look (roughly) like this:

- 1 chicken breast, leg or two thighs
- 1 fish fillet
- 150g (usually half a pack) of tofu
- 110g–150g beef, pork, lamb, turkey or venison
- 2–3 eggs
- 120g–150g cooked chickpeas, lentils or beans (a 400g tin contains 240g drained)

WHAT PROTEIN CAN I EAT?

All fish, such as salmon, mackerel (including tinned in spring water or brine), sea bass, sole, bream, brill, sardines (including tinned), turbot, plaice, cod, haddock, halibut, mullet

All seafood, such as prawns, scallops, crab, squid

All poultry, such as chicken, turkey, duck

Leaner cuts of meat, such as pork fillet, lamb fillet and steak, beef fillet and sirloin, lean roast beef, venison

All pulses, such as chickpeas, butter beans, haricot beans, cannellini beans, black beans, red lentils

Soy, such as tofu, tempeh, edamame

All nuts and seeds (NB: these are lower protein), such as pumpkin seeds, sunflower seeds, almonds, chia seeds

Protein powder. Whey protein isolate or pea protein (vegan).

WHAT IF I'M VEGAN OR VEGETARIAN?

There's no doubt it's easier to get the amount of protein you need on the plan if you eat meat, fish or eggs. Animal proteins are high quality or 'complete' proteins, which means they contain more of the essential amino acids, the building blocks of the body. However, lots of people find it's possible to do the plan as a vegan or vegetarian. The best quality vegan proteins are the non-GMO soy products and pea protein powders.

2. FIBRE

In the gut, fibre from vegetables regulates hunger hormones and helps you feel full. It also helps feed and multiply good bacteria as well as clear out used hormones. Plus, vegetables are packed with essential vitamins, minerals and phytonutrients, which help all our body systems work well.

Vegetable portion size: 110g–150g raw weight vegetables per lunch and dinner, ideally made up of at least two different types of vegetables per meal

3. CARBOHYDRATES

This is a lower carbohydrate diet. But it's not a zero-carb diet as, technically, vegetables are carbs. Too severe carb restriction puts you into ketosis, which affects thyroid metabolism and can impact stress hormones.

However, you will be limiting carbohydrate. One reason is to stop blood sugar spikes, which prompt the release of the fat-storage hormone insulin, and lead to the hunger hormones button being permanently switched on. High levels of insulin are also inflammatory.

Six of the seven Metabolic Types (all except the Insulin Type) will include a portion of carbohydrates with dinner, mainly starchy vegetables but also fruits and some grains.

Carbohydrate portion sizes: Up to 100g sweet potato or new potatoes, butternut squash or parsnips or pumpkin (raw weight).

OR 30–50g wild or basmati rice or quinoa, or rice or buckwheat noodles (uncooked weight). This is usually 2–4 tablespoons.

4. HEALTHY FATS

Fat has recently come back into food fashion. For years, people talked about it as the worst thing you could eat. That's why the supermarket shelves are filled with pots and packets labelled as 'low fat', from yoghurts to crisps to oat bars.

We now know better: that we need to eat fat for so many processes.

It provides the building blocks of cell walls, it helps us make hormones and we need it in order to absorb vitamins A, D, E and K.

We also know that some fats are better quality than others. These are the fats on the plan – extra virgin olive oil and coconut oil – as well as fats in your food from fish, nuts, seeds and avocado.

Fat portion size: You'll be including one tablespoon of added fat to your lunch and dinner, either for cooking or as a dressing or sauce. You'll also get some fats from food.

HAPPY FATS

Our cell walls are made of fat, which is a good reason to eat high-quality fat. The brain is also made up of 60 per cent fat and needs good fats to support mood, cognition, learning and memory. Good fats also nourish our bodies and eating them can help with weight loss through lowering blood sugar and insulin levels, and encouraging the burning of fat, rather than storing it.

You can have too much of a good thing, though. Fat contains a lot of energy, so on this plan you will be limiting intake. These are the types of fats you will be eating on the plan:

FOR DRESSINGS AND BAKING

Extra virgin olive oil. Research suggests that minimally processed extra virgin olive oil provides the greatest health benefits by increasing HDL (healthy cholesterol) and decreasing oxidative damage. You'll get the same benefits from whole olives, too.

(continued overleaf)

FOR SAUTÉING

It used to be thought that extra virgin olive oil shouldn't be used at high temperatures but more recent research has shown it's a good choice. Coconut oil is rich in medium-chain fatty acids (MCFAs), which help restore gut health. It also has antioxidant and antimicrobial properties that help support the immune system, as well as antifungal, antibacterial and antiviral benefits. Ghee has a very high smoking point, which makes it excellent for high temperature cooking.

FOR EATING

Omega-3 oils are anti-inflammatory and help make healthy cell membranes. They're found in cold-water fish such as salmon and sardines, as well as in flax and hemp seeds, walnuts, Brazil nuts and sea vegetables. Nuts and seeds also contain omega-6 oils.

BUILDING A DELICIOUS BREAKFAST

Breakfasts follow similar rules to lunches and dinners but are a little smaller. There are recipes to try in chapter 14 but if you want to build your own, follow one of these guidelines:

- 1–2 eggs – omelette, boiled, poached, fried – with 50–70g vegetables.

- 50–70g tofu, smoked salmon or other protein with 50–70g vegetables.

- A smoothie: one portion of protein powder, a small handful of leafy greens, 2 tablespoons of berries or a small pear, 1 tablespoon of chopped nuts or seeds with your non-dairy milk of choice

Troubleshooting

Everyone's body is different and not everything always goes to plan. It may take a while to get used to the PCM, to find your favourite recipes from the ones included here or to work out how to adapt your own recipes (which is another reason a Prep Week can be helpful!). If you feel like something's not quite working, read down for some solutions to common problems...

I'M STILL HUNGRY!

It's perfectly normal to feel a little hungry when you start the plan. Your body needs a few days to adapt. You might feel hungry because you're used to filling up with a lot of carbs. But after a few days of eating plenty of protein and fibre to keep your blood sugar even, you'll find you're able to get through to the next meal without feeling hungry. However, if you can't, check these things:

Are you weighing your food? If you've stopped, start again. You may not be giving yourself your full required portion.

Are you very active? If you are losing weight, you can try upping your protein portion by 10–20g, towards the higher end of the scale.

Are you doing cardio for too long? This will increase your appetite. Switch away from endurance and hard cardio to strength training, Pilates, yoga and gentler exercise such as walking and swimming.

Are you drinking enough water? It's easy to mistake thirst for hunger.

Are you sleeping 7.5–9 hours? Not getting enough sleep can affect the levels of your fullness hormones and make you crave more carbohydrates.

Are you prioritising your bedtime routine? A good bedtime wind-down is more likely to lead to a good night's sleep. Have a relaxing evening of no-screens reading, bath and/or calm chatting. When you do this, do you feel less hungry the next day?

Are you stressed? Having high levels of the stress hormone cortisol can lead to appetite changes. What can you do to decrease your stress, whether it is walking, mindfulness, yoga, meditation, having a bath or just resting? Add this into your day.

I'M NOT LOSING WEIGHT!

For one person, weight loss might start to happen quickly, for another it might be slower, two weeks or more. Here are some things to check if you feel weight loss is slow to kick in:

Are you weighing your food? If you've stopped, start again. The weights you are guessing may be higher than you need.

Do you need to reduce your portion size? If you are eating at the higher end (150g) of protein, try coming down by 20–30g per meal. This is often enough to kickstart weight loss. This may not be news to you, but some clients find that as they get older, and especially during perimenopause, they simply need less food.

Are you getting a lot of detox symptoms, such as nausea, headaches or tiredness? Your body may need a few days to adjust to this new way of eating before you start to lose weight.

CHAPTER 14

The Recipes

BREAKFASTS

In all the following recipes, all oven temperatures refer to fan temperatures.

Matcha Tea, Spinach and Kiwi Smoothie

The L-theanine in matcha is thought to reduce levels of cortisol and to help induce a state of calm.

Serves 1
(Di, I, C, De, T, O, S)

10g baby spinach
1 kiwi, peeled and chopped
1 teaspoon matcha tea powder

100ml non-dairy milk
1 serving of pea or whey protein
   powder

Put all the ingredients in blender and blitz into a smoothie.

Baked Portobello Mushroom and Poached Egg

Eggs are a good source of choline, which is essential for making flexible cell membranes. And these are necessary for the thyroid hormone T3 to get into cells to do its job.

Serves 1
(Di, I, C, De, T, O, S)

1 portobello mushroom
1.5 tsp coconut oil or ghee, melted
4–5 cherry tomatoes
1 tsp balsamic vinegar
1 small shallot, finely sliced

1 small garlic clove, minced
55g fresh spinach
1 large egg
1 tsp fresh parsley, chopped
Salt and pepper
Pinch of chilli flakes (optional)

Preheat the oven to 200°C. Wipe off any soil from the mushroom with a dry paper towel but don't wash it as it will take on water. Remove the stem, then place the mushroom rounded side up onto one side of a baking tray. Brush with ½ a teaspoon of coconut oil and bake for 8 minutes. Flip the mushroom over, then place the cherry tomatoes on the other side of the baking tray and drizzle over the balsamic vinegar. Add a pinch of salt and pepper and cook for 5 more minutes. Meanwhile, heat the remaining coconut oil in a non-stick frying pan, then add the shallot and garlic. Sauté, stirring often, for 2–3 minutes or until softened. Add the spinach and 1 tablespoon of water and continue to cook until the spinach has wilted and the water has evaporated. Season to taste.

Bring a small pan of water to the boil and poach the egg. Spoon the spinach onto the mushroom, then top with the poached egg. Serve alongside the roasted tomatoes. Top with the chopped parsley, salt and pepper and a pinch of chilli flakes, if you like.

Chia Yoghurt Breakfast Bowl

Ginger and lemon zest both contain great antioxidants to support detoxification. Chia seeds are high in fibre which can help prevent constipation – so those toxins don't hang around! Brazil nuts are a source of selenium, needed to convert T4 to T3 thyroid hormones.

Serves 1
(Di, De, T, O, S)

100g coconut, almond or
   organic soya yoghurt
15g chia seeds
1cm piece of fresh ginger,
   peeled and finely grated

Zest of ½ unwaxed lemon
2 tbsp blueberries and
   raspberries
3 Brazil nuts, chopped

Mix the yoghurt, chia seeds, ginger, orange juice and unwaxed lemon zest in a small bowl. Cover and refrigerate overnight. When ready to serve, top the chia yoghurt mix with the blueberries, raspberries, chopped Brazil nuts and orange zest.

Chocolate Tofu Bowl with Cherries and Coconut

Cacao may increase levels of serotonin, the feel-good hormone, due to the serotonin and L-tryptophan it contains. Cherries contain melatonin, the sleep hormone.

Serves 1
(Di, I, C, De, O, S)

50g organic silken tofu
2 tsp raw cacao powder
1 tsp flaked almonds

1 tbsp coconut flakes, toasted
30g cherries, fresh or frozen,
   de-stoned

Blitz the silken tofu and cacao together in a blender or mini food processor until smooth, then transfer to a serving bowl. Add the flaked almonds, coconut flakes and cherries on top.

Detox Smoothie

Beetroot contains betalains, a type of antioxidant that's good for detoxification.

Serves 1
(Di, I, C, De, T, O, S)

1 small pear (75g), cored and roughly chopped

1 small cooked beetroot (30g), peeled and roughly chopped

1cm piece of fresh ginger, peeled and roughly chopped

3cm piece of cucumber, roughly chopped

Juice of ½ lime

1 serving pea or whey protein powder

6 ice cubes

Put everything in a high-powered blender and blend until smooth. Add cold water to reach your desired consistency.

Griddled Asparagus with Lemon and Poached Egg

Research has shown that eating asparagus may help prevent insulin spikes and protect against diabetes.

Serves 1
(Di, I, C, De, T, O, S)

65g asparagus
1 tsp extra virgin olive oil
1 large egg

zest and juice of 1 unwaxed lemon
Salt and pepper

Brush the asparagus with olive oil and cook on a hot griddle for 3 minutes. Turn over and cook for a further 3 minutes or until tender.

Meanwhile, poach the egg. Transfer the asparagus to a serving plate and squeeze over the lemon juice and zest. Top with the poached egg and plenty of salt and pepper.

Almond and Flaxseed Porridge with Smashed Berries

Flaxseeds are a great source of lignans, which are phytoestrogens. And because they're full of soluble fibre, they can also help regulate blood sugar and insulin levels.

Serves 1
(Di, I, De, T, O, S)

2 tbsp whole almonds
1.5 tbsp flaxseeds
250ml dairy-free milk

½ tsp ground cinnamon
20g blueberries, smashed
20g raspberries, smashed

Grind the almonds and flaxseeds in a spice grinder or blender, or use pre-ground flaxseeds and almonds. Place in a small pan with the milk and warm through on a medium to low heat, stirring regularly, for 5 minutes until thickened. Add the cinnamon and warm through for another minute. Finally, add the smashed berries and extra milk if desired.

Miso-glazed Tenderstem Broccoli with Spinach and Poached Egg

Fermented foods such as miso are a good source of both prebiotics and probiotics, making them brilliant for your gut.

Serves 1
(Di, I, C, De, T, O, S)

50g Tenderstem broccoli
1.5 tsp white miso paste
15g spinach

1.5 tsp almond butter
1 egg
Sea salt and black pepper

Blanch the Tenderstem broccoli in salted boiling water for 3 minutes, then drain, reserving 100ml of the water.

Heat a frying pan over a medium heat and add the miso and half of the reserved cooking water and stir well. Add the broccoli to the pan and toss to coat in the glaze, then transfer to a bowl and mix in the spinach. Turn the heat to low, then add the almond butter to the frying pan and mix with the miso glaze. Add a splash more water as needed to create a smooth glaze.

Poach the egg and place on top of the vegetables on a plate. Drizzle over the glaze and add a sprinkle of salt and pepper.

Smoked Salmon with Pear and Watercress

Salmon is a good source of amino acids and omega-3 oils, to balance blood sugar and reduce inflammation. This recipe can work well as either a breakfast or a lunch.

Serves 1
(Di, I, C, T, O, S)

60g watercress
100g smoked salmon
1 small pear, thinly sliced
2 tbsp walnuts, chopped
Juice of ½ lemon

1 tsp dill, finely chopped
  (optional)
Flaked sea salt and fresh
  cracked pepper

Arrange the watercress on a plate and top with the smoked salmon and sliced pear. Scatter the chopped walnuts and squeeze the lemon juice over the top. Season with salt, cracked black pepper and a sprinkle of dill, if desired.

Breakfast Smoothie Bowl

Oregano has antimicrobial and antifungal properties. Warding off the bad bugs will help your good gut bacteria thrive.

Serves 1
(Di, C, De, T, O, S)

1 small pear, peeled and cored
20g rocket
1 sprig of fresh oregano, leaves
   only

60g kefir or yoghurt (dairy free)
1 serving of pea or whey protein
   powder
20g blueberries

Simply blitz all the ingredients except the blueberries together in a blender or processor, then scatter with blueberries.

Spicy Beans on Cumin Aubergine

Kale is cruciferous, from the family of vegetables that support the liver's detox function.

Serves 4
(De, T, O, S)

For the spicy beans:
1 tsp coconut oil or ghee
50g white onion, peeled and
    finely chopped
½ tsp ground cumin
½ tsp ground coriander
½ tsp chilli flakes
½ tsp flaked sea salt
100g sun-dried tomatoes,
    roughly chopped
400g tin cannellini beans,
    drained and rinsed

For the cumin aubergine:
1 medium aubergine
½ tsp ground cumin
1 garlic clove, minced
1 tsp coconut oil or ghee

To serve:
120g kale, chopped
Juice of 1 lemon
Salt and pepper

Put the coconut oil or ghee into a frying pan over a medium heat. Once melted, add the onion and cook for 3 minutes. Add the cumin, coriander, chilli flakes and salt and cook for a further 3 minutes, allowing the spices to release their flavour. Turn the heat to low and add the sun-dried tomatoes. Cook for 10 minutes, stirring occasionally, until the onions are soft. Add the beans, stir to coat in the spices and cook gently for a further 10 minutes.

While the beans are cooking, prepare the aubergine. Cut into 1cm slices, then use a sharp knife to score the flesh diagonally one way then the other. Rub the cumin and garlic into the flesh on both sides.

Heat the coconut oil or ghee over a medium heat in a frying pan. Once hot, fry the aubergine for 4 minutes on each side or until golden and soft then remove from the pan and keep warm.

Tip the kale into the frying pan, add the lemon juice and season with salt and pepper. Cook, stirring frequently until wilted.

To serve, plate a slice of aubergine and top with a quarter of the bean mix and kale.

Stewed Apples with Yoghurt and Almonds

This is a marriage made in heaven for the gut, with the prebiotic fibre in the apple and the probiotics in the yoghurt.

Serves 3
(Di, De, O, S)

3 apples, peeled, cored and diced
2 tsp ground cinnamon

150g coconut, almond or organic soya yoghurt
1 tbsp toasted flaked almonds

Put the apples into a heavy-based saucepan along with the cinnamon and 60ml of water. Cover with a lid and cook over a low heat, stirring occasionally, for 10 minutes or until the apples have broken down but still have some texture. Spoon 50g yoghurt into a bowl and top with a third of the stewed apple and a sprinkle of toasted almonds.

LUNCHES

Beetroot and Kale Salad with Gremolata

This salad contains some super detox-boosting vegetables, such as rocket, parsley, kale and beetroot, plus anti-inflammatory omega-3 fats from the walnuts. You can substitute these vegetables for any on your list. Try watercress instead of rocket, spinach instead of kale and Jerusalem artichokes instead of beetroot. Serve with one portion of your chosen protein (see pages 152–3).

Serves 2
(Di, C, De, O, S)

For the gremolata:
100g flat-leaf parsley, leaves
   and tender stalks only
30g rocket
2 garlic cloves, roughly chopped
Juice of ½ lemon

2 tsp extra virgin olive oil
1 tsp salt
30g kale
100g cooked beetroot, cut
   into wedges
30g walnuts

To make the gremolata, put the parsley, rocket, garlic, lemon juice, oil and salt into a blender and blitz until it reaches a pesto-like consistency. Add a little cold water if necessary.

Shred the kale with your fingers and add a heaped tablespoon of gremolata, massaging it in to soften and wilt the leaves. Top with the beetroot, walnuts and your chosen protein.

Cauliflower and Rosemary Soup

Cruciferous vegetables such as cauliflower are great for supporting oestrogen detoxification. Rosemary has great anti-inflammatory properties too. Serve with one portion of your chosen protein (see pages 152–3).

Serves 4
(Di, I, C, De, T, O, S)

2 tbsp extra virgin olive oil
3 shallots, peeled and sliced
4 garlic cloves, sliced
½ leek, white part, sliced
1 stick of celery, sliced
Salt and pepper
1 cauliflower, cut into small
   florets

2 sprigs of rosemary
600ml vegetable stock
100g pine nuts and/or pumpkin
   seeds, toasted, for garnish
2 spring onions, thinly sliced
   for garnish

Heat the olive oil in a large saucepan over a medium heat. Add the shallots, garlic, leek and celery, season well, then cook gently for 5 minutes, stirring frequently. Add the cauliflower and rosemary, stir together and cook for a further 15 minutes. Add the vegetable stock and simmer over a low heat for 20 minutes or until the cauliflower is soft. Remove one of the rosemary sprigs and blitz or hand blend to get a smooth consistency – add a little boiling water to thin down as desired. Taste for seasoning and adjust if needed. Serve 200ml of soup per portion and top with 25g of toasted pine nuts and/or pumpkin seeds and some spring onion.

Chicken and Shiitake Broth

There are variations of chicken broths around the world, often fed to people when they're not well. That's because it nourishes and heals the gut lining and reduces inflammation. It's also easy to digest, so you get the benefits of its protein and minerals. My version contains added gut superfoods such as shallots, leeks and carrots.

Serves 1
(Di, C, De, T, O, S)

400ml chicken stock

10g dried shiitake mushrooms

1 chicken leg

20g shallot, diced

20g leek, sliced

20g kale, sliced

20g carrot, sliced

20g cauliflower, cut into
 small florets

Pour the chicken stock into a deep saucepan with the dried shitake and chicken leg. Top up with water as needed to cover the chicken. Cover the pan with a lid and cook over a low heat for 30 minutes or until the chicken is tender and can be pulled apart. Strain through a sieve, keeping the stock. Shred the chicken from the leg and chop the shiitake mushrooms, then put aside until later.

Pour the stock back into a saucepan along with the shallot, leek, kale, carrot and cauliflower florets. Bring to a simmer and cook for 5 minutes or until the vegetables are al dente. Add the shredded chicken and chopped shiitake mushrooms. Simmer for a further 2 minutes, then serve.

Chinese Cabbage Salad with Edamame and Ginger

Radishes are a bitter food, which help digestion and detoxification. Edamame are a phytoestrogen source, which means they help balance out oestrogen levels.

Serves 1
(Di, I, C, De, O, S)

Juice of ¼ lime

1 tbsp tamari

50g Chinese cabbage, shredded

50g edamame

½ tsp grated ginger

½ avocado, peeled and sliced

3 radishes, quartered

Chilli flakes and sesame seeds (optional)

Whisk the lime juice and tamari together, then pour over the cabbage. Massage the dressing into the leaves, then leave for 5 minutes. Add the edamame to the cabbage and toss to coat in dressing. Transfer to a serving plate and top with the avocado and radishes. Sprinkle over chilli flakes and sesame seeds to garnish, if you like.

Coronation Chickpea Salad

This salad is another level, with its creamy curry dressing. This recipe also works very well with leftover roast chicken. Radishes not only give a pop of colour but also stimulate bile flow to help eliminate toxins from the body.

Serves 2
(C, De, T, O, S)

125g coconut, almond or organic soya yoghurt

2–3 tsp curry powder

2–3 dried apricots, finely chopped

2 tbsp coriander, finely chopped

400g tin chickpeas, drained and rinsed

200g watercress or romaine lettuce

3 radishes, thinly sliced

¼ cucumber, thinly sliced

½ red onion, thinly sliced

1 tbsp flaked almonds, toasted

Mix together the yoghurt, curry powder, apricots and coriander. Add the chickpeas and stir through. Arrange the watercress, lettuce or radishes, cucumber and red onion on a serving plate and top with the chickpea mix. Sprinkle over the flaked almonds and serve.

Warm Mediterranean Cauliflower Salad

Cauliflower is a cruciferous vegetable high in antioxidants and supports detoxification in the liver. It is also a great source of fibre, which improves digestion and can improve insulin sensitivity. Capers and red onions are rich in a flavonoid called quercetin which has anti-inflammatory and anti-histamine properties.

Serves 2
Suitable for all types

250g cauliflower, cut into florets

2 tablespoons capers in brine, chopped

2 tablespoons pitted green olives

½ red onion, finely diced

4 tablespoons parsley, chopped

1 lemon, juice

2 tablespoons extra virgin olive oil

½ teaspoon ground cumin

Salt and pepper to taste

2 Portions of cooked protein

Steam the cauliflower briefly so still crunchy. Finely chop by hand or in a food processor. Place in a bowl.

Add the other ingredients and mix well. Serve with choice of protein.

Store in the fridge for up to 3 days.

Leek and Watercress Soup with Balsamic Onions

Watercress, like other leafy greens, contains magnesium, a mineral that helps to reduce cortisol levels and fights inflammation. Serve with protein portion of your choice (see pages 152–3). The onions can be stored for up to 3 days in the fridge, or kept in the freezer for up to 3 months.

Serves 4
(Di, I, C, De, T, O, S)

For the soup:
2 tsp extra virgin olive oil
400g leeks, sliced
2 shallots, sliced
1 stick of celery, sliced
1 garlic clove, thinly sliced
500ml vegetable stock
200g watercress
Salt and pepper

For the balsamic onions
  (batch recipe):
1 tbsp extra virgin olive oil
500g white onion, sliced
200ml balsamic vinegar

Heat the olive oil in a deep saucepan over a medium heat. Add the leeks, shallots, celery and garlic and toss to coat in the oil. Turn the heat to low and cook for 10 minutes, stirring occasionally, until the vegetables are soft. Add the stock and cook for a further 20 minutes. Add the watercress and 200ml hot water. Blend with a hand blender until smooth, adding extra water if needed. Add salt and pepper to taste.

To make the balsamic onions, heat the oil in a heavy-based saucepan and add the onions. Cook over a low heat for 45 minutes, stirring occasionally until the onions are soft and golden. Add the balsamic vinegar and cook for a further 15 minutes or until the onions have absorbed all the liquid. Serve the soup topped with a tablespoon of the balsamic onions.

Raw Vegetable Salad

Chopping or chewing raw cruciferous vegetables results in the release of enzymes that support liver detoxification. Serve with a protein portion of your choice (see pages 152–3).

Serves 1
(Di, I, C, De, O, S)

For the salad:
30g avocado, diced
30g Tenderstem broccoli,
    finely sliced
30g radishes, cut into wedges
30g red cabbage, shredded
30g watercress, spinach or
    rocket leaves (or
    a combination)

1 tsp hazelnuts, chopped
1 tsp pumpkin seeds

For the dressing:
2 tsp extra virgin olive oil
1 tsp apple cider vinegar
½ tsp lemon juice
Salt and pepper

Whisk together the dressing ingredients until emulsified. Toss the salad ingredients with the dressing in a bowl, then serve immediately.

Smoked Mackerel Niçoise

Oily fish, such as mackerel and anchovies, is one of the best sources of omega-3 fatty acids, essential for making healthy cell membranes.

Serves 1
(Di, I, C, T, O, S)

30g green beans, halved

1 medium egg, room
    temperature

1 smoked mackerel fillet

½ romaine lettuce, shredded

8 black olives

3 anchovies

¼ small red onion, peeled
    and chopped

5 basil leaves, torn

Juice of ½ a lemon

Salt and pepper

Bring a small pan of water to the boil and cook the green beans for 3 minutes. They should be tender but still have bite. Use tongs to remove the beans from the water and drop into a bowl of cold water until you're ready to serve.

Carefully lower the egg into the water and boil for 7 minutes. Remove from the heat and transfer the egg into a bowl of iced water. Once cool, peel the egg and cut it into quarters.

Heat a large frying pan and fry the mackerel fillet for 2 minutes on each side to warm through.

Drain the beans. Place the shredded lettuce on a plate, top with the egg and sprinkle over the green beans, olives, anchovies, red onion and basil. Add the mackerel fillet, a squeeze of lemon juice and season with salt and pepper.

Smoked Mackerel, Beetroot and Orange Salad

Oranges are packed full of vitamin C, essential support for immune function.

Serves 4
(Di, C, O, S)

2 tbsp extra virgin olive oil

Juice of 1 lemon

1 tbsp fresh chopped parsley

Zest of 1 orange

180g kale, tough stalks removed
and leaves chopped

4 smoked mackerel fillets

2 oranges, peeled and sliced

4 radishes, thinly sliced

4 cooked beetroot, cut
into wedges

2 tbsp pumpkin seeds, toasted

Whisk together the olive oil, lemon juice, parsley and half of the orange zest. Then pour this over the kale. Massage the dressing into the kale for a few minutes until it starts to wilt. Set aside.

Heat a large frying pan and fry the mackerel fillets for 2 minutes on each side to warm through.

Tip the sliced orange, remaining orange zest, radishes, beetroot and 1 1 tablespoon of pumpkin seeds into the kale and toss together. Divide the salad between four plates and flake over one mackerel fillet per portion. Sprinkle over the remaining pumpkin seeds.

Spicy Green Beans and Broccoli with Charred Spring Onions

The rendang paste is full of antioxidant spices. It makes about four servings and can be frozen for later use.

Serves 1
(Di, I, C, De, T, O, S)

For the rendang paste (batch recipe):

1 medium white onion, peeled and chopped

3 red chillies, deseeded and roughly chopped

1 lemongrass stalk, roughly chopped

3 garlic cloves

2cm piece of fresh ginger, peeled

2 tsp ground coriander

2 tsp ground cumin

1 tsp ground turmeric

2 tsp tamarind paste

For the dish:

2 eggs

65g green beans

65g broccoli, cut into small florets

2 spring onions

20g cashews, toasted and roughly chopped

¼ red chilli, deseeded and thinly sliced

Blend the rendang paste ingredients together. Place the eggs into a pan of boiling water for 6 minutes. Transfer to a bowl of iced water. Meanwhile, cook the green beans and broccoli in a pan of boiling water for 4 minutes or until al dente. Drain, reserving 50ml of the cooking water. Heat a frying pan over a high heat and cook the spring onions whole for 30 seconds on each side. Add 1 teaspoon of rendang paste and the reserved cooking water and stir. Add the beans and broccoli, cook until warmed through. Plate the vegetables and top with the egg, sliced in half. Garnish with toasted cashews and red chilli.

Spicy Tempeh Rainbow Salad

Tempeh is a great source of protein and the salad is high in fibre. Eating these together will help keep blood sugars and insulin balanced.

Serves 2
(Di, I, C, De, O, S)

For the salad:
240g tempeh, sliced into
   1cm cubes
2 tbsp tamari
Juice of 1 lime
1cm piece of fresh ginger,
   peeled and grated
1 garlic love, minced
1 tsp smoked paprika
½ tsp cayenne pepper
½ tsp flaked sea salt
1 tsp coconut oil

60g rocket
60g radishes, thinly sliced
60g red cabbage, shredded
2 spring onions, cut into thin
   strips
1 medium carrot, cut into ribbons

For the dressing:
1.5 tbsp extra virgin olive oil
Juice of 1 lime
¼ tsp cayenne pepper
½ tsp flaked sea salt

Steam the tempeh for 10–15 minutes until it's soft and warmed through. Meanwhile, make the marinade. Whisk together the tamari, lime juice, ginger, garlic, smoked paprika, cayenne and salt. Add the steamed tempeh and leave to marinate for at least 1 hour, ideally overnight.

Heat a griddle or heavy-based frying pan, add the coconut oil and cook the tempeh over a high heat for 5 minutes. Turn and cook for a further 5 minutes. Combine the rocket, radishes, red cabbage, spring onions and carrot in a large bowl. Whisk together the dressing ingredients, pour over the salad and gently toss together. Transfer the salad to a serving plate and top with the tempeh.

Bean Patties with Courgette and Preserved Lemon Salad

All beans and pulses are a great source of fibre. Garlic has natural antibacterial properties. For the Courgette and Preserved Lemon Salad, please see page 183.

Serves 4
(C, De, T, O, S)

For the bean patties:

1 tbsp chia seeds

2 tsp ghee or coconut oil

40g red onion, finely peeled and chopped

50g chestnut mushrooms, finely chopped

85g red pepper, deseeded and finely chopped

2 garlic cloves, finely chopped

1 tsp smoked paprika

1 tsp ground cumin

½ tsp chilli flakes

½ tsp flaked sea salt

2 x 400g tin mixed beans, drained and rinsed

Begin by preparing the courgette salad. Once prepared, leave to allow the flavours to develop while you prepare the patties.

Stir the chia seeds together with 3 tablespoons of water and leave to one side. This makes a 'chia egg' to bind the patties.

Heat a frying pan over a medium to low heat and add 1 teaspoon of ghee or coconut oil. Once hot, add the onion, mushrooms, red pepper and garlic with a pinch of salt. Cook gently for 5 minutes, stirring occasionally, until softened. Stir in the paprika, cumin, chilli flakes and remaining salt and cook for a further 2 minutes, then remove from the heat.

In a mixing bowl, use a fork to mash the beans into a coarse puree.

Add the 'chia egg' and mix. Tip the vegetables into the bowl and stir well to bring everything together. Divide into eight and shape into small patties.

Heat the remaining teaspoon of ghee or coconut oil in the frying pan and cook the patties for 3 minutes on each side or until golden and crisp, in batches. Serve 2 patties per portion alongside the courgette salad.

DINNERS

All Metabolic Types (except Insulin Type) can add a carb side with your dinner, to help you sleep better and to support your hormones. However, this isn't the case if the recipe already contains pulses, lentils, beans or chickpeas, as these already contain enough carbs.

Beef and Mushroom Stew and 'Cheesy' Cauliflower Mash

Beef is a good source of iron and B12, both needed for thyroid function. For a vegan option, switch the beef for 600g cooked mixed tinned beans, use 400ml vegetable stock and reduce cooking time to 30 minutes.

Serves 4
(Di, I, C, De, T, O, S)

For the beef stew:
1 tsp ghee
500g braising steak, chopped
½ white onion, chopped
1 stick of celery, finely sliced
100g chesnut mushrooms
   (left whole)

2 bay leaves
1.5 tbsp tomato purée
1 tbsp Worcestershire sauce
650ml beef stock

Preheat the oven to 160°C. Heat an oven- and flame-proof casserole dish over a medium/high heat and add the ghee. Once hot, cook the beef until browned well on all sides. Remove the meat from the pan with a slotted spoon and place on a plate to one side.

   Tip the onion, celery, mushrooms and bay leaves into the pot and cook over a low heat for 5–10 minutes, or until the mushrooms have browned and any water released from them has evaporated. Add the tomato purée and Worcestershire sauce, stir to combine, then tip in the beef along with any juices on the plate. Pour in the stock and bring to a simmer. Cover with a lid and cook in the oven for 3 hours. Check on the stew every hour or so, give it a good stir and top up with a little extra water if it's looking dry. Optional carb: add 160g chopped sweet potato at the same time as the cooked beef (NB: not for the vegan option).

Serve with cheesy cauliflower mash (see page 220).

Bombay Cauliflower Steak with Roasted Onion Bhaji

This dish is full of anti-inflammatory spices. Coriander in particular contains liver and bile-supporting detox antioxidants.

Serves 1
(Di, I, C, De, T, O, S)

For the cauliflower steak:
1 tsp ground turmeric
1 tsp ground coriander
1 tsp black mustard seeds
1 tsp ground cumin
½ tsp flaked sea salt
120g cauliflower steak
1 garlic clove, minced

For the onion bhaji:
½ tsp ghee or coconut oil
1 medium onion, sliced
1 red chilli, deseeded and finely sliced
1 tsp ground turmeric
2 tbsp gram flour
50ml vegetable stock
fresh coriander to serve

Preheat the oven to 180°C. Blend the spices, salt and garlic together, then add 1 tablespoon of water to make a paste. Rub the paste over the cauliflower steak and roast in the oven for 15–20 minutes or until tender.

Heat the ghee in a saucepan and add the sliced onion and a pinch of salt. Cook over a low heat for 5 minutes or until softened. Add the chilli and turmeric and cook for a further 2 minutes. Take off the heat, mix in the gram flour to coat the onions, then gradually add the vegetable stock to create a sticky batter holding the onions together. Divide into 3 patties on a lined or greased baking tray and press down to flatten. Bake for 10 minutes or until golden and crisp. Serve garnished with fresh coriander. Optional carb: serve with 3 tablespoons of basmati or wild rice.

Cauliflower, Kale and Red Pepper Dhal with Lime Yoghurt

Lentils are packed full of B vitamins, magnesium and zinc, all needed to support serotonin, the feel-good hormone.

Serves 4
(Di, I, C, De, T, O, S)

1 tsp ground turmeric

½ tsp cumin seeds

1 tsp garam masala

¼ tsp chilli flakes

1 tbsp coconut oil

1 red onion, diced

½ cauliflower, cut into small florets

1 red pepper, deseeded and diced

2 large garlic cloves, minced

200g red lentils, rinsed

500ml veg stock

20g kale, shredded

40ml coconut, almond or organic soya yoghurt

Zest and juice of 1 unwaxed lime

2 tbsp coriander leaves, finely chopped

Place a heavy-based saucepan over a medium heat, then add the turmeric, cumin seeds, garam masala and chilli flakes and toast for 30 seconds until fragrant. Add the coconut oil and heat through. Tip in the diced red onion and fry gently for 5 minutes. Add the cauliflower, red pepper and garlic, stir, then cook for 10 minutes. Add a splash of stock if the vegetables are sticking to the pan. Add the red lentils and the rest of the stock and cook for 15 minutes or until the lentils are tender. Take off the heat and stir in the kale, then transfer into serving bowls.

Mix the yoghurt, lime zest and juice together and dollop on top of the dhal with a sprinkle of coriander.

Chargrilled Chicken with Pumpkin Seed Pesto

Basil is a rich source of folate, a B vitamin which helps in daily detoxification. For a vegan option use 120g of tofu instead of chicken and follow the same method. The pumpkin seed pesto can be stored for up to 3 days in the fridge.

Serves 1
(Di, I, C, De, T, O, S)

For the chicken:
Juice of ½ lemon
¼ tsp extra virgin olive oil
Pinch of salt and pepper
120g chicken breast
80g watercress
50g cucumber, thinly sliced

For the pumpkin seed pesto (batch recipe):
30g pumpkin seeds
1 garlic clove
25g basil, leaves only
15g parsley, leaves and tender stems only
Juice of 1 lemon
½ tsp flaked sea salt
60ml extra virgin olive oil

Whisk together the lemon juice, olive oil and salt and pepper. Butterfly the chicken breast (slice the breast horizontally and open it in half) and lay on a plate. Pour over the lemon juice mixture and flip the chicken over to fully coat it. Leave to marinate for 30 minutes.

Heat a griddle pan over medium/high heat and add the chicken. Cook for 3 minutes on each side, or until charred and cooked through. Cover loosely with foil and leave to rest while you prepare the pesto.

Heat a frying pan over a medium heat, then add the pumpkin seeds. Cook for a few minutes, tossing every now and then, until the seeds start to pop. Tip into a food processor.

Add the garlic, basil, parsley, lemon juice and salt to the food processor and blend until finely chopped. With the processor still going, slowly add the olive oil. Check for seasoning and adjust as needed. Arrange the watercress and cucumber on a plate and top with the chicken and 1 teaspoon of pumpkin seed pesto. Optional carb: 75g cooked quinoa.

Store the pumpkin seed pesto in the fridge for up to 3 days

Chicken Tagine

Chicken is a great source of key amino acids and B vitamins. The red pepper and tomatoes provide vitamin C, a nutrient easily depleted by stress and is important for the function of the adrenal glands. For a vegan option, use 800g of chickpeas and remove the chicken.

Serves 4
(C, De, T, O, S)

2 tsp coconut oil or ghee
8 chicken thighs, skinless and boneless
1 red onion, peeled and finely chopped
1 red pepper, deseeded and finely chopped
2 garlic cloves, minced
½ tsp ground cinnamon
½ tsp ground turmeric

½ tsp ground cumin
½ tsp ground coriander
½ tsp smoked paprika
400g tin chopped tomatoes
300ml chicken stock
Salt and pepper
400g tin chickpeas, drained and rinsed
Mint and parsley to serve

Heat the ghee in a flameproof casserole dish over medium/high heat and fry the chicken thighs for 2–3 minutes on each side until golden. Transfer the chicken to a plate and put to one side. Tip in the onion, pepper and garlic. Cook over a low heat for 5–6 minutes until starting to soften. Add the cinnamon, turmeric, cumin, coriander and paprika and cook for another minute until fragrant. Put the chicken back into the dish along with the tomatoes and stock. Season to taste, then bring to the boil. Turn down to a simmer, cover with a lid and cook for 35 minutes. Remove the lid, add the chickpeas and turn the heat up to medium/high. Cook for a further 15 minutes or until the sauce has thickened. Serve with mint and parsley.

Chickpea Tagine with Jewelled Cauliflower rice

This dish is high in vegetable fibre, which makes it great for detoxing.

Serves 6
(C, De, T, O, S)

For the tagine:

2 tsp coconut oil

1 red onion (80g), peeled and finely chopped

2 garlic cloves, minced

2cm piece of fresh ginger, peeled and finely grated

1 tsp ground turmeric

1 tsp ground cinnamon

1 tsp cayenne pepper

1 tsp smoked paprika

100g red pepper, deseeded and chopped

100g yellow pepper, deseeded and chopped

100g aubergine, chopped

150g courgette, chopped

150g tomatoes, chopped

Pinch of saffron (optional)

4 dried apricots, chopped

2 x 400g tins chickpeas, drained and rinsed

400ml vegetable stock

Salt and pepper

1 tbsp fresh parsley, leaves only, finely chopped

For the cauliflower rice:

1 small cauliflower (200g), cut into florets

1 tsp coconut oil

2 shallots (50g), finely sliced

40g pomegranate seeds

2 tbsp fresh parsley, leaves picked and finely chopped

Heat the coconut oil in a heavy-based saucepan or casserole dish over a medium heat. Sauté the onion and garlic for 5 minutes or until softened but not coloured. Add the ginger, turmeric, cinnamon and cayenne and cook for a further 1–2 minutes until fragrant.

Add the vegetables and 60ml of water, then stir to coat the vegetables in the spices. Cook for 5 minutes until starting to soften and brown. Add the saffron (if you have it), apricots, chickpeas and stock. Season to taste, then cover with a lid and simmer over a low heat for 30 minutes or until the vegetables are soft.

Meanwhile, make the cauliflower rice. Tip the cauliflower florets into a food processor and pulse until you achieve rice-like grains. Heat the coconut oil in a large frying pan and add the shallots. Cook for 5 minutes or until softened. Tip in the cauliflower rice and stir everything through. Cook for a further 5 minutes, or until cooked to your liking, then remove from the heat and stir in the pomegranate seeds and parsley. Season to taste. Serve the tagine alongside the cauliflower rice and top with a sprinkle of fresh parsley. Optional carb: 3 tablespoons of cooked basmati rice instead of the cauliflower rice OR stir in three tablespoons of cooked basmati rice into the cauliflower rice and reduce the portion size of the tagine.

Cottage Pie with Cauliflower Mash

Beef is an excellent source of protein. Protein helps slow digestion and prevents post-meal blood sugar spikes, as well as increases feelings of fullness. Choose lean beef mince. Cauliflower mash is a great low GI alternative to regular potato mash. For a vegan option, use 500g cooked Puy lentils instead of the beef, adding them 10 minutes before the end of cooking time. Reduce cooking time to 25 minutes.

Serves 4
(Di, I, C, De, T, O, S)

½ tsp ghee or coconut oil

500g lean beef mince

2 sticks of celery, peeled and finely chopped

100g white onion, finely chopped

100g leek, halved lengthways and finely sliced

2 garlic cloves, finely chopped

1 tbsp tomato purée

750ml beef stock

400g cauliflower, cut into florets

1 tsp wholegrain mustard

1–2 tbsp plant-based milk

Salt and pepper

Heat the ghee or coconut oil in a large heavy-based saucepan, then tip in the beef mince. Cook over a medium/high heat for 10–15 minutes or until well browned. Use a slotted spoon to transfer the beef to a plate, leaving the beef fat in the pan. Add the celery, onion, leek and garlic to the pan and cook over a low heat for 30 minutes until well softened. Stir the vegetables every now and then to avoid them sticking to the bottom of the pan. Return the beef to the pan and stir in the tomato purée and beef stock. Bring to the boil, then turn down to a simmer and cook for 40–45 minutes or until the stock has reduced to a fairly thick gravy. Tip into an ovenproof dish.

While the beef mix is cooking, prepare the cauliflower mash topping. Steam the cauliflower for 7–8 minutes or until soft. Remove from the heat and leave to cool.

Preheat the oven to 180°C. Tip the cooled cauliflower into a food processor along with the wholegrain mustard. Blend until smooth, adding milk as necessary to create a smooth mash. Season to taste. Spoon the cauliflower mash on top of the beef mixture. Leave the texture quite rough with plenty of peaks to get a crispier topping. Cook in the oven for 30 minutes or until golden and bubbling. Optional carb: add 160g finely chopped sweet potato at step 2.

Courgette and Kale Pakoras with Minted Yoghurt

Red onions are a good source of quercetin. For some people who break down the feel-good hormone serotonin too fast, quercetin acts to help increase levels.

Serves 1
(Di, I, C, De, T, O, S)

For the pakoras:
60g kale, tough stems removed
    and leaves shredded
85g courgette, grated
120g red onion, sliced
1 tsp garam masala
1 tsp ground turmeric
1 tsp chilli powder
½ tsp flaked sea salt

70–80g gram flour
1 tsp ghee

For the minted yoghurt:
1 tbsp coconut, almond or
    organic soya yoghurt
¼ tsp fresh mint, chopped
Salt and pepper

Mix together the ingredients for the yoghurt, then set to one side whilst you make the pakoras. Preheat the oven to 180°C. Mix the vegetables, spices and salt. Gradually add the gram flour and mix in with your hands – the moisture in the courgettes should be enough to bring it together into a sticky mix without adding extra water. There shouldn't be extra batter, just enough to hold the vegetables together. Divide the mixture, about a heaped tablespoon each, and squeeze into rough balls. Heat a non-stick frying pan over a medium heat and add the ghee. Once melted, place the pakoras into the pan and press down gently to flatten them. Cook for 2 minutes on each side or until golden and crisp. Transfer to a lined or greased baking tray and bake for 5 minutes. Serve the pakoras with the minted yoghurt.

Falafel with Spiced Slaw

Carrot fibre helps prevent the reabsorption of oestrogen in the gut. Don't peel the carrots as that is where the fibre is! For the Spiced Slaw recipe, please see page 223.

Serves 2

(C, De, O, S)
For the falafel:
60g red onion, peeled and
  roughly chopped
400g tin chickpeas, drained and
  rinsed
2 garlic cloves, roughly chopped
1 tbsp sesame seeds

2 tbsp coriander, leaves only
2 tbsp parsley, leaves only
1.5 tsp ground cumin
2 tbsp gram flour
Salt and pepper
Extra virgin olive oil

Preheat the oven to 200°C. Tip the falafel ingredients, except the olive oil, into a food processor and blend until finely chopped but not puréed. Divide the mixture into eight and shape into balls. Place onto a lined baking tray and press gently to flatten them. Drizzle each falafel with ⅛ teaspoon of oil, then flip over and repeat on the other side. Bake for 15 minutes, then flip them over and bake for a further 10–15 minutes or until golden and crisp.

While the falafel are baking, prepare the slaw. Serve the falafel alongside the slaw. Garnish with dried rose petals if desired.

Fish Curry with Fenugreek

Research looks promising that fenugreek can lower blood glucose levels and so potentially have anti-diabetic benefits. You can make a vegan option by swapping the fish with 240g of tofu or 300g of drained, tinned chickpeas.

Serves 2
(Di, I, C, De, T, O, S)

1 tsp ghee or coconut oil
80g white onion, peeled
   and chopped
2 garlic cloves, minced
2cm piece of fresh ginger,
   peeled and minced
1 red chilli, deseeded and finely
   chopped
1 tsp black mustard seeds
½ tsp cumin seeds

1 tsp dried fenugreek leaves
½ tsp ground turmeric
½ tsp chilli flakes
190g ripe tomatoes, chopped
1 tsp tamarind paste
150ml coconut milk
Juice of ½ lime
30g spinach
240g cod (or other meaty white
   fish), cut into chunks

Heat the ghee in a large saucepan over a medium heat then fry the onion, garlic, ginger and chilli for 5 minutes or until softened and starting to colour. Using a pestle and mortar, crush the black mustard seeds and cumin, together with the fenugreek, turmeric and chilli flakes. Add the spices to the onion and stir and cook for 2 minutes. Add the tomatoes, tamarind paste, coconut milk and lime juice, bring to a simmer and cook for 10 minutes or until the tomatoes have broken down and the sauce has thickened a little. Add the spinach and fish to the sauce and simmer gently until the fish has cooked through.

Lemon and Garlic Salmon Traybake

Salmon provides anti-inflammatory omega-3 oils, which help make healthy cell membranes.

Serves 4
(Di, I, C, De, T, O, S)

80g red onion, peeled and
    cut into 8 wedges
80g leek, thickly sliced
80g red or yellow pepper,
    deseeded and chopped
80g radishes
4 garlic cloves, unpeeled,
    crushed
4 x 120g salmon fillets
100g cherry tomatoes
80g Tenderstem broccoli

80g courgette, sliced

For the lemon dressing:
1 unwaxed lemon
2 tbsp extra virgin olive oil
20g shallot, peeled and
    finely chopped
2 tsp fresh parsley, finely
    chopped
Salt and pepper

Preheat the oven to 190°C. Tip the onion, leek, pepper, radishes and garlic into a deep roasting tray. Zest half of the lemon, then slice the whole lemon into 8 slices. Mix the olive oil, lemon zest, shallot, parsley and salt and pepper and toss 1 teaspoon of the mix into the vegetables. Roast for 30 minutes, turning the tray and giving the vegetables a good shake halfway through. Carefully remove the garlic cloves from the tray and squeeze the flesh into the dressing. Nestle the salmon fillets in between the vegetables, spoon the remaining dressing over the fish and lay two lemon slices on each fillet. Add the cherry tomatoes, broccoli and courgette to the tray and return to the oven for 15 minutes or until the salmon is cooked through.

Pan-fried Liver with Crispy Sage and Celeriac Mash

Liver is a good source of vitamin A which helps support thyroid function. For the Celeriac Mash recipe, please see page 220.

Serves 1
(Di, C, De, T, O, S)

For the liver:
6 sage leaves
1 tbsp gram flour
140g sliced lamb's liver

1 tsp ghee or extra virgin
olive oil
1 shallot, sliced
Salt and pepper

Begin by making the celeriac mash. Add the celeriac, garlic and shallot to a saucepan and cover with water. Bring to the boil and simmer for 15–20 minutes or until tender.

Finely chop three of the sage leaves and mix into the flour along with a little salt and pepper. Tip this mix onto a plate, then lay the sliced liver into the flour and coat both sides. Heat the ghee in a non-stick frying pan and add the shallot. Cook over a low heat for 5 minutes or until softened and starting to colour. Push the shallots to the side of the pan, then lay the liver in the centre. Cook for 2 minutes on each side. Transfer the liver and shallots to a plate, cover loosely with foil and leave to rest. Add the remaining sage leaves into the frying pan and fry for a few seconds on each side until crisp.

Prepare the celeriac mash. Serve the liver with the celeriac mash, shallots and crispy sage. Optional carb: mash the celeriac with 40g cooked sweet potato.

Miso Cod Fillet with Tenderstem Broccoli

Miso is made from soy beans and fermented, which makes it both probiotic and prebiotic..

Serves 1
(Di, I, C, De, T, O, S)

120g cod fillet
2 tsp white miso paste
2 tbsp tamari
Juice of 1 lime
120g Tenderstem broccoli
¼ tsp coconut oil

½ red chilli, deseeded and
   finely chopped
1 garlic clove, finely chopped
1cm piece of fresh ginger,
   peeled and grated
½ tsp sesame seeds

Whisk together the miso, a tablespoon of the tamari and the lime juice in a bowl. Lay the fish in the bowl and turn to coat in the marinate. Cover and leave to marinate in the fridge for at least 2 hours. Remove from the fridge 30 minutes before cooking. Heat the grill to its highest setting, then place the fish onto a foil-lined tray. Grill for 6–8 minutes or until the flesh flakes easily. The cooking time will depend on the thickness of the fillet.

Meanwhile, blanch the broccoli in boiling water for 2 minutes, then transfer to a bowl of iced water. Heat a large frying pan over a medium heat and add the coconut oil. Once hot, add the chilli, garlic and ginger and cook for 2 minutes, stirring frequently. Drain the broccoli and add to the pan along with the remaining tablespoon of tamari and the sesame seeds. Toss everything together and cook until the broccoli is al dente. Serve the broccoli with the grilled cod and pour over any remaining sauce from the pan. Optional carb: mix cooked buckwheat noodles into the sauce with the broccoli. (For all optional carb weights, refer to page 154).

Nori Wrap

Nori, like all sea vegetables, is high in iodine, which is needed for good thyroid function.

Serves 1
(Di, I, C, De, T, O, S)

65g cauliflower, cut into florets
1 tsp extra virgin olive oil
2 sheets of nori
Salt and pepper
25g red cabbage, shredded
25g carrot, cut into thin strips

25g cucumber, cut into thin strips
120–150g choice of protein
Avocado or tahini dressing to serve (optional)

In a food processor, process the cauliflower into a rice-like consistency. Heat the oil in a large saucepan over a medium heat. Add the cauliflower, stir together with the oil and cook for 1 minute. Turn the heat down a little and add 2 tablespoons of water to the pan. Cover with a lid and cook for 4–5 minutes, stirring regularly, or until the cauliflower is tender. Season with salt and pepper to taste.

Lay out one sheet of nori, shiny side down, and spread the cauliflower rice over the bottom third of the nori. Arrange the half of the cabbage, carrot and cucumber in rows on top of the cauliflower. Add half of your chosen protein, then roll up the nori. Use a little water to dampen the top edge and seal the roll. Repeat with the remaining ingredients. Slice each roll in half. This can be served with avocado or tahini dressing (see pages 224 and 225).

Orange and Balsamic Chicken Traybake

Chicken provides the amino acid tryptophan which is needed for serotonin production. When the body is in a state of inflammation, cruciferous vegetables such as broccoli can help prevent this tryptophan being 'stolen'. You can also make this with fish or chickpeas/beans.

Serves 4
(Di, I, C, De, T, O, S)

For the chicken:
80g red onion, peeled and
   cut into 8 wedges
80g leek, thickly sliced
80g red or yellow pepper,
   deseeded and chopped
80g radishes
4 garlic cloves, unpeeled,
   crushed
½ orange, cut into 4 wedges
4 x 120g skin-on chicken thighs

Salt and pepper
100g cherry tomatoes
80g Tenderstem broccoli
80g courgette, sliced

For the balsamic dressing:
2 tbsp balsamic vinegar
2 tbsp extra virgin olive oil
Juice of ½ orange
½ tsp flaked sea salt

Preheat the oven to 190°C. Tip onion, leek, pepper, radishes, garlic and orange wedges into a deep roasting tray. Whisk together the dressing ingredients and pour 3 tablespoons over the vegetables, tossing to evenly coat in the dressing. Season the chicken with salt and pepper and rub into the skin. Nestle the chicken in between the vegetables and pour the remaining dressing over the skin. Roast for 30 minutes, turning the tray and basting halfway through. Add the tomatoes, Tenderstem and courgette to the tray and give everything a good shake to make sure nothing is sticking. Cook for a further 15 minutes or until the chicken is golden and cooked through.

For fish: add the fish fillets to the tray with the broccoli and tomatoes and baste with dressing from the pan. Cook as above.

For chickpeas/beans: add with the broccoli and tomatoes and cook as above.

Poached Salmon with Braised Fennel

Fennel contains manganese, which helps regulate glucose metabolism and may help prevent insulin resistance.

Serves 1
(Di, I, C, De, T, O, S)

½ tsp fennel seeds

1 star anise

600ml fresh vegetable stock

¼ fennel bulb

150g salmon fillet

50g chard or other leafy green veg, chopped

10g capers

Add the star anise and fennel seeds to the vegetable stock in a pan just large enough to fit the fennel and salmon in and bring to the boil. Place the fennel (whole, not sliced) into the stock and simmer for 15 minutes. Add the salmon to the pan and cook gently for 7 minutes or until the salmon is cooked through.

Heat a small frying pan over a medium heat and add the chard and 2 tablespoons of the veg stock. Stir until the chard has wilted and the stock cooked away. Remove from the heat and add the capers. Take the salmon and the fennel out of the stock, drain well then plate with the cooked chard.

Prawn Hot and Sour Broth

Bok choy is packed with nutrients that support oestrogen detoxification in the liver. For a vegan version, you can switch the prawns for tofu.

Serves 3
(Di, C, De, T, O, S)

1 litre vegetable stock

2 tbsp tamari

4cm piece of fresh ginger, peeled and sliced

2 red chillies, deseeded and roughly chopped

1 tbsp rice wine vinegar

Juice of 1 lime

25g dried shiitake mushrooms

100g mixed mushrooms (left whole)

100g carrot, thinly sliced

360g raw king prawns

2 bok choy (200g)

Pour the vegetable stock into a large saucepan along with the tamari, ginger, chillies, rice wine vinegar, lime juice and shiitake mushrooms. Bring to the boil, then simmer for 15 minutes. Strain the stock into a jug, then tip back into the saucepan. Pick out the shiitake mushrooms, chopping them and returning them to the pan with the stock but discard the rest of the strained ingredients. Add the fresh mushrooms and carrot, bring back to the boil and simmer for 3 minutes. Add the prawns and bok choy and simmer for 3–4 minutes until the prawns are completely pink. Optional carb: add cooked buckwheat noodles with the prawns. (For all optional carb weights, refer to page 154).

Red Lentil Dhal

Red lentils are very high in fibre. Cooking them until soft makes them easier to digest.

Serves 1
(Di, C, De, T, O, S)

1 tsp coconut oil or ghee
20g white onion, peeled and
    chopped
1 garlic clove, minced
1cm piece of fresh ginger,
    peeled and grated
1 tsp ground turmeric
1 tsp ground coriander
1 tsp paprika

½ tsp flaked sea salt
50g red lentils, rinsed
250ml vegetable stock
30g spinach
100ml coconut, almond or
    organic soya yoghurt
Juice of ½ lemon
Fresh coriander, chopped (to
    garnish)

Place a large saucepan over a medium heat and add the coconut oil or ghee. Once hot, add the onion, garlic, ginger, spices and salt and stir together. Turn the heat down to low and cook for 5 minutes until fragrant and the onion is softening. Add the lentils and cook for a further 2 minutes, then pour in the vegetable stock. Bring to a simmer, cover with a lid and cook for 15–20 minutes or until the lentils are tender. Once the lentils are cooked, stir in the spinach until wilted, then remove the pan from the heat and add the yoghurt and lemon juice. Taste for seasoning and adjust as necessary. Serve the dhal with fresh coriander to garnish.

Roasted Chicken Breast with Charred Tenderstem Broccoli

This is super simple and a great recipe for when you are short of time. It will also work well with salmon or a meaty white fish like cod. Adding the clove of garlic will add in sulphur to support detoxification.

Serves 1
(Di, I, C, De, T, O, S)

150g chicken breast
Juice of ½ lemon
Sprig of thyme
1 garlic clove, sliced
70g Tenderstem broccoli

30g carrot, sliced into
    matchsticks or ribbons
20g radishes, sliced
10g cashews, toasted and
    roughly chopped

Preheat the oven to 180°C. Line a baking tray with foil, then grease-proof paper. Lay the chicken breast on the greaseproof and squeeze the lemon juice over it. Add the thyme and garlic, then bring the foil together to create a purse so the chicken will steam. Bake for 20–25 minutes until the chicken is cooked through and the juices run clear.

Heat a frying pan or griddle over a medium to high heat. Add the Tenderstem broccoli and fry for 3–4 minutes on each side until the broccoli is charred and tender. Transfer to a plate and add the carrot, radish, sliced chicken breast, cashews and a few extra thyme leaves.

Roasted Pork Loin with Sauerkraut and Cauliflower

Sauerkraut improves the friendly bacteria in our gut, which in turn can have an impact on mood too. Some clients report feeling happier when eating it regularly.

Serves 1
(Di, I, C, De, T, O, S)

60g sauerkraut (see page 222)
120g pork loin
Salt and pepper
1 tsp ghee
½ red onion, peeled and
    finely chopped

1 garlic clove, minced
60g cauliflower, cut into small
    florets
1 sprig of thyme leaves, finely
    chopped
1 tsp fresh sage, finely chopped

Preheat the oven 180°C. Line a baking tray with foil, then greaseproof paper. Spoon the sauerkraut onto the greaseproof and spread out to around the size of the pork loin. Place the pork on top and season with salt and pepper. Fold the foil up to create a purse. Cook for 20 minutes or until cooked through, then leave to rest while you cook the vegetables.

Heat the ghee in a saucepan over a medium heat, then add the onion, garlic, cauliflower and a pinch of salt. Cook, stirring regularly, for 5 minutes or until the vegetables are tender. Remove from the heat and stir in the herbs. Slice the pork and serve with the cauliflower. Optional carb: add cooked basmati or wild rice to the pan once the vegetables are nearly cooked to warm through. (For all optional carb weights, please see page 154).

Roasted Salmon Niçoise

A twist on the traditional tuna niçoise. Because tuna can be high in mercury (a toxin we want to reduce exposure to) I have swapped it for salmon.

Serves 1
(Di, I, C, De, O, S)

120g salmon fillet
¼ tsp extra virgin olive oil
Salt and pepper
30g red onion, peeled,
    quartered and layers divided
    into petals

60g spinach
30g apple, sliced
10g black olives
10g capers
1 soft-boiled egg
Lemon wedges to serve

Preheat the oven 180°C. Drizzle the salmon with the oil and season well. Roast for 10 minutes, then add the onion petals to the tray and cook for further 3–5 minutes or until the salmon is cooked through and flakes apart easily.

Toss together the spinach, apple, olives, capers and red onion and arrange on a plate. Top with the roasted salmon and boiled egg. Serve with lemon wedges.

Salmon Sushi Bowl

A lower carb version of the traditional sushi, this is packed full of antioxidants and nutrients such as iodine, which many people are lacking in their diet. You can substitute the salmon here for any firm white fish.

Serves 1
(Di, I, C, De, T, O, S)

Extra virgin olive oil

1 tbsp tamari sauce

Juice of ½ lime

1 tsp red chilli, deseeded
   and finely chopped

120g salmon fillet

20g cucumber, deseeded and
   chopped

¼ tsp sesame seeds

½ tsp rice wine vinegar

90g cauliflower

Salt and pepper

20g radishes, cut into wedges

1 tbsp pickled red cabbage

½ nori sheet, cut into squares

2 tsp avocado dressing
   (see page 224)

Mix the tamari, lime juice and red chilli and pour over the salmon. Leave to marinate for at least 30 minutes. Stir together the cucumber, sesame seeds and rice wine vinegar and leave to pickle while you prepare the rest of the ingredients.

In a food processor, chop the cauliflower into a rice like consistency. Heat the oil in a large saucepan over a medium heat. Add the cauliflower, stir together with the oil and cook for 1 minute. Turn the heat down a little and add 2 tablespoons of water to the pan. Cover with a lid and cook for 4–5 minutes, stirring regularly, or until the cauliflower is tender. Season with salt and pepper to taste.

Preheat the grill to high and grill the salmon for 10 minutes or until golden and cooked through. Place a saucepan over a medium heat. Add the cauliflower rice, a pinch of salt and pepper and two tablespoons of water. Cook, stirring often until tender. Plate the cauliflower rice with the radishes, cucumber, pickled cabbage and nori, then flake the salmon over the top. Serve with 2 teaspoons of avocado dressing. Optional carb: mix cooked basmati or wild rice into the cauliflower rice, adjusting the portions accordingly. (For all optional carb weights, refer to page 154).

Smoky Black Bean 'Tacos' with Zesty Yoghurt Dressing

Black beans are a great source of fibre and resistant starch. Resistant starch ferments in the large intestine and feeds our good bacteria. It can help you feel full for longer too! The yoghurt dressing can be stored for up to 3 days in the fridge.

Serves 2
(Di, C, De, T, O, S)

1 tbsp extra virgin olive oil

2 shallots, peeled and finely chopped

1 carrot, finely diced

2 sticks of celery, finely diced

1 garlic clove, finely chopped

100g tomatoes, chopped

1 tbsp tomato purée

2 tsp smoked paprika

½ tsp cayenne pepper

400g tin black beans, drained and rinsed

200ml vegetable stock

Baby gem lettuce

For the yoghurt dressing (batch recipe):

250g coconut, almond or organic soya yoghurt

1 tsp Dijon mustard

Small bunch of coriander

Small garlic clove

Juice of 1 unwaxed lime

Salt and pepper

Preheat the oven to 160°C. Heat the olive oil in a casserole dish over a medium heat, then add the shallots, carrot, celery and garlic. Give it a stir, then turn the heat down to low and cook for 15 minutes, stirring regularly. Add the tomatoes, tomato purée, smoked paprika and cayenne pepper, stir and cook for a further 5 minutes. Add the black beans and vegetable stock, stir everything together, then cover with a lid and transfer to the oven for 45 minutes, stirring halfway through.

To make the dressing, add all the ingredients to a food processor and blend until smooth. Taste and add more seasoning or lime juice if needed. Separate the leaves of the baby gem lettuce and fill each 'cup' with the bean mixture, adding a drizzle of yoghurt dressing on top.

Dressing can be stored in the fridge for up to 3 days.

Sumac Chickpea Traybake

Sumac is packed with antioxidant plant compounds – anthocyanins, tannins, flavonoids, and others – that have anti-inflammatory effects. You can also make this with chicken or fish.

Serves 4
(C, De, T, O, S)

80g red onion, peeled and cut into 8 wedges

80g leek, thickly sliced

80g red or yellow pepper, deseeded and chopped

80g radishes

4 garlic cloves, unpeeled, crushed

100g cherry tomatoes

80g Tenderstem broccoli

80g courgette, sliced

2 x 400g tins chickpeas, drained and rinsed

For the sumac dressing:

2 tsp sumac

1 tsp smoked paprika

½ tsp ground cumin

1 tsp flaked sea salt

Juice of 1 lemon

3 tbsp extra virgin olive oil

Preheat the oven to 190°C. Tip the onions, leek, pepper, radishes and garlic into a deep roasting tray. Whisk together the dressing ingredients, pour over the vegetables and roast for 30 minutes. Add the tomatoes, broccoli, courgette and chickpeas to the tray and toss everything together to coat in the spiced oil. Return to the oven for 15 minutes, then serve.

For chicken: season the chicken thighs, add to tray with the onions and leek and cook as above, basting halfway through.

For salmon: season the salmon fillets and add to the tray with the tomatoes and broccoli, spooning over some of the oil from the tray. Cook as above.

Toasted Cauliflower Green Tabbouleh

Add your protein portion of choice (see pages 152-3).

Serves 4
(O, Di, C, De, S)

250g cauliflower

3 tsp extra virgin olive oil

Salt and pepper

60g asparagus, finely chopped

80g broad beans

80g peas, fresh or frozen

Zest and juice of ½ unwaxed
   lemon

2 tsp flaked almonds, toasted

Preheat oven to 200°C. Pulse the cauliflower in a food processor into a rice-like consistency. Stir in 1 teaspoon of the oil and season with salt and pepper. Spread out into an even layer on a baking tray and roast for 10 minutes, stirring halfway through, until tender and starting to brown.

Meanwhile, blanch the asparagus, broad beans and peas in a pan of boiling water for 2 minutes, then refresh in cold water. Pod the broad beans to remove their leathery skins, then stir the vegetables into the cauliflower along with the remaining 2 teaspoons of olive oil and the lemon juice. Taste and add salt and pepper as needed. Serve scattered with toasted almonds. Optional carb: add cooked quinoa.

(For all optional carb weights, please see page 154).

Turkey Mince Wraps with Brussels Sprout Slaw and Avocado Dressing

Turkey is the food with the highest level of the amino acid tryptophan, needed for making serotonin. For the Brussels Sprout Slaw, please see page 219.

Serves 4
(Di, I, C, De, T, O, S)

2 tsp coconut oil or ghee

500g turkey mince

80g red onion, peeled and
   finely chopped

1 garlic clove, finely chopped

1 tsp tomato purée

3 tbsp vegetable stock

To serve:

2 baby gem lettuce

Avocado dressing
   (see page 224)

Heat a non-stick frying pan over a medium heat and add the coconut oil or ghee. Once this is hot, add the turkey mince, onion and garlic and cook until the meat is well browned. Add the tomato puree and stock and cook until reduced and sticky.

Meanwhile, prepare the slaw. For recipe, see page 219.

To serve, cut the base from the baby gem lettuce and divide the leaves. Add a tablespoon of slaw to each leaf and top with the turkey mince. Drizzle with 2 teaspoons of avocado dressing per serving. Optional carb: add cooked quinoa to the slaw. (For all optional carb weights, please see page 154).

Turkey, Bok Choy and Shiitake Mushroom Sweet and Sour Broth

Turkey is a great source of lean protein, full of amino acids which are the building blocks of our bodies.

Serves 1
(Di, I, C, De, T, O, S)

2 tsp coconut oil

150g turkey mince

300ml fresh chicken stock

10ml rice vinegar

1 tbsp tamari

40g shiitake mushrooms, sliced

10g bamboo shoots, sliced

½ small red chilli, deseeded and thinly sliced

½ spring onion (sliced)

30g bok choy, sliced

Heat the coconut oil in a large saucepan over a medium heat, then add the turkey mince. Cook, stirring frequently, until well browned. Add the chicken stock, rice vinegar, tamari and shiitake mushrooms, then bring to a simmer. Add bamboo shoots, chilli, spring onion and bok choy and cook until the bok choy has wilted. Remove from the heat and serve. Serve with an optional carb portion. (For all optional carb weights, please see page 154).

Turmeric Chicken

Turmeric is a powerhouse of a spice, with anti-inflammatory and antioxidant properties.

Serves 1
(Di, I, C, De, T, O, S)

50g coconut, almond or organic
   soya yoghurt
2 tsp ground turmeric

Pinch of salt
150g chicken breast

Mix the yoghurt, turmeric and salt together. Place chicken breast into the mixture and leave to marinate in the fridge for at least 3 hours. Remove from the fridge 20 minutes before cooking.

Preheat the oven to 180°C. Put the chicken breast on a baking tray lined with baking paper or foil (this will prevent the turmeric staining the tray) and roast for 20 minutes or until cooked through. Serve with your choice of side dish and optional carb portion. (For all optional carb weights, please see page 154).

Vegetable Stir-fry

A stir-fry is such an easy mid-week dinner option. Adding fresh ginger can aid digestion, relieve constipation and reduce inflammation. It's an all-round winner ingredient. Add your choice of protein (see pages 152–3).

Serves 4
(Di, I, C, De, T, O, S)

3 tbsp tamari

1 tbsp tomato purée

1 garlic clove, minced

1cm piece of fresh ginger, peeled and grated

100ml vegetable stock

1 tsp coconut oil

1 red chilli, deseeded and thinly sliced

4 spring onions, cut into 4cm lengths

1 red pepper, deseeded and cut into thick matchsticks

1 yellow pepper, deseeded and cut into thick matchsticks

1 carrot, peeled and cut into matchsticks (omit for insulin types, replace with another courgette)

70g Tenderstem broccoli, each stalk cut into 3 pieces

1 courgette, cut into thick matchsticks

80g mangetout

Mix the tamari, tomato purée, garlic, ginger and vegetable stock, then set aside. Heat the coconut oil in a wok or large frying pan over a high heat. Add the chilli, spring onions, peppers, carrot, broccoli, 2 tablespoons of water and stir-fry for 4 minutes. Add the courgette and mangetout and cook for another 4 minutes, or until the vegetables are cooked but still crisp. Add the sauce and toss together. Cook for another minute to heat the sauce through. Serve with your chosen protein. Optional carb: add cooked basmati or wild rice with the courgette and mangetout. (For all optional carb weights, please see page 154).

SIDES

Brussels Sprout Slaw

Serves 3
(O, Di, De, S, C)

2 tsp extra virgin olive oil
1 tbsp apple cider vinegar
2 tsp wholegrain mustard
Salt
200g Brussels sprouts, finely
   shredded

60g radishes, thinly sliced
120g carrot, grated
40g red onion, finely sliced
2 tbsp pumpkin seeds

Whisk together the olive oil, vinegar, mustard and a pinch of salt until emulsified. Mix the vegetables and pumpkin seeds, then pour over the dressing. Toss to coat the slaw. Taste and adjust the seasoning if necessary.

Celeriac Mash

Serves 1
(Di, C, De, T, O, S)

140g celeriac, peeled and
    chopped into 2cm chunks
1 garlic clove, peeled

1 shallot, peeled and halved
Salt and pepper

Put the celeriac, garlic and shallot into a saucepan and cover with water. Bring to the boil and simmer for 15–20 minutes or until tender. Drain, saving a cupful of the water, then tip into a food processor along with the garlic and shallot. Blend until smooth, adding the reserved cooking water as necessary to get your desired consistency. Season to taste.

'Cheesy' Cauliflower Mash

Serves 4
(Di, I, C, De, T, O, S)

500g cauliflower, cut into small
    florets
2 tbsp nutritional yeast

3–4 tbsp plant-based milk
40g spinach
Salt and pepper

Tip the cauliflower into a large saucepan along with 3 tablespoons of water and a pinch of salt. Cover with a lid and steam for 5 minutes or until the cauliflower is tender. Tip the cooked cauliflower into a food processor and add the nutritional yeast. Blend until smooth, adding the milk gradually until the mixture reaches a creamy consistency. Scoop the mash back into the saucepan and place over a low heat to heat back through, then add the spinach. Stir until wilted then taste for seasoning.

Courgette and Preserved Lemon Salad

Serves 2
(Di, I, C, De, T, O, S)

250g courgettes

2 tsp extra virgin olive oil

Juice of ½ lemon

1 tsp preserved lemon skin,
   finely chopped

2 tsp fresh mint, finely chopped

½ tbsp pumpkin seeds

½ tbsp flaxseeds

Salt and pepper

Top and tail the courgettes, then use a vegetable peeler to slice them into ribbons. Discard the central seedy part of the courgettes. Whisk together the olive oil and lemon juice until emulsified, then stir in the preserved lemon, mint, seeds and salt and pepper. Pour the dressing over the courgettes and toss to combine.

Sauerkraut

(Batch recipe)
(All types, especially Di, S)

1kg white cabbage, thinly
    shredded, 1 outer leaf
    reserved

1.5 tbsp flaked sea salt
1 tsp pink peppercorns
1 tsp caraway seeds

Tip the cabbage into a large mixing bowl, mix in the salt and leave to sit for 10 minutes.

Massage the salt into the cabbage for 10–15 minutes; by this time, the cabbage should be soft and reduced in volume by half. There should be a pool of brine in the bottom of the bowl.

Stir in the peppercorns and caraway seeds, then transfer the cabbage and brine to a large clean jar and pack tightly. Cut the reserved outer cabbage leaf to fit inside the jar and lay it over the top of the shredded cabbage. Place a weight into the jar, such as a ramekin or egg cup, to press down the cabbage so it is covered in the brine. Seal the jar tightly.

Leave to ferment in a cool, dark place for 7 days. Loosen the lid once a day to release any gases that have built up through the fermentation process. Give it a stir, then reseal. Taste the sauerkraut after 7 days; once the flavour is to your liking, transfer to smaller jars and store in the fridge to slow down the fermentation. It can be stored in the fridge for up to 4 weeks.

Sesame Greens

Serves 1
(Di, I, C, De, T, O, S)

½ tsp ghee or coconut oil
1 garlic clove garlic, minced
1 tsp sesame seeds

120g rainbow chard, chopped
(or other leafy green veg,
such as kale or collard greens)
½ tsp toasted sesame oil

Heat the ghee or coconut oil in a frying pan and fry the garlic for 1 minute or until softened. Add the sesame seeds and cook for a further minute. Add the chard and 1 teaspoon of water to the pan and cook until wilted. Transfer to a serving plate and drizzle with sesame oil.

Spiced Slaw

Serves 2
(O, Di, De, S, C, I)

4 tsp extra virgin olive oil
2 tsp apple cider vinegar
2 tsp ras el hanout spice mix
120g sweetheart cabbage,
shredded
80g carrot, coarsely grated

80g red onion, finely sliced
2 tsp preserved lemon skin,
finely chopped
Dried rose petals to garnish
(optional)

Whisk together the olive oil, apple cider vinegar and ras el hanout. Combine the cabbage, carrot, onion and preserved lemon in a mixing bowl and pour over the dressing. Toss to coat the vegetables in the dressing.

SAUCES AND DRESSINGS

These are all batch recipes. These sauces and dressings are suitable for all metabolic types. All of them can be stored in fridge for up to 3 days, and all are added fats which can be included with any meal.

Avocado Dressing

½ avocado, roughly chopped

2 tbsp extra virgin olive oil

5 tbsp water

Juice of 1 lime

1 tbsp fresh parsley, chopped

½ tsp chilli flakes

Salt and pepper

Blend everything together, taste and adjust the seasoning as needed.

Lemon Gremolata

20g fresh parsley, leaves only, finely chopped

1 tsp grated unwaxed lemon zest

1 tsp freshly squeezed lemon juice

1 garlic clove, minced

2 tbsp extra virgin olive oil

Salt

Stir everything together and season with salt to taste.

Pumpkin Seed Pesto

30g pumpkin seeds

1 garlic clove

25g basil, leaves only

15g parsley, leaves and tender
stems only

Juice of 1 lemon

½ tsp flaked sea salt

60ml extra virgin olive oil

Add the pumpkin seeds, garlic, basil, parsley, lemon juice and salt to the food processor and blend until finely chopped. With the processor still going, slowly add the olive oil. Check for seasoning and adjust as needed.

Tahini Dressing

80ml tahini

1 tbsp lemon juice

1 garlic clove garlic, minced

4–5 tbsp cold water

Salt and pepper

Whisk together the tahini, lemon juice, garlic and a pinch of salt and pepper. Add the water a spoonful at a time to achieve your desired consistency. Taste for seasoning and adjust as needed.

Chimichurri

3 garlic cloves, crushed
2 spring onions, finely sliced
1 tbsp chilli flakes
3 tbsp white wine vinegar
½ tsp salt
25g flat-leaf parsley, leaves
    chopped

Handful of coriander, leaves
    chopped
3 oregano sprigs, leaves
    chopped
5 tbsp extra virgin olive oil

Combine all the ingredients and mix well. Goes well with steak.

Everyday Dressing

Juice of ½ lemon
1 tbsp apple cider vinegar
1 tsp Dijon mustard
Zest of 1 unwaxed lemon

5 tbsp extra virgin olive oil
Salt and pepper
1 tbsp freshly chopped parsley
    or basil

Put all ingredients into a jam jar and shake to mix well.

Hummus

1 tin chickpeas

3 tbsp tahini

Juice of 1 lemon

1 very small garlic clove,
   crushed

3 tbsp best extra virgin olive oil

½ tsp salt

To serve – extra virgin olive oil
   and sweet or spicy paprika

Drain the chickpeas but keep half the chickpea water. Blend all the ingredients, including the chickpea water, together in a food processor to your desired consistency. Add a little water if needed. Drizzle over olive oil and paprika to serve. Can be served with carrots, cucumber, cauliflower, etc.

Miso Dressing

1 tsp brown miso paste

2 tsp apple cider vinegar

1 tsp tamari

2 tbsp extra virgin olive oil

Mix all the ingredients together in a small bowl.

Oil-Free Pesto

Large handful of fresh basil

1–2 garlic cloves (adjust as desired)

1 tbsp sunflower seeds, soaked for 1 hour OR ½ avocado

Salt and pepper

Place all the ingredients in a food processor and pulse until the mixture is roughly chopped

Salsa Verde

1 bunch of parsley

1 bunch of basil leaves

Handful of mint leaves

2 garlic cloves, crushed

2 anchovies (optional)

2 tbsp capers

2 tbsp red wine vinegar

1 tsp Dijon mustard

Sea salt and pepper

½ red onion, diced

4–5 tbsp extra virgin olive oil

Place all the ingredients for the salsa verde in a food processor, except for the oil, and pulse until the mixture is roughly chopped. Gradually add the oil and pulse to combine. Serve as a dressing or sauce for fish and meat.

Thai Chilli Lime Dressing

100ml lime juice

1 garlic clove, crushed

20g fresh ginger, grated

2 tbsp fish sauce

2 tbsp warm water

½ tsp fresh chilli, deseeded and
finely chopped (to taste)

Mix the dressing ingredients together in a bowl or jar.

Smoky BBQ Marinade

200g tomato purée

4 tbsp apple cider vinegar

4 tbsp apple juice

1 tbsp honey

2 tbsp coconut aminos or tamari

2 tsp fish sauce

1 tsp sea salt

½ tsp black pepper, freshly
ground

1 tsp sweet paprika

1 tsp chipotle chilli powder

1 tsp Dijon mustard

2 garlic cloves, crushed

1 onion, deseeded and finely
chopped

Put all the ingredients in a blender and blend until well combined. Use the marinade for chicken pieces or other meat. Marinate overnight or for at least an hour. (You can also make this into a sauce by adding 4–6 tablespoons of water before blending, then simmering over a medium/high heat for about 20 minutes.)

CHAPTER 15

How to Create Your Own Meals

This is where you get stuck in. If you don't want to stick exactly to the meal plan in your Metabolic Type chapter, these guidelines will help you go freestyle. They will allow you to adapt dishes you already cook and use foods you already like to fit in with the PCM. There are only two rules: make it delicious and savour every bite.

How to build a salad

Choose your base: a leafy green, such as rocket or watercress.
+ Sulphur food: red onion, garlic, leeks, asparagus
+ Bitter food: radish, endive
+ Fibre: artichokes, Brussels sprouts, broccoli, kale, beetroot,
   carrots (skin on), parsnips, avocado, pulses
The greens and veg above to add up to 110–150g.
+ Texture: 1 teaspoon of nuts or seeds
+ Protein: 110–150g fish, tofu, chicken, eggs, meat

+ Dressing: apple cider vinegar or lemon juice, 1 tbsp extra virgin olive oil (if not cooking with oil)
+ If You Only Do One Thing: Add the one thing from your Metabolic Type

How to build a plate

1 portion of protein (chicken, fish, tofu) cooked without oil
+ 110g–150g varied vegetables/salad
+ 1 tablespoon of dressing/sauce (see pages 224–9)
OR
1 portion protein cooked in 1 tbsp oil
+ 110–150g varied vegetables/salad

+ for dinner, 1 optional carb portion (not for Insulin Type).

Your plate might look like...

- Any fish baked in a baking parchment parcel with a drizzle of extra virgin olive oil. Steamed broccoli, shredded cabbage.

- A grilled chicken breast. Cauliflower mash, 1 tablespoon of miso dressing.

- A tin of sardines in water or brine. A bag of rocket (about 150g), slices of red onion, dressing of choice.

- Mixed peppers, onions, kale, asparagus (or other leftover veg) sautéed in a pan. Two eggs cracked into wells made in the mixture and cooked for 7 minutes with the lid on the pan.

- Prawns with spinach, watercress, rocket, chopped tomatoes, chopped cucumber, 1 tablespoon of salsa verde. (see page 228)

- Steamed salmon with wilted chard, steamed asparagus and 1 tablespoon of Thai chilli lime dressing (see page 229).

- Traybake of chickpeas, red onion, cherry tomatoes, courgettes and two whole unpeeled garlic cloves roasted in smoked paprika with 1 tablespoon of extra virgin olive oil. Squeeze out garlic to serve.

- Ready-cooked Puy lentils warmed through in a pan with leftover roasted vegetables served with one tablespoon of lemon gremolata (see page 224).

- Turkey mince with onion and garlic and ground cumin, pan-fried in 1 tablespoon of ghee served on cauliflower and broccoli rice.

- Cod on a bed of spinach and bok choy topped with 1 tablespoon of tamari, Chinese five spice mix and a squeeze of lime. Bake in a baking parchment parcel.

- Homemade beef burger made with lean beef mince, garlic and onion powder cooked on a barbecue or grill, served with avocado in baby gem lettuce, and a side of slaw.

- Chicken thighs marinated overnight in smoky BBQ marinade (see page 229) served with roasted red peppers and aubergine.

- Grilled tempeh with cauliflower cut into steaks and roasted with 1 tablespoon of extra virgin olive oil and ground turmeric.

- Grilled sirloin steak with 1 tablespoon of chimichurri dressing (see page 226) and Tenderstem broccoli. Served with diced beetroot roasted in extra virgin olive oil and chilli flakes.

PROTEIN PORTION CALIBRATION

I have included a range of protein portion size because people do vary a lot in their needs. It will depend on your size, activity level and metabolism. If you are eating 120g, for example, and you still feel hungry, then try adding 20g and see how you feel. You may do better on the higher amount.

Making a plan for the week

Is it all feeling a bit overwhelming? The secret is in planning and keeping things as simple as suits you. Think through your days in advance; what will work for you?

- Look at the recipes – which ones do you like? Mark the ones that appeal to you as they won't all be to your taste. What will the family like, or what can you adapt for them? (Usually by adding extra carbs.)

- Make a list of three easy breakfasts, three easy lunches, and three dinners you can tweak with different vegetables.

- Find the simplest recipe for your Metabolic Type and save the ingredients on your phone, or stock up on the ingredients, so you have it as your stand-by.

- Is there a dish you can make at the weekend and batch-freeze for later in the week?

- Is there any dish you already know off by heart that you can adapt to the plan – by cutting the oil, measuring out portions, or adding more vegetables?

- What is the simplest breakfast you can make for yourself? You might want to plan to have a protein shake all week, then a delicious dish that takes longer at the weekend.

- Make your lunch as tasty as you can. This is often the meal that people bolt, while working or looking at a screen. What can you do to make it a little more special? Can you make a new sauce or dressing? Or repurpose yesterday's leftovers? Eat seated at a table, and remember to chew and savour.

- Make stewed apple for breakfast and portion it in the freezer. Or make up to 3 portions of the Chia yoghurt breakfast bowl and keep in the fridge. Pre-boil your breakfast eggs – they will keep for up to 7 days in the fridge.

- Make dressings and sauces, and store them in jam jars. Most will keep for 7 days in the fridge. When you have zero time or energy, poach a piece of fish straight from the freezer (make sure it's cooked through), steam some vegetables and add a dressing.

- If you don't want to think about different herbs and spices, buy three or four premixed spice mixes and sprinkle on protein portions before cooking.

- Double cook. Cook two portions of whatever protein you're having for dinner and save a piece for lunch, to be sliced in your salad.

SMOOTHIE TIP

Add the nuts, seeds or cacao nibs at the very end, to leave it a little textured. Then, instead of gulping your smoothie, chew it for better digestion.

Stocking up

When people begin the plan, often they easily get the hang of breakfasts and lunches but find dinners difficult. If you can stock up on some of the below, you can always put a meal together.

FREEZER FILLERS

Fish fillets (buy and freeze individually, or buy frozen)
Chicken breasts (buy and freeze individually, or buy frozen)
Beef and turkey mince (buy and freeze, or buy frozen)
Veggies: beans, cauliflower, broccoli, spinach, stir-fry mix, broad beans, Brussels sprouts

STORE CUPBOARD STAPLES

Tins of fish
Tins of chickpeas and lentils
Packets of tempeh and/or tofu
Packets of microwaveable rice
Long-life vegan milk (one without additives)
Flavourings and seasonings

IF YOU HAVE A FEW OF THESE INGREDIENTS YOU CAN MAKE ANY MEAL TASTE GOOD

Garlic, ginger, lemons, limes, chilli, sumac, harissa, cumin, sweet paprika, turmeric, coriander (fresh and dried), parsley, basil, miso paste, tahini, artichoke paste, pesto, tamari, coconut aminos, unpasteurised apple cider vinegar, Dijon mustard.

COOKING WITH LESS FAT

As you're using your fat portion for either dressings or cooking, you may find this list useful. Within a few days of preparing food with less oil you'll notice your taste buds adapt and you'll have a new-found appreciation for the natural textures and flavours of the ingredients.

- *Oil-free salad dressing: apple cider vinegar or freshly squeezed lemon, salt, pepper. This is also good on steamed veggies.*

- *Sauté in stock for flavour. You can make this by boiling a chicken carcass or beef bones and freezing the liquid in ice-cube trays.*

- *Bake fish and chicken 'en papillote' – or wrapped in a parchment parcel. Add sea salt and black pepper, chilli flakes, lemon juice and your favourite herbs.*

- *Pulse meat in a food processor to make into patties. These can be sautéed in a non-stick pan or baked in the oven.*

- *Soups are easy to make without oil. Make a large batch and freeze in portion sizes.*

WHAT WILL I DO WHEN I GO OUT?

During the 21-day eating plan, you're going to stick to the rules as much as possible. There's more on what you'll do after the 21 days in chapter 16. But for these first 21 days, if you're going out, stick as closely to the plan as you can. Look at the menu in advance to work out your options.

- *Stick to the principles: protein + veg + tablespoonful dressing or sauce on the side. The simplest way is to order a small starter (if other people are having starters), such as a plain asparagus or a light broth or soup. Then a main course of plain grilled protein (fish, meat, chicken, eggs or tofu) without sauce. Ask for no carbs and an extra side of steamed vegetables, and an extra side salad with no dressing. You can dress it yourself with olive oil.*

- *Don't be embarrassed about adapting your food to suit you. It's better than eating something you don't want to eat and feeling bad afterwards. You could even call the restaurant and ask in advance, so you don't have to order in front of people.*

- *The same is true of not drinking: do not be embarrassed. You don't need an excuse.*

YOUR EMERGENCY KITS

This is what to keep on stand-by:

Protein powder, some long-life vegan milk and a shaker at work for emergencies. It can be a last-resort meal or to have before a less ideal meal to keep your blood sugar balanced.

A bag of walnuts in your handbag in case it looks as though you might need to skip a meal. This will save you when the only other food on offer is meeting-room biscuits or cornershop sweets and crisps.

Extra virgin olive oil and apple cider vinegar at work for a basic dressing. For a speedy lunch, go to a supermarket and a buy a pre-cooked protein portion – e.g., a salmon fillet or chicken breast – and a bag of rocket leaves.

The final secret of success: your diary

Keep filling in your Food and Mood diary as you go along. Write down the foods that work for you. Write down the recipes that make you feel full and the ones that leave you wanting more, whether you prefer a sweet or savoury breakfast, the ingredients that make your smoothie feel filling.

Write your meal plans for the week and tick them off. Record what hasn't gone well too – how you feel after a late bedtime or drinking or a Social Meal (see pages 242–3). Make a note of your feelings when someone offers you cake you don't want and you take it. And your feelings when you don't. Follow my Instagram @pippacampbell and write down whatever speaks to you. Keep learning about you!

You'll find it so useful to have all this information to refer to. It's so easy to forget what you've learnt. By looking back at your notebook, you can remember how good you felt when you were losing weight and addressing your symptoms. Write down what you wore, how you felt, your energy levels. Then, if you feel as if you're not sure where to go next, you can open your book and start planning for the food that makes you feel good. This knowledge is now all yours. You have the power to feel in control of what you are eating. It's all in your notebook!

CHAPTER 16

Beyond 21 Days

Congratulations! You did it! You have spent three weeks looking after your body and by now you should be feeling healthier – and you should have lost weight too. Be very proud of yourself, as it's taken a lot of focus and effort.

So what happens next? It's likely that the last time you lost weight or came to the end of a regime you slipped back into your old eating habits because it wasn't sustainable for you and/or you didn't have a real strategy. This might have happened gradually or all at once. This time, that's not going to happen.

The difference with the PCM is that how you've been eating for the past 21 days will now form the basis of your new way of eating for life. What this will look like for you, for the foreseeable future at least, will depend on where you are with your weight loss.

Do you want to lose more weight?

If you aren't yet the weight you want to be, you can stay on the 21-day plan. It's fine to continue because it is a healthy eating programme. I know that, for some people, 21 days is not long enough to balance a body system completely. The longer you've been out of balance, the longer it will take to improve some symptoms.

So, keep on with the plan and the 5 Foundations. Continue to experiment with more new recipes, adding more vegetables and finding more foods you like.

However, you will need to take a break every so often. This is good for your metabolism, as it stops it from going into save-every-calorie survival mode. You may have heard of the concept of treat meals, regular splurges that you have religiously, once a week. The PCM version is slightly different. We call it the 'Social Meal' because you plan it to fit in with your social life.

WHAT DOES A SOCIAL MEAL LOOK LIKE?

On page 238, there are guidelines about going to a restaurant when you're sticking to the plan. This is different: it's the moment you decide to eat the foods you miss and love. What have you been missing? For most clients, it's usually carbs. So you have carbs, but you choose the ones you really love.

One client who was in the middle of losing a lot of weight told me about ordering a chocolate pudding at the end of her Social Meal. A friend commented, 'How can you eat that – it's full of sugar?!' I asked my client, 'Do you love chocolate pudding?' And she said, 'Yes it's my absolute favourite, and I was really looking forward to it.' My answer? 'Make sure you are eating the chocolate pudding!'

She enjoyed her chocolate pudding but she didn't have the bread or the potatoes, and she had one glass of wine. She could have had the bread and the chips, or two glasses of wine. She enjoyed herself but she decided what she'd do in advance and so didn't go completely off plan.

The point at a Social Meal is to look forward to having the thing you love and leave out the rest. If what you love is cream, fruit and meringue, choose the pavlova. If you're not that interested in the chips, leave them.

Can I exercise more?

Yes, after 3 weeks, you can gradually increase the amount and intensity of exercise you do. But slowly is the key. You have learnt to listen to your body when it comes to food, so why not do it with exercise too? If you are tired, then rest and sleep.

In particular, don't go all out with cardio. Remember, too much will make you crave carbohydrates, especially if it raises your levels of cortisol, the stress hormone. To make sure your appetite doesn't spike after working out, stick to weights, yoga, Pilates and more gentle exercise, such as swimming and walking.

If you used to have a run-the-junk-off attitude to working out, don't get back into that pattern. You can't out-exercise a bad diet. Instead, keep eating the foods that suit you and do exercise you like because it makes you feel good or you love it, not to burn calories.

What happens when life gets in the way?

If you have read the client testimonials in the book, you'll know that you can't keep losing weight, all of the time.

A client called me at the end of a half-term holiday; she said her children had been driving her to distraction and she felt so stressed that she didn't have the headspace to cook for herself, so she ended up eating their pizza and snacks every day. She was upset and felt completely out of control.

When we talked, I explained that it's not what you eat sometimes that matters, it's what you do every day. She hadn't undone all her previous good work. It was a blip, part of her learning curve.

We talked about what she might do for the next school holiday, which was to go into Maintenance Mode. If you are having a stressful period in your life, this is one approach you can take so you don't slip back into patterns that make you feel unhappy and unhealthy.

WHAT IS MAINTENANCE MODE?

The idea of Maintenance Mode is to roll with your life instead of fighting against it. You accept that, this week, you're not going to lose weight. But if you do gain weight in Maintenance Mode, it will be minimal. Then, as soon as life gets back to normal, you know how to get back on track.

For example, you're going on holiday. You know you're going to be eating out, at the airport, on the plane, at the beach, so you plan to loosen the rules during the holiday. You will eat the food you love; it's about deciding what that is so you don't feel deprived and you enjoy your holiday – maybe a pain au chocolat one day, or a delicious pasta carbonara the next – but not abandoning your new way of eating to the point where your symptoms return and you feel unhealthy.

This is what Maintenance Mode looks like:

- You make a conscious choice that this is a temporary solution.

- If possible – such as for holidays, school holidays, or being at a work conference – you decide to go into Maintenance

Mode in advance. Plan ahead for the times when you will be able to stay on-plan, such as taking your own food for the journey.

- You enjoy what you eat that's off the plan. This is really important as there is no point going off plan for things you don't like that much! With the client who was struggling with half term, we discussed that for the next school holidays, she'd stock up on carbs she absolutely loves – for example, her favourite dark chocolate – and have that at the end of dinner, rather than the kids' leftover pizza or chips at teatime.

- The rest of the time, you stick to the 5 Foundations: two bites of protein first and enough protein at every meal, water, all the veggies, chewing and gaps between meals. You keep eating some foods that suit your Metabolic Type. By now, you also know what a great plate looks like, the portions and proportions of protein, carbs, fat and veggies you need, too.

- You keep being aware of your reactions to foods. You'll learn a lot about yourself from eating off-plan. For example, if you eat sugar after not having it for a while, it will seem incredibly sweet – often, clients say, too sweet. This direct message from your brain and body, in reaction to what you've eaten, helps you to make the choices that suit your body better.

- And remember, you are in control. When life is back to normal, you can calmly go back to the meals that fit the eating plan and make you feel good.

You are at your happy weight

Well, even bigger congratulations! You have achieved your desired weight and overall well-being. Now, you're going to be in Maintenance Mode for life. In the past, you might have been all or nothing, strict or binge. It can feel scary, staring down the barrel of no strict rules, not needing to lose weight, but not wanting to put on weight either. The good news is that because the 5 Foundations are now already second nature (or becoming so), you know exactly what to do to maintain your new weight and well-being.

Maintenance Mode has been tried and tested in clinic, so that it's now just as much a part of the PCM as the weight-loss part of the plan. We call it 80:20 because you stick to the plan 80 per cent of the time and go off it 20 per cent. That way, you can enjoy every type of celebration or party because you make the right choices. You plan to loosen up for social occasions and holidays – and during stressful and other tricky times – but you never leave the plan completely.

You'll plan events into your food diary to help you get the 80:20 right. Over the next few months, you will tweak it. Your aim is to make sure your 80:20 works so that:

1. You stay at a weight that makes you feel good.

2. Your signs and symptoms do not return.

3. You know what to eat for your body and Metabolic Type.

4. You feel in control of your eating.

I've seen clients do 80:20 in various ways. Which of the following options do you think might suit you best? You can work out your own version too.

- You eat roughly four meals out of five exactly to the plan, then one-off plan.

- You add back some of the things you were missing. You might have a couple of squares of dark chocolate every day after lunch, for example. Or a glass of wine with dinner a couple of nights a week.

- You might like to increase portion sizes or add more fats. So, you have extra dressing or sauce or avocado, or add a handful of nuts or seeds or an extra vegetable portion.

- You might eat according to the plan all week and then be looser at the weekend. (This is the option that most of my clients choose.)

NB: This might sound obvious, but choose one not all of the above!

Even if you have the weekend off, it's not about 5 days strict, 2 days binge. Think balance. For example, if you are going to your favourite restaurant one night, and a birthday party the next night, decide which one is your night. Eat your favourite food the first night and at the party, stick broadly to the 5 Foundations, with may be one addition, such as a drink. Then, when you go to the buffet, choose some protein and fill your plate with vegetables. The key is, choose what you love.

Or perhaps, on Friday night, you might be planning to have a glass of wine and a takeaway. If it's an Indian, perhaps you might order the tandoori, no sauce, then you can have a poppadum. But if you really love the korma, then have the korma. But don't finish the bottle of wine and get stuck into the ice cream as well. Or you might make quinoa to go with the korma and have some ice cream. Be mindful that if you do have half a bottle of wine *and* the korma with poppadum, rice *and* ice cream, the next morning your blood sugar will be all over the place, and you'll crave toast. And by mid-morning, you'll be feeling exhausted and bloated. So think balance. What do you love and what won't you miss?

But, that said, if you do eat everything, make sure you flipping well enjoy every moment, savour it and do not feel guilty. Then, calmly, at the next meal, go back to the 5 Foundations.

Help! My symptoms are back!

When you've had a Social Meal – or perhaps a weekend off – be prepared that some of your old symptoms might come back. It might be that you feel bloated or full of wind, have a headache or feel overtired. A lot of clients tell me their cravings return. You'll probably find you can no longer drink nearly as much as you did previously and that the hangover symptoms are worse. Don't worry, you aren't back to square one. You haven't undone all your good work. Now you know your body better, you can feel what doesn't work for it. Over time, you will find your way to eat food you enjoy at social occasions but not end up with symptoms.

You may notice you get particularly strong symptoms from a specific food when you reintroduce it. During the 21 days of not eating this food, you have effectively been on an elimination diet, which is how functional medicine diagnoses a food sensitivity. So, when you reintroduce it, your body reacts in a negative way. It's not that you're more sensitive to that food, it's that you're noticing your sensitivity. It's advisable to reintroduce foods one by one, to make it clear which foods are an issue (see page 249).

HELPFUL, HAPPY LIFE HABITS

We have talked a lot about balance in food but balance in life is important too! These habits will help you find that.

1. Early, regular bedtime, most of the time. *Eating late and going late to bed will make you more likely to put on weight.*

And our bodies need routine – they love to get the better-quality sleep that comes in the earlier part of the night.

2. Move every day. *Even if you don't have time to do formal exercise, take the stairs instead of the lift, walk or cycle instead of taking the car or getting a bus, take a lunchtime walk, get off the bus one stop earlier, park at the far end of the car park.*

3. Take part in proper physical activity at least two to three times a week. *Regular exercise will help maintain your weight and will optimise your health and well-being.*

Can I add foods back in?

Yes, now is the perfect time to do that. The reason that dairy and gluten aren't included in the plan is that they are the foods that most often cause reactions or intolerances. Bring them back one at a time. If you've been missing dairy the most, for example, add it in first.

Day one: Eat the food two to three times. Then wait 72 hours to see if you have a reaction. Use your food diary to keep track of any symptoms. These might be in any body system: digestion, joint and muscles, headache, congestion, bladder, skin, energy level, sleep, or any others.

End of day three: At the end of day three, if there are no symptoms, you can keep eating the food. You can also reintroduce another food. If you are not sure if you had a reaction, repeat the test.

Helen, 58, now knows how to eat to nurture her body

'I love food and I always have. I was brought up in a northern family, and every celebration, holiday, success or event involved food – lots of food! There would be a buffet: sandwiches, cakes, pastries, sausage rolls, pork pies. And so I came to associate food with feeling secure and happy.

I didn't have a problem with my weight until I left university and moved to London for my first job. It was in an advertising agency and involved a *lot* of client lunches and wine. When things felt stressful or difficult, I would turn to food for comfort or reward.

As I started to gain weight, I tried many different kinds of diet. I'd lose weight but at the end, I'd go back to eating 'normally'. And 'normally' for me was a huge plate of pasta and a lot of cheese washed down with a few glasses of Malbec! I yo-yo dieted through my thirties and forties, going between size 10 and size 18. When I hit my early fifties and menopause, I was overweight and exhausted and size 18. But when I started HRT aged 54, my energy came back. And so I restarted my slimming plan regime and exercising, and, over eight months, went down to a size 10/12.

But then lockdown hit. I couldn't get to the gym. I started to eat cakes, biscuits, anything comforting to lift the boredom of working from home. Within four months, I was back to size 16. I couldn't even find the energy to diet again. I was tired all the time, had brain fog, migraines and indigestion. When I tried to exercise, my joints ached, I had hardly any strength. As a part-time singer who fronts a band, looking good and having a lot of energy is pretty important to me. I was worried my days of performing were over.

Then in January 2022, I started working with Pippa. She gave me an eating plan but more than that, she gave me an education.

I have always cooked but I hadn't thought about the fact that some foods I was eating, like the gravy granules and diet drinks that are allowed on most diets, are processed. Pippa taught me how the body finds it hard to digest and detox processed foods. Before, I hadn't understood why when I ate a diet yoghurt with artificial sweeteners, I'd want to eat three more half an hour later, but Pippa explained that sweeteners can trigger cravings.

I cut out sugar, caffeine, gluten, alcohol and dairy. I stopped snacking too, which wasn't easy at first. For the first three days, I had terrible headaches as my body got rid of all those toxins. After three days, I suddenly started to feel so much better. I had loads more energy, started to sleep really well and so could exercise more effectively too. In the first week, I lost over 3.5kg.

I noticed that the better I felt, and the more weight I lost, the more motivated I became. I kept preparing my meal plans and writing my food diary. I realised that when I ate less carbs, I had more energy. My skin began to look clearer and my eyes looked brighter, probably from cutting out the alcohol and increasing my water intake.

Now, five months later, all my symptoms have pretty much resolved and I'm a size 12, the right size for me. My migraines have gone completely, which is such a relief. People have said I look well, younger, less tired. One friend even said I looked happier. It's not surprising – I'm no longer carrying around 13kg of extra weight.

I live according to Pippa's 80:20 maintenance rule: I stick to the plan strictly 80 per cent of the time and I can do what I want 20 per cent of the time. I have found swaps that work for me. Instead of cheese, I'll now have a bit of coconut yoghurt with fruit and seeds. Instead of crisps, I've become a bit addicted to seaweed thins. Kombucha has replaced my glass of wine. I am in the gym at least three times a week, where I do weights, cardio, spin classes and Pilates. I'm still strict about avoiding additives, sugar and gluten, and try to keep meals as natural, fresh and healthy as they can be. I make everything from scratch and buy organic when I can. I've learnt to make the protein and vegetables the biggest part of the meal and to eat the right amount of good carbs for my body. My portion sizes have decreased because eating the right amount of protein makes me feel full much more quickly.

The interesting thing is, though, that I don't want to eat the kind of food I ate before. I like the way this food makes me feel. It's a sustainable way of eating for me. I now know that we should nurture our bodies with the food that we eat, rather than eat for weight loss. I am keen to be fit and healthy into my sixties, and eating this way will not only help me do that but allow me to continue enjoying my music, too.'

Stacey, aged 41, *has found ways to make the plan suit her*

'For most of my twenties and thirties, I was a slim size 8 to 10 and under 57kg. I was pretty fit. I competed as a runner to quite a high level when I was young and I worked as a PE teacher.

We struggled to conceive our first child and, when I had IVF, I began to put on weight. Luckily, I then fell pregnant naturally. But after having my two children, I couldn't seem to lose the baby weight. I tried a slimming club but it left me hungry all the time. I tried keto too but it didn't suit me because it was so restrictive.

Two years ago, when the children were aged two and four, I was 68.5kg and a size 12 to 14. It may not sound big, but I'm only 5 feet, 2 inches. And I didn't feel well. I was lacking in energy and unmotivated. I had brain fog. I was often bloated and constipated. I had bad PMT, sometimes angry, sometimes crying or anxious. Each month, I had ovulation pains and more than a week of period pain. I craved sweets and chocolate or carbs too. On bad days, I'd eat white toast with butter and jam, a sandwich and a packet of crisps and a chocolate bar for lunch.

When I saw Pippa, she explained that my symptoms were down to me not detoxing oestrogen; both my liver and digestion were sluggish. The first change I made was to my breakfast. I switched to eating eggs or smoked salmon with spinach instead of my usual toast. I started drinking a lot more water throughout the day too. It wasn't easy to stop eating bread for that first 3 weeks. Afterwards, when I tried eating it again, my stomach blew up so much that I looked pregnant, so I rarely eat it now. For lunch, I'll eat a big salad with as many varied vegetables as possible, plus lentils, pulses or quinoa. In the evenings, I like to follow Pippa's recipes – tonight, I've made a shepherd's pie with sweet potatoes on top. Or I might eat salmon, chicken or steak with at least one cruciferous vegetable, as they help with oestrogen detoxing. I also eat broccoli sprouts for this every day.

Now, I do still get a little bit of PMT but nothing like before. And I'm just under 63.5kg. Pippa's plan was different from any other weight-loss plan I've tried because I was able to make it into a way of life. The children like a lot of the food too. And it's helped me get to know my body better. I know that if I don't eat well, I'll feel miserable and lethargic again. But I also know exactly what I need to eat to feel motivated, energetic, ambitious and happy.'

LIFT YOURSELF UP

If you've lost a significant amount of weight, remind yourself what an incredible job you've done. If you go to the gym, next time you are there, find a weight or kettlebell that's the same as the amount you've lost. Can you pick it up? That is what you have been carrying around with you all those years.

Look how far you've come

When women tell me how they feel so different about themselves on the PCM, it's so moving. Some of their stories are so inspirational.

If you want to get in touch with other women doing the plan, there are often chats underneath my Instagram posts. I do Instagram Lives, where you can ask questions (I answer as many as I can but may not manage all of them, sorry). There's also my Female Food Club, a (paid-for) online group that's about health as well as weight loss, that takes you through all the stages of the PCM as a group. Women say they get a lot from posting what they eat there, as well as learning and getting support from the other women. You could also get a group of friends and work through the book together. You'll not only encourage each other but you can cook for each other too.

Doing the PCM is making real change. And that takes energy and dedication, so it's testament to your courage that you've done it. One encouraging thing my clients often say is that the more they do the PCM, the better they feel. And the better they feel, the more motivated they feel and the easier it gets. Good luck and keep in touch.

Appendices

Optional supplement recommendations

This is not an exhaustive list of supplements that I find useful, but some you might consider. For more bespoke recommendations, I suggest working with a practitioner.

FOR ALL TYPES

Vitamin D3 + K2
Pippa Campbell Health Complete Women's Multi or a good multivitamin and mineral complex
Or Pippa Campbell Health B Complex
Pippa Campbell Health Super Greens

If you don't eat meat: Pippa Campbell Health Just B12
If you are constipated: When you change what you eat, it's very common to get constipated. One supplement that's very helpful for this is Pippa Campbell Health Magnesium Complex .

DIGESTION TYPE

Pippa Campbell Health Digest, Pippa Campbell Health Just
HCL & Pepsin,

Pippa Campbell Health Repopulate

Prebiotics such as inulin

OX bile

L-glutamine

Pippa Campbell Health Just Aloe Vera Juice

INSULIN TYPE

Pippa Campbell Health B Complex

Pippa Campbell Health Meta-Boost

Inositol

Alpha-lipoic acid

CORTISOL TYPE

Pippa Campbell Health Just Ashwagandha

Holy basil

Rhodiola

Pippa Campbell Health Chill

Pippa Campbell Health B Complex

DHA/EPA

Vitamin C

Pippa Campbell Health Magnesium Complex Magnesium citrate
or glycinate

DETOX TYPE

Pippa Campbell Health Detox

Pippa Campbell Health Super Greens

Dandelion root extract

Milk thistle
BodyBio Phosphatidylcholine (see my website for 15% off).

THYROID TYPE

Pippa Campbell Health Meta-Boost
Pippa Campbell Health Just Ashwagandha
NAC
Pippa Campbell Health Magnesium Complex
Vitamin D
Vitamin A

OESTROGEN TYPE

Broccoli seed extract
Pippa Campbell Health Detox
Pippa Campbell Health B Complex
NAC
Pippa Campbell Health Magnesium Complex
Ca D-Glucarate
BodyBio Phosphatidylcholine (see my website for 15% off) GLA

SEROTONIN TYPE

Pippa Campbell Health Mood & Sleep
Pippa Campbell Health Magnesium Complex
Pippa Campbell Health Just B12
Folate

For more information on the PCM, see pippacampbellhealth.com or follow Pippa on Instagram @pippacampbell_health. For group support, Pippa's Female Food Club is a monthly membership with expert lessons on how to support your journey.

Source Notes

CHAPTER 1: WHY CAN'T I LOSE WEIGHT?

13 For example, people who have anxiety often have gut issues too; there's a two-way superhighway between the brain and the gut that's key to mood: Carpenter, Dr. Siri, *That gut feeling: With a sophisticated neural network transmitting messages from trillions of bacteria, the brain in your gut exerts a powerful influence over the one in your head, new research suggests [American Psychological Association;* September 2012, Vol 43, No. 8]; Available from: https://www.apa.org/monitor/2012/09/gut-feeling#:~:text=Gut%20bacteria%20also%20produce%20hundreds,both%20mood%20and%20GI%20activity

CHAPTER 2: THE TRUTH BEHIND BODY SIZE

17 But let's look at the latest UK government figures. They show that in the UK, 28 per cent of adults are obese and a further 36 per cent are overweight: UK Government; Available from: https://commonslibrary.parliament.uk/research-briefings/sn03336/

20 Michael Moss, in his book *Salt Sugar Fat: How the Food Giants Hooked Us*, writes: Moss, Michael, *Salt Sugar Fat: How the Food Giants Hooked Us.* W.H. Allen, 2014. p. xxvii.

22 Long-term inflammation is thought to contribute to the development of heart disease: Clark, A. (27 August 2021); *Ultra-processed food is associated with cardiovascular disease*; British Heart Foundation; Available from: https://www.bhf.org.uk/what-we-do/news-from-the-bhf/news-archive/2021/august/ultra-processed-food-is-associated-with-cardiovascular-disease

22 cancer: Pasquazzi, K; (12 August 2019); The Link Between Processed Foods and Cancer; Lifespan; Available from: https://www.lifespan.org/lifespan-living/link-between-processed-foods-and-cancer

22 Alzheimer's: Alzheimer's Research UK; (27 July 2022); Available from: https://www.alzheimersresearchuk.org/diet-high-in-ultra-processed-foods-linked-to-a-higher-risk-of-dementia/

22 and autoimmune illnesses: Whiteman, H.; (6 January 2016); *Could processed foods raise the risk of autoimmune diseases?*; Medical News Today; Available from: https://www.medicalnewstoday.com/articles/304645

23 They're high in the wrong oils: Veerman, J.L.; (12 April 2016); **Dietary fats: a new look at old data challenges established wisdom**; BMJ; Available from: https://doi.org/10.1136/bmj.i1512

CHAPTER 4: THE 5 FOUNDATIONS

41 Importantly, chewing thoroughly helps you to eat less: Zhu, Y. and Hollis, James H.; (9 November 2013); *Increasing the number of chews before swallowing reduces meal size in normal-weight, overweight, and obese adults*; PubMed.gov; Available: https://pubmed.ncbi.nlm.nih.gov/24215801/

41 Importantly, chewing thoroughly helps you to... feel fuller, faster: Ikeda, A., Miyamoto, J., Usui, N, Taira, M and Moriyama, K; (8 February 2018); Chewing Stimulation Reduces Appetite Ratings and Attentional Bias toward Visual Food Stimuli in Healthy-Weight Individuals; PubMed Central; Available: https://www.ncbi.nlm.nih.gov/pmc/articles/PMC5809478/

42 One study showed that babies begin to like a food after eight tries: Maier, A., Chabanet, C., Schaal, B., Issanchou, S., Leathwood, P.; *Effects of repeated exposure on acceptance of initially disliked vegetables in 7-month old infants*; Elsevier Press; [Food Quality and Preference, Volume 18, Issue 8, December 2007]; Available from: https://www.sciencedirect.com/science/article/pii/S0950329307000523

CHAPTER 5: DIGESTION TYPE

49 Obese people have been shown to have less variety of microorganisms in their guts than non-obese people: Robertson, R.; (13 February 2018); *How Your Gut Bacteria Can Influence Your Weight*; Healthline; Available from: https://www.healthline.com/nutrition/gut-bacteria-and-weight#TOC_TITLE_HDR_3

49 More recent research shows your gut microbiome affects how well you respond to trying to lose weight, too: American Society for Microbiology; (14 September 2022); *Gut Microbiota Influences the Ability to Lose Weight*; Available from: https://asm.org/Press-Releases/2021/September/Gut-Microbiota-Influences-the-Ability-to-Lose-Weig#:~:text=The%20findings%20were%20published%20this,study%20author%20Christian%20Diener%2C%20Ph

55 It's full of probiotic good bacteria as well as prebiotics that feed good bacteria: Mohammed, M.; (17 February 2022); *Fermented food: why eating sauerkraut helps your gut stay healthy;* The Conversation; Available from: https://theconversation.com/fermented-food-why-eating-sauerkraut-helps-your-gut-stay-healthy-175980

CHAPTER 6: INSULIN TYPE

65 Avoiding high levels of fructose, found in fizzy drinks and fruit juice, sweetened yogurt, sauces and salad dressing, for example, is also key for blood sugar control: Horst, K.W.T., Schene, Merle R., Holman, R., Romijn, Johannes A., Serlie, Mireille J.; *Effect of fructose consumption on insulin sensitivity in nondiabetic subjects: a systematic review and meta-analysis of diet-intervention trials;* [*The American Journal of Clinical Nutrition;* 9 November 2016, 104(6):1562-1576]; Available from: https://pubmed.ncbi.nlm.nih.gov/27935520/

65 And 'eating a rainbow' – the polyphenols found in different colour plant foods have been shown to increase insulin sensitivity: Munir, K.M., Chandrasekaran, S., Feng, G., and Quon, M.J.; *Mechanisms for food polyphenols to ameliorate insulin resistance and endothelial dysfunction: therapeutic implications for diabetes and its cardiovascular complications;* [Am J Physiol Endocrinol Metab. 2013 Sep 15; 305(6): E679–E686.]; Available from: https://www.ncbi.nlm.nih.gov/pmc/articles/PMC4073986/

66 Finally, there's good research that chillies are good for regulating insulin too: Sanati, S., Razavi, B.M., and Hosseinzadeh, H.; A review of the effects of Capsicum annuum L. and its constituent, capsaicin, in metabolic syndrome; [Iran J Basic Med Sci. 2018 May; 21(5): 439–448.]; Available from: https://www.ncbi.nlm.nih.gov/pmc/articles/PMC6000222/

68 it makes your tissues more sensitive to insulin. And the bigger your muscles, the more glucose they burn, even at rest: Paquin, J., Lagacé, J.C., Brochu, M., Isabelle J. Dionne; *Exercising for Insulin Sensitivity – Is There a Mechanistic Relationship With Quantitative Changes in Skeletal Muscle Mass?;* [Front. Physiol., 12 May 2021, Sec. Exercise Physiology]; Available from: https://www.frontiersin.org/articles/10.3389/fphys.2021.656909/full

68 Just a single night of bad sleep can make your body more resistant to insulin: Donga, E., van Dijk, M., van Dijk, J.G., Biermasz, N.R., Lammers, G.J., van Kralingen, K.W., Corssmit, E.P.M., Romijn, J.A.; *A single night of partial sleep deprivation induces insulin resistance in multiple metabolic pathways in healthy subjects;* [J Clin Endocrinol Metab. 2010 Jun;95(6):2963-8.]; Available from: https://pubmed.ncbi.nlm.nih.gov/20371664/

68 just three minutes of walking up and down stairs had an impact on both blood glucose and insulin levels: Halsey, G. (20 January 2022); *Blood Glucose Down, Insulin Sensitivity Up with 10 Minutes of Moderate-intensity Stair Stepping*; Patient Care Online; Available here:https://www.patientcareonline.com/view/blood-glucose-down-insulin-sensitivity-up-with-10-minutes-of-moderate-intensity-stair-stepping

Moore, J., Bartholomae, E., Ward, K., Hooshmand, S.; *Three minutes moderate-intensity stair walking improves glucose and insulin but not insulin sensitivity or total antioxidant capacity;* [October 2021, Nutrition, metabolism, and cardiovascular diseases: NMCD 32(Suppl 2)]; Available here: https://www.researchgate.net/publication/355740160_Three_minutes_moderate-intensity_stair_walking_improves_glucose_and_insulin_but_not_insulin_sensitivity_or_total_antioxidant_capacity

68 ACV has been shown to lower blood-sugar levels after eating: Shishehbor, F., Mansoori, A., Shirani, F.; Vinegar consumption can attenuate postprandial glucose and insulin responses; a systematic review and meta-analysis of clinical trials; [Diabetes Res Clin Pract. 2017 May;127:1-9]; Available here: https://pubmed.ncbi.nlm.nih.gov/28292654/

68 ...and so keeps insulin levels more stable too: Mitrou, P., Petsiou, E., Papakonstantinou, E., Maratou, E., Lambadiari, V., Dimitriadis, P., Spanoudi, F., 2 Raptis, S.A., Dimitriadis, G.; *Vinegar Consumption Increases Insulin-Stimulated Glucose Uptake by the Forearm Muscle in Humans with Type 2 Diabetes*; [J Diabetes Res. 2015; 2015: 175204]; Available here: https://www.ncbi.nlm.nih.gov/pmc/articles/PMC4438142/

68 There's also promising evidence ACV may help with weight loss, too: Khezria, S.S., Saidpour, A., Hosseinzadeh, N., Amiri, Z.; *Beneficial effects of Apple Cider Vinegar on weight management, Visceral Adiposity Index and lipid profile in overweight or obese subjects receiving restricted calorie diet: A randomized clinical trial*; [Journal of Functional Foods Volume 43, April 2018, Pages 95-102]; Available here: https://www.sciencedirect.com/science/article/abs/pii/S1756464618300483

CHAPTER 7: INSULIN TYPE

76 The HPA response is supposed to be a short-term fix, lasting for 20 – 40 minutes: Dickerson, S.S., Kemeny, M.E.; Acute stressors and cortisol responses: a theoretical integration and synthesis of laboratory research; [Psychological Bulletin, 2004 May;130(3):355-91; Available here: https://pubmed.ncbi.nlm.nih.gov/15122924/

77 Instead, it's been shown that high levels of cortisol make it more likely you will reach for sweet foods and carbs: Epel, E., Lapidus, R., McEwen, B., Brownell, K.; Stress may add bite to appetite in women: a laboratory study of stress-induced cortisol and eating behavior; Psychoneuroendocrinology, 2001 Jan;26(1):37-49]; Available here: https://pubmed.ncbi.nlm.nih.gov/11070333/

80 And in some studies, consuming high levels was shown to decrease stress hormones: *Scientists Say Vitamin C May Alleviate The Body's Response To Stress*; (23 August, 1999); American Chemical Society; Available here: https://www.sciencedaily.com/releases/1999/08/990823072615.htm

80 These are important to counter brain inflammation caused by stress: Mehta, V., Parashar, A., Udayabanu, M.; *Quercetin prevents chronic unpredictable stress induced behavioral dysfunction in mice by alleviating hippocampal oxidative and inflammatory stress*; [Physiolical Behaviour. 2017 Mar 15;171:69-78]; Available here: https://pubmed.ncbi.nlm.nih.gov/28069457/

80 All vegetables contain antioxidants, but some that are particularly rich are: Carlsen, M.H., Halvorsen, B.L., Holte, K., Bøhn, S.V., Dragland, S., Sampson, S., Willey, C., Senoo, H., Umezono, Y., Sanada, C., Barikmo, I, Berhe, N., Willett, W.C., Phillips, K.M., Jacobs Jr, D.R., Blomhoff, R.; *The total antioxidant content of more than 3100 foods, beverages, spices, herbs and supplements used worldwide*; [Nutr J. 2010; 9: 3., 22 January 2010]; Available here: https://www.ncbi.nlm.nih.gov/pmc/articles/PMC2841576/

82 It's been shown in animal studies that there is a lot of communication between the gut and the HPA axis: Rosin, S., Xia, K., Azcarate-Peril, M.A., Carlson, A.L., Propper, C.B., Thompson, A.L., Grewen, K., Knickmeyer, R.C.; *A preliminary study of gut microbiome variation and HPA axis reactivity in healthy infants*; [Psychoneuroendocrinology. 2021 Feb;124:105046]; Available here: https://pubmed.ncbi.nlm.nih.gov/33254059/

Misiak, B., Łoniewski, I., Marlicz, W., Frydecka, D., Szulc, A., Rudzki, L., Samochowiec, J.; *The HPA axis dysregulation in severe mental illness: Can we shift the blame to gut microbiota?*; [Prog Neuropsychopharmacol Biol Psychiatry. 2020 Aug 30;102:109951]; Available here: https://pubmed.ncbi.nlm.nih.gov/32335265/

82 Even moderate exercise has been shown to raise cortisol: Hill, E.E., Zack, E., Battaglini, C., Viru, M., Viru, A., Hackney, A.C.; *Exercise and circulating cortisol levels: the intensity threshold effect*; [J Endocrinol Invest. 2008 Jul;31(7):587-91.]; Available here: https://pubmed.ncbi.nlm.nih.gov/18787373/

83 This herb has been shown to work on the stress pathways to the brain: Cohen, M.M.; *Tulsi - Ocimum sanctum: A herb for all reasons*; J Ayurveda Integr Med. 2014 Oct-Dec; 5(4): 251–259; Available here:https://www.ncbi.nlm.nih.gov/pmc/articles/PMC4296439/

83 Although you might think alcohol calms you, in fact it raises cortisol levels: *Chronic drinking increases levels of stress hormones, leading to neurotoxicity*; (9 September 2010); Alcoholism: *Clinical & Experimental Research*; Available here: https://www.sciencedaily.com/releases/2010/09/100907163313.htm

84 Slow, deep breathing has been shown to get you out of fight-flight state into a slower, steady, relaxed one, while improving emotional control and mood too: https://www.ncbi.nlm.nih.gov/pmc/articles/PMC6137615/

85 Pumpkin seeds are a good source of the calming mineral magnesium, which helps to regulate cortisol: Zaccaro, A., Piarulli, A., Laurino, M., Garbella, E., Menicucci, D., Neri, B., Gemignani, A.; *How Breath-Control Can Change Your Life: A Systematic Review on Psycho-Physiological Correlates of Slow Breathing*; [Front Hum Neurosciencce, 7 September 2018; 12: 353.]; Available here: https://www.health.harvard.edu/blog/nutritional-strategies-to-ease-anxiety-201604139441

85 And research shows that eating a diet high in walnuts can improve your physical reaction to stress: West, S.G., Krick, A.L., Klein, L.C., Zhao, G., Wojtowicz, T.F., McGuiness, M., Bagshaw, D.M., Wagner, P., Ceballos, R.M., Holub, B.J., Kris-Etherton, P.M.; *Effects of diets high in walnuts and flax oil on hemodynamic responses to stress and vascular endothelial function*; [Journal of the American College of Nutrition, 2010 Dec;29(6):595-603.]; Available here: https://pubmed.ncbi.nlm.nih.gov/21677123/

92 ...increasing evidence that if you have a high toxic load, you are more likely to be obese and even to develop diabetes: Pizzorno, J.; *Is the Diabetes Epidemic Primarily Due to Toxins?*; [Integr Med (Encinitas). 2016 Aug; 15(4): 8–17.]; Available here: https://www.ncbi.nlm.nih.gov/pmc/articles/PMC4991654/

CHAPTER 8: DETOX TYPE

96 Lemon zest (from an unwaxed lemon): high in limonene, which studies suggest may help reduce fat in the liver: Jing, L., Zhang, Y., Fan, S., Gu, M., Guan, Y., Lu, X., Huang, C., Zhou, Z; Preventive and ameliorating effects of citrus D-limonene on dyslipidemia and hyperglycemia in mice with high-fat diet-induced obesity; Eur J Pharmaco. 2013 Sep 5;715(1-3):46-55.]; Available here: https://pubmed.ncbi.nlm.nih.gov/23838456/

97 The Dirty Dozen and the Clean 15 lists come from yearly US research: EWG's Shopper's Guide to Pesticides in Produce; Available here: https://www.ewg.org/foodnews/dirty-dozen.php

98 The thermal paper they're printed on is coated in BPA, a chemical that's been shown to act as a hormone disruptor: Flynn, V.; *Till receipts no longer contain BPA but they could still be a health hazard*; The Times; 2 September 2021; Available here: https://www.thetimes.co.uk/article/till-receipts-bpa-health-hazard-environment-comment-zsrzrms9k

CHAPTER 9: THYROID TYPE

108 Studies have shown high mobile phone usage changes levels of thyroid hormones: Alkayyali, T., Ochuba, O., Srivastava, K., Sandhu, J.K., Joseph, C., Ruo, S.W., Jain, A., Waqar, A., Poudel, S.; *An Exploration of the Effects of Radiofrequency Radiation Emitted by Mobile Phones and Extremely Low Frequency Radiation on Thyroid Hormones and Thyroid Gland Histopathology*; [Cureus 13(8): e17329.]; Available here: https://www.cureus.com/articles/66244-an-exploration-of-the-effects-of-radiofrequency-radiation-emitted-by-mobile-phones-and-extremely-low-frequency-radiation-on-thyroid-hormones-and-thyroid-gland-histopathology

109 Fluoride and chlorine both affect thyroid function: Kheradpisheh, Z., Mirzaei, M., Mavhi, A.H., Mokhtari, M., Reyhane, A., Hossein F., Ehrampoush, M.H.; *Impact of Drinking Water Fluoride on Human Thyroid Hormones: A Case-Control Study*; [Sci Rep. 8 February 2018; 8: 2674]; Available here: https://www.ncbi.nlm.nih.gov/pmc/articles/PMC5805681/

109 The thyroid system is very responsive to stress: Helmreich, D.L., Tylee, D.; *Thyroid Hormone Regulation by Stress and Behavioral Differences in Adult Male Rats*; [Horm Behav. 2011 Aug; 60(3): 284–291]; Available here: https://www.ncbi.nlm.nih.gov/pmc/articles/PMC3148770/

110   particularly young women, pregnant women and the over 55s: Bath, S.C., Steer, C.D., Golding, J., Emmett, P., Rayman, M.P.; Effect of inadequate iodine status in UK pregnant women on cognitive outcomes in their children: results from the Avon Longitudinal Study of Parents and Children (ALSPAC); [Lancet. 2013 Jul 27;382(9889):331-7]; Available here: https://pubmed.ncbi.nlm.nih.gov/23706508/

Vanderpump, M.P.J., Lazarus, J.H., Smyth, P.P., Laurberg, P., Holder, R.L., Boelaert, K., Franklyn, J.A., British Thyroid Association UK Iodine Survey Group; Iodine status of UK schoolgirls: a cross-sectional survey; [Lancet. 2011 Jun 11;377(9782):2007-12.]; Available here: https://pubmed.ncbi.nlm.nih.gov/21640375/#:~:text=Urinary%20iodine%20measurements%20indicative%20of,%25%2C%20n%3D135

Watutantrige-Fernando, S., Barollo, S., Bertazza, L., Sensi, F., Cavedon, E., Censi, S., Veronese, N., Ceccato, F., Federica, V., Boscaro, M., Nacamulli, D., Camozzi, V., Mian, C.; Iodine Status in the Elderly: Association with Milk Intake and Other Dietary Habits; Journal of Nutritional Health & Food Science; 27 February 2017; Available here: https://symbiosisonlinepublishing.com/nutritionalhealth-foodscience/nutritionalhealth-foodscience89.php

German Federal Institute for Risk Assessment; *Veganism: Vitamin B12 is well supplemented, iodine is a matter of concern*; (31 August 2020); Available here:https://www.bfr.bund.de/en/press_information/2020/28/veganism_vitamin_b12_is_well_supplemented_iodine_is_a_matter_of_concern-259482.html

CHAPTER 11: SEROTONIN TYPE

127   serotonin is also our natural appetite suppressant: Yabut, J.M., Crane, J.D., Green, A.E., Keating, D.J., Khan, W.I., Steinberg, G.R.; *Emerging Roles for Serotonin in Regulating Metabolism: New Implications for an Ancient Molecule*; [Endocrine Reviews, Volume 40, Issue 4, August 2019, Pages 1092–1107]; Available here: https://academic.oup.com/edrv/article/40/4/1092/5406261

128   The key building block of serotonin is an amino acid called tryptophan: Friedman, M.; *Analysis, Nutrition, and Health Benefits of Tryptophan*; [Int J Tryptophan Res. 2018; 11: 1178646918802282]; Available here: https://www.ncbi.nlm.nih.gov/pmc/articles/PMC6158605/

130   salmon and eggs. The best vegan source is tofu, but you can also get some tryptophan from edamame, pumpkin seeds, peanuts and peanut butter, almonds and almond butter, sesame seeds and tahini: Whitbread, Daisy; Top 10 Foods Highest in Tryptophan; (26 September 2022); My Food Data; Available data: https://www.myfooddata.com/articles/high-tryptophan-foods.php

132   Getting enough sleep is not only essential for health... it's also a great weight-loss habit: Koren, D., Dumin, M., Gozal, D.; *Role of sleep quality in the metabolic syndrome*; [Diabetes Metab Syndr Obes. 2016; 9: 281–310]; Available here: https://www.ncbi.nlm.nih.gov/pmc/articles/PMC5003523/

134   GPs often prescribe antidepressants when HRT might be more beneficial: Joffe, H., Cohen, L.S.; *Estrogen, serotonin, and mood disturbance: where is the therapeutic bridge?*; Biological Psychiatry Volume 44, Issue 9, 1 November 1998, Pages 798-811; Available here: https://www.sciencedirect.com/science/article/abs/pii/S0006322398001693

135   You need tryptophan to make serotonin and melatonin: Jenkins, T.A., Nguyen, J.C.D., Polglaze, K.E., Bertrand, P.P.; Influence of Tryptophan and Serotonin on Mood and Cognition with a Possible Role of the Gut-Brain Axis; [Nutrients. 2016 Jan; 8(1): 56.]; Available here: https://www.ncbi.nlm.nih.gov/pmc/articles/PMC4728667/

CHAPTER 14: THE RECIPES

164   Research has shown that eating asparagus may help prevent insulin spikes and protect against diabetes: Diabetes.co.uk; 22 November 2012; Available here: https://www.diabetes.co.uk/news/2012/nov/asparagus-may-have-anti-diabetic-benefits-99047861.html

Acknowledgements

I'd like to thank all of these lovely people for helping me bring the book together, for their inspiration, support, work, friendship and love, and for being on my life team!

Thank you to my husband James, for all his support during training, and for forgiving me when work takes over. Thank you to my daughter Poppy and son Josh, my favourite recipe testers. To my parents, Philip and Antonia, who paid for my first diploma. And especially to my mother, who inspired me to love food and to try everything. Thank you for making me a confident cook.

Thank you to the dedicated, hard-working PCH practitioners – Laura MacDonald, Lu Mieville, Claire Dilliway and Emma Hammond – for all our illuminating and in-depth client discussions and insights. And especially to Kate Leigh-Wood, for saving me when the clinic waiting list went up to four to six months! She is such an empathetic coach, who knows how to keep clients on track on our nutrition programmes. To my old schoolfriend Jo de Burgh Galwey, clinic manager and marketing coordinator, who not only organises my life but makes me laugh.

Thank you to my agent, Becca, for believing in me and telling me I could write a book. Thank you to Hollie Rutter, the marketing whizz who runs the Female Food Club and who listens to endless voice notes.

Thank you to my mentor, friend and functional medicine practitioner Antony Haynes, who taught me not to look at the obvious in consultations, but instead to dig deep into root causes. To Dr Christina O'Brien from Dutch Test who continues to teach me how women work. To Emma Beswick from our DNA laboratory, the brilliant gene geek.

Thank you to Brigid Moss, who structured my thoughts and translated them onto the page with finesse. Thank you to Jen Rich for recipe testing and for her beautiful photographs.

Thank you to the team at Lagom, Isabel Smith, Francesca Eades, and Sophie Nevrkla, and to Annie Arnold for the beautiful cover. And finally to Michelle Signore, my editor, for finding me on Instagram and having faith in me and my work.

Index